Pelican Book A883
Risinghill: Death of a Comprehensive School

Leila Berg, born in Salford, has written many children's books
for various ages which are read in most countries, including the
U.S.A. and the Soviet Union, and are frequently broadcast. (One
of them, *Little Pete Stories*, is a Young Puffin, *The Penguin who
Couldn't Paddle* is in the new Puffin i.t.a. series and her poetry
anthology *Four Feet and Two* is a Puffin.) Her writings on children
and other people have appeared in *Where*, the *Guardian*, the
Teacher, *Anarchy*, and elsewhere. She has been children's books
editor, children's books reviewer, and given talks to children,
parents, teachers, and children's librarians. She has had Youth
Campaign for Nuclear Disarmament meetings, folk song sessions
and a nursery school running in her house simultaneously. She
is married, with an adult son and daughter.

Risinghill

Death of a Comprehensive School

Leila Berg

All I have is a voice . . .

Penguin Books

Penguin Books Ltd, Harmondsworth, Middlesex, England
Penguin Books Inc., 3300 Clipper Mill Road, Baltimore 11, Md, U.S.A.
Penguin Books Australia Ltd, Ringwood, Victoria, Australia

First published 1968
Copyright © Leila Berg, 1968

Made and printed in Great Britain by
Cox & Wyman Ltd, London, Reading and Fakenham
Set in Monotype Plantin

Contents

Announcement   No flowers by request   **7**

Birth 1960   The children   9
                    The head   25
                    The place   44
                    The teachers   61
                    The labour   83

Growth 1961   Anxieties   101
                    Delights   112
                    First warning   118
                    Sniping from inside   126

Attack 1962–5   First blow from outside   129
                    Re-grouping   134
                    First blow from inside   137
                    Second blow from outside   152
                    Rallying   167
                    Fighting back   177
                    Desperation   192
                    Death blow   199

Death 1965   Dissolution   211
                    Waste   233

Obituary   Last words – for the moment   247

Appendix 1   Pages from an official document   281

Appendix 2   Risinghill and the problem before us   283

The names of all Risinghill children, parents and teachers (except Michael Duane, Zvia, and Bob Redrupp) are disguised.

The quotations which head the chapters are from the Newsom Report (*Half our Future*), prepared at the request of the Ministry of Education and presented to the government in 1963.

In memory of Susan Isaacs, George Sampson, Anton Makarenko, Homer Lane and Alex Bloom, and dedicated to all those adults – parents, teachers and others – who respect and delight in the growing child.

Announcement

No flowers by request

In 1964 and 1965, out of one of the dirtiest, ugliest, most despised parts of London where two prisons bar the streets like warning fingers, a co-educational comprehensive school shot into the newspaper headlines. WILD SCHOOL IS TAMED BY LOVE – DOES SPARING THE ROD BREED CRIME? – THAT OTHER FOUR-LETTER WORD – PARENTS WILL FIGHT MOVE TO CLOSE SCHOOL – HEAD ASKED TO GIVE UP TEACHING.

All over England, and outside it, people were disturbed by Risinghill School. Not only the children who marched through the drab streets, not only the parents themselves who had rarely known gentleness, but psychologists, social workers, teachers and lecturers throughout England, and educationists and politicians from new emerging countries, felt personally vindicated or defeated when the Government finally closed the school.

To those who may query my right to record this history, let me say openly and willingly I am not a teacher, a psychologist, a sociologist, an anthropologist, a politician, or even a journalist on the staff of a paper. I am merely a writer, a parent, and a fully-paid-up member of a well-known democracy.

February 1966

This book was documented and completely written in the twelve months of 1965. Although two years have passed before its publication, I have made no attempt to disguise the date of its writing, and would indeed wish to underline it.

November 1967

Birth 1960

The children

Corporal punishment is likely to delay, rather than promote, the growth of self-discipline, and it is humiliating to staff and pupils.

Islington is not, on the whole, a district of delight. Delight is a private matter, and like wild flowers carolling on bomb sites can spring from secret encounters; but it had never broken out in the Risinghill area. Risinghill Street used to have a school, a primary school. And when, years ago, these children were dispersed to other schools, still in the same grimy decrepit Islington but a few streets away, the teachers said 'We never had any hooliganism . . . never had any trouble . . . never had any nastiness . . . till those Risinghill children came.' The parents of many of today's children grew up, in this mean district, under the stigma of coming from the part that was meanest of all – Risinghill.

In March 1960, a new comprehensive school was opened on this spot. If you can imagine a puppy born with a tin can fastened to its tail, that was Risinghill School.

To it were drafted the children from four Islington secondary schools, and with them were put a group of younger children straight from Islington primary schools. Many of these children had not had much grace in their upbringing. But when they were five they had gone to school. They described what they had experienced of education – or to be accurate and fair, of a certain aspect of their primary-school education (before they came to Risinghill).

A girl with a gold crucifix round her neck said:

I got beat up by one teacher. She kicked me up the stairs, banged my head against the door, and pushed me into her office.

We were clearing out our classroom, you see. I was sitting in the desk and I put my necklace in there, and it's 22-carat gold, you know. My mum would have gone mad if I lost it. So I went over to get it.

She says 'Sit down!' So I said 'I want to get my necklace.' And so she says 'I'm going up to Miss Gard about you.'

She says 'Come on up there with me.' I said 'No I ain't going up there.' I says 'I want my necklace first' – cos there are a lot of thieves in that class.

So she dragged me upstairs. And then Miss Gard came out. And she pushed me up the stairs. She started kicking me up the stairs, going 'Get up! Get up!' And I kept falling up the stairs.

And then she just pushed me into the door. She knew that door was locked.

I went into her office. She started talking to me. And then she says 'Get down to your lesson', she says, 'I want so many sums done time I get down there.' And there was only about ten minutes left of that lesson, and so I had to do all them sums.

And after, when the bell went, I went up to her office, and she said to me 'Ooh! Wash your face, wash your face!' So she made me wash my face, so my face weren't red where I'd been crying.

And all the girls in the class knew that I'd been crying. She just didn't want my mum to know. She knows my mum. If anybody hits me, she knows my mum'd come up and hit them.

The London education authority does not call this kind of thing corporal punishment. The Press Officer at County Hall said to me 'Hitting, slapping and pushing children, ordinary things like that . . . Mr Duane talks as if that kind of thing is corporal punishment!'

Miss Jones, she just got a piece of wood and hit me round the leg with it. And my mate started to laugh. Well, she didn't know there was a nail in there. Then she hit my mate with it too, and the nail dug in her leg, and we had to take her down to the medical to pull the nail out, out of her leg. I went up to the headmistress, and I told her about it. . . .

I told my mum to come up the school. And my mum come up the school telling her to leave me alone and that, and that she should hit me with her hand and not with a piece of wood.

This second girl, her friends all agreed, was 'always getting hit'. She said herself, another time:

It was a day before we was breaking up, and I went to put all my books away. Well, I left my maths book out, or some book or other, you know. And I was bending over to try and fit in the book I left out and someone *nearly* fell, but they didn't. There was a pile, and they *nearly* fell over, but they didn't. And she came up and said 'What are you doing there?' and smacked me ever so hard while I was bending over. And so I just . . . I just started to cry, and I ran home, and my mum was in, and I told her about it, and my mum come up to the school again and told Miss Gard – that's the headmistress – all about it.

A boy said 'I used to get caned for stealing.' What did he steal? 'Used to steal ink.' Ink? 'Yeah, used to fill my pen. Got six for that.'

This boy said he 'stole'. These children are educated to think themselves criminals or devils. In a similar way another boy said he 'locked' children in classrooms, and only with a little questioning did the milder truth emerge.

I used to get it. For being bad. Well, I mean like locking the boys in the classroom and that. Not letting them out and that. We used to hold it, just used to hold the handle. And then you'd go down to the headmistress, and then she used to ask Mr Ross, one of our teachers, to cane us, and he'd give us one on each hand.

The children are aware that being hit – or how much or how hard they are hit – has little connexion with what they do, that what they do is merely a flashpoint. 'They just used to hit you when they were in the mood,' said one. And another, later on, said the same thing in more detail.

I was caned by the teacher, but never by the headmaster. I got caned whenever she was in a bad mood. She was only a little woman and all. She had a long bamboo cane. And she'd cane you for talking and mucking about. How many, it would depend what mood she was in. She was funny like that. If she was in a good mood, she'd only hit you once. Bad mood, about four times. She was old. She didn't have a book.*

But most children who came to Risinghill had been hit most repeatedly for talking. 'We had the ruler on our knuckles for talking,' and 'I was talking to this boy in church, and I got caned for that.'

The development of such children is astonishing. When they cry as babies – their first attempt at communication – they are

*i.e. a Punishment Book. This is explained later (see p. 21).

hit, and told 'Stop that row!' When they first learn to speak, they are either met with tight-lipped silence or told 'Shut up!' and clouted. At twelve months, earlier or later, some of them go to crowded under-staffed day nurseries where the children are grouped rigidly according to age, and where anyone who is able to put more than three words together is an adult and has no time to speak to them; the rest stay imprisoned in flats as conducive to creative spontaneous chatter, to the actions that flow from words or lead into them, as a jail. At five they are hurled into a huge screaming reception class, where the teacher, however willing and warm-hearted, if she talked incessantly could only give each individual child two minutes' conversation. And yet somehow, though they have never in their lives had the whole-hearted attention of an adult who thinks that what they are saying or trying to say is important, they nevertheless manage to prove their humanity by stringing words together. It is a tremendous achievement. And so, at seven, they are still being hit for 'speaking'.

'He used to give us poetry,' said a boy. 'And when you're talking and he's drawing on the board, he turns round and throws a bit of chalk at you. And he says "Pick it up!" And you pick it up, and he kicks you up the backside.' An inspiring teacher. (But perhaps, to be fair, his nerves were screaming, because he was too limited to align poetry with stinking basements and law-breaking.)

If these children's indomitable delight still tended to burst out in little leaks, then they were hit for 'larking about'.

'I was running about, and shouting,' a boy said. 'So one of the teachers, he got hold of me, and he took me to the headmaster, and he gave me the cane three times on the backside.'

'Larking about' is, in fact, the second main thing these children were hit for. What this child says, all of them said with slight variations.

They have no playing space, these children, except, some of them, the dark, breaking stairs of an unlit tenement. They have never had a room to themselves. Luckier children have their own room – even sometimes their own for day, their own for night; but these children share two rooms, often, with the whole family, eating, sleeping, and fucking, and sometimes the ceiling comes down in one of them, and then there is only one room and only one bed and only one lot of floor space for everyone.

Their whole environment is hostile to ordinary human growth; it spits at them. You climb over a wall – and are pinched for trespassing. You race down the street together – and are dangerous hooligans. You linger and become absorbed a little – and you are plotting something. You congregate on a street corner to talk quietly, because you have no home to talk in, no fields to walk in, no grass to sit on – and a policeman settles down to watch you over the road, knowing you are likely to break the law and waiting for it. You need to be private or you need to be adventurous, but the only place to be quiet or adventurous is an abandoned car with splintered windows that both cradles you and gives you power, or an empty rat-ridden house with fantasy clouds of swirling secretive magic mist that is the dust of masonry falling. Everything you do, the most natural act that translates the most natural emotion, is, in areas like this, delinquent, or potentially so, and every human upsurge of the spirit, you have already proved by the time you are about a year and a half old, is a danger to yourself.

It is not wicked that children in these wretched districts lark about in the classroom. It is amazing. We should give thanks that by some irrational means they still manage to keep joy and hope-fulness alive, and can still use their muscles to express this joy and hopefulness, not merely to do permitted work like harnessed cart-horses. But authoritarians always flinch and stiffen when children even move out of their desks, and when the children move faster they see them as potential rioters.

'When you gets out at playtime, start running down the corridor, and he pokes his head out of the door –' A boy starts to talk then shrugs it off. Then there's trouble, Johnny; three for that – or is it four ?

Being late, too, is something they were regularly hit for.

If you come in late – you'd only have to come in a couple of minutes late, and you have to stand out. And he gave you the cane on each hand. I must have come in late plenty of times. Lots of kids! And I used to get it.

Why does no one ever find out what the children do before they arrive at school? Do they clean up the room, look after a baby, take the washing round to the launderette, do a newspaper round, hang round a betting shop, knock something off in the market? Do they play in that empty disintegrating house, or on the bomb site? Did their father beat up their mother last night, was Mum taken to hospital, or did she go off with another man, is there a new baby and no one to look after the kids, did Nan die last night, did the roof fall in? Nobody knows or cares.

Boys and girls just the same, they was always getting caned for being late. Every day they used to come in late. And then they got the cane. It didn't make any difference. They'd still do it. Still get the cane. Dicky Clegg was always late.

Dicky Clegg was always late. . . . What utter futility! (The same boy goes on, after a little while, 'It's better at home now. Bit better clothes and that. Of course I don't see my mum at all. She writes to me when it's my birthday, and she wrote me at Christmas. She sent me ten shillings. I put it towards my boots. It's two years since I saw my mum – no, not that, about a year and a half.')

And then of course the children 'fight'. The little ones tumble about, like puppies; it is part of their still miraculously surviving high spirits. But adults see everything they do as evil. When a baby of three months bites with his growing teeth on his mother's breast, when a baby of twelve months reaches out a hand to that extraordinary still yet moving object, the human eye, when a one-and-a-half-year-old grabs at a fellow baby, he is hit, hard, by his fearful parents for 'being spiteful'. Seeing these small schoolchildren rolling about in the playground, the teacher (who, after all, also has his fears and anxieties and humiliating memories) is resolved that all physical touching must be understood to be bad, hurtful, hostile and dangerous, never larking about, never friendly or hopeful, or companionably just.

'We was out in the playground and Terry kept calling me names, so I grabbed hold of him and I whacked him. And the headmaster took me up in his office and hit me with the cane,' said a boy.

So the small children are bewildered and terribly limited – and frightened by the 'evil' quality in adults who see evil always, constantly, in them. They are brutalized or made indifferent by the adult's demonstration that might is right, and that the person you hit should always be much smaller than you because then you are bound to beat him down. (Teachers stop hitting the children when they are big enough to hit back – unless the child goes to a so-called 'good' school, where the children have been successfully conditioned to the middle-class sado-masochistic pattern, called by those who approve it, or had to give in to it, learning to obey in order that you will lead.)

Talking, larking about, fighting, being late, these were the main occasions when these children who came to Risinghill had been hit at other schools. Of course they were not the only occasions; there were plenty of others. With some children the occasions ran so rapidly together they were hit all the time.

My mate Billy was always getting the cane. He got it for everything. Swearing at the teachers, throwing ink, fighting. . . . Sometimes he got a slap, sometimes he got the cane, and sometimes he got the slipper. Specially off Mr Barton. Anybody who talked, you got that. About four times on the bottom you got it.

And another boy said:

I got the cane for playing the hop. And then I was with my mates in a fight, having a fight with St Peter's. And I stepped outside the school cos there was school dinners. No, twice I think I was outside the school, playing with this old cronk . . . an old car, you know, a wreck. I had to get caned for that, playing in the car. And then I had to get caned for going outside the school when there was dinners. Playing the hop, and fighting, that was four times I got the cane.

Someone else said:

We used to get the cane for playing up with the teachers, fighting, breaking windows. And if you swore at a teacher you'd get it about eight times. I never got it. No, I never got the cane at all. I got the ruler. Used to get the ruler, but not the cane. Never had the cane in that school.

There was one boy in our class [said another], he used to get it nearly every day. He used to go out of school at dinnertime when you're not supposed to. He used to run. He used to get the cane for that. When he used to talk, he used to get it. He used to get it for practically everything. Sometimes he'd get it three times on each hand, and sometimes six on each hand.

And a child commented with a laugh 'Bound to pick up a grudge against you.'

Some children, every teacher knows, become scapegoats – 'that one', or 'that lot'. They get knocked about for everything; and they begin to say 'I'll be blamed anyway, so what does it matter.' (A teacher said to me, 'This is where you get the breakdown of real discipline.')

Girls are caned as well as boys in Islington. 'Miss said no one should come in the class during the dinnertimes. And I did. I forgot, and I got caned.'

At some schools 'the girls didn't get caned, they just got hit.' At such a school, a girl said:

I used to get hit with a ruler. Once I was in the corridor on the stairs, with a lot of my friends. They were doing a rehearsal for a puppet show, and I stayed in and watched. And then the headmaster come in and he said 'What are you doing down there?' So I said 'I'm watching the rehearsal for the puppet show.' So he said 'Come up to my office.' It was a wet day. We went up. I had some elastic bands in my hand, and he said 'What are you doing with them?' So I says 'They're mine.' And then he got the ruler and hit me across the hand, on the knuckles.

Someone else said:

This girl, her name was Shirley. When we had P.E. and went down to the playground for a game of rounders, if she was running and she knocked something over or something and she went straight on and then she got a rounder, well our teacher used to say 'That wasn't a rounder.' And if she said it was, she used to cane her. She used to hit her with a ruler and say 'You shouldn't tell lies to me.'

But a boy who said 'She caned the girls too, on the hand . . . for the same thing – talking and that', added, 'She never used to cane the girls so much, though.'

Girls have other terrors. To be shouted at is a recurring nightmare to them.

When we didn't know how to do our sums . . . when I didn't know how to do long division . . . I weren't quite sure of it . . . she used to shout at you, and it used to frighten you, and so I used to do everything wrong.

And another said, on quite a different occasion:

Once we had the headmaster for writing, you know. And we had to start italic. And you must have an italic nib. If you didn't you'd get told off. I had my own pen – it was an Osmiroid, you know. It had an italic nib. And it didn't seem anything wrong with it. And then the headmaster he come up behind me, and he says 'Your writing's slanting.' You know, I didn't say anything, I just kept on writing. He says 'You'll have to do that again.' And he kept shouting at me and that, you know. I was nearly crying, you know . . . the way he shouts at you and that . . . '

But – 'Never caned the girls so much', said the boy. So a feeling grows up among the boys, which they take with them into adult life, that girls lead boys into trouble and boys suffer for it, and the girls get off (with the addendum: so make the girls suffer whenever you can; it's getting your own back). And among the girls a dreadful anxiety grows ('Frightened all the time you'd get into trouble') and a terror of witnessing another's violence and another's suffering – or else an acceptance of the role of sly causer of pain. (Do adults never think what it does to a child, a child who has committed no fault, a child who *since* she has managed to commit no fault is perhaps intelligent, sensitive and aware, to see and hear another's pain? But of course they do. They say it is 'an example'; it is 'good' for children.)

Sometimes, with sardonic chivalry, the boys were separated from the girls in order to be caned.

A boy said:

The headmaster he took all the girls out of the class and brought all the boys into one class, and gave the boy six whacks with the cane on his backside. I think he threw some paint.

(But this may be because they do not think it seemly for a girl to see a boy beaten on his bottom. They are often very prim and fastidious, these beaters.)

But while the boys and the girls are in this genteel seclusion, sometimes a little girl gazes abstractedly out of the classroom window, and her vision suddenly focuses. 'I was looking out of the window in the classroom,' said a girl, 'and I saw him through the other window, and he was hitting him, the headmaster was, with a cane.'

Girls like this are haunted. And let no fool say the solution is one-sex schools.

Later on these same children talked about marriage, and the boys said they wouldn't ever help their wives, because women have everything easy, don't they.

But the main hate is against the teacher, only this is a hate that dare not be pinned on its object. A boy said 'When he used to give me the stick on the backside I used to go in the toilet and pull my trousers down and try to have a look at it. There used to be a big red mark across my backside. We used to plot against him, you know. Say we were going to hit him or something.' But they didn't hit him, and such a hate becomes destructive to others, or, turning in on itself, self-destructive.

Sometimes, rapidly, bedlam grows – panic and chaos and despair.

A teacher named Mr Stead, you know, well you know he was a bit mad. A big fat geezer. He'd put his hands under your ribs and pick you up, you know, like that. Or he'd pick you up with two fingers poking into your chin. Pick you up by the ears. By the nose. He used to stretch it and pull you up – if you talked, anything. He had a go at Mick Martin once. Picked him up like that, and his nose started bleeding, so he kicked him. I mean this kid named Mick Martin kicked Mr Stead. So Mr Roberts grabbed the kid and hit him with a big wooden spoon.

Then the children create their own hopeless counter-attack of clowning, the threatened dog rolling over on its back and acting the fool.

'Mr Carter, he was a madman. And he used to have a tennis ball and he used to call the table. He used to say "Six tens!" and throw it up to the wall. And if you didn't get it he used to slipper you. What? No, it wasn't a joke. There used to be a boy named – what's his name? – Bill Robins. He used to come into school and say "Carter, smack my arse, Carter, smack my arse, smack my arse, Carter!" And he used to slipper him about twelve times.' How close are force and farce; how ennobling is our education.

The girls began to describe how a teacher 'threw' a small boy. Threw him? – how do you mean? 'He *threw* him!' they insisted, refusing any other word. 'He *threw* him. He was only a little boy, and he threw him, and he went right across the room and landed up against the radiator.' I remember that then for the first time there was a rising emotional note in these reports; these two children were getting a little excited and edged with hysteria and with only the slightest hint of sensational response would begin to egg each other on. I saw the whole scene, sickeningly and clearly, the teacher hauling the child up and hurling him away so that he staggered against the wall. I saw it so clearly because I remembered it clearly from my own childhood, the outrage and the shock of it. This was the moment when my optimism faltered, I felt very tired, and I did not want to hear any more for a while.

Perhaps then this may be a good moment, before we return again to these Islington children, to review the whole position and see how these things can be, a century and a half after Blake and a century after Dickens.

*

The public is told – and was told over and over again during 'the Risinghill row' – that there is no corporal punishment in L.C.C. schools. The L.C.C. in fact issues a cautiously progressive booklet for the public to read, which says things like:

Most teachers will agree that the use of corporal punishment should be considered only when the actions of individuals seriously threaten their well-being or that of class community, and then, as a rule, only after other methods have been tried and have failed. But before this exceptional last-resort method is used, there is still another question to ask: if other methods have failed, is corporal punishment likely to succeed? Some heads, after studying records in the Punishment Books, have concluded that the efficacy of corporal punishment is, with many children, so doubtful that, after consulting with their staffs, they have abandoned it altogether. It is a plan worth considering, at least as an experiment, especially when corporal punishment has already been reduced almost to vanishing point.

And:

Whatever opinions we may hold on such matters – and it cannot be denied that there are many opinions – it is clear that the discouragement of all forms of physical punishment for girls can foster that respect for womanhood which is one of the marks of a civilied society. Furthermore, its discouragement for both sexes (especially important in mixed schools) may help to foster an appreciation of the dignity of human beings, and ultimately make some contribution to an increased respect for humanity as a whole.

Personally I have read this booklet through many times, with genuine hope and concern, but I still have no idea what it is saying. It seems to me it would make an excellent English language exercise of the most deadly kind – 'Précis this, giving the gist of the argument.' It is redolent of the terror of being thought to hold an opinion that keeps the teaching profession as motionless as a well-trained dog.

Mr James Young, then chairman of the L.C.C. Education Committee, in a letter to the *Guardian* during the Risinghill row (15 February 1965), boldly claimed that such passages meant that 'thirteen years ago many London schools had, undramatically, abolished corporal punishment, and the movement away from its use has continued over the years', and took pains to emphasize that this remarkable booklet was issued as far back as 1952.*

Though enthusiastic about dates, Mr Young does not mention 1959. In this year the L.C.C. issued a rather different booklet – not for the public, but marked 'Confidential within the London Teaching Service'. Right up to this year, 1965, this booklet was still being issued to new teachers as part of their 'Welcome to Teaching'. I most recently saw one in the possession of a teacher starting at Risinghill School. (She was an American. Had no one ever told the L.C.C. that other countries – Holland, Israel, Norway, U.S.A. – have made corporal punishment illegal, and that people from these countries are astounded to know such barbarity exists here ?)

This confidential booklet tells teachers what they should hit the children with (one of two canes of an 'approved pattern'),

---

* Something more courageous was also published in 1952, which was a better year for education than the L.C.C. might lead us to believe. In that year the West Riding Education Authority published a booklet which anyone can obtain from their offices in Wakefield, giving the results of a small survey of theirs which showed that the schools which had the most caning produced most delinquency – a very humane piece of work combining statistics, scholarship and vision.

and on what part of the body. It also lays down all rules for the administration of this punishment.

At a meeting I had at County Hall, which I describe in detail later, I asked why this booklet was confidential, and was told that it was not parents' business. At this meeting, Mr Turner, Assistant Education Officer, pressed, admitted to me 'Corporal punishment has not been abolished in London schools.' I asked him helpfully, 'But the Council would like to see it abolished?' and this he refused to say. Does this surprise Mr Young? Does the chairman of the Education Committee know no more than the parents?

The confidential booklet lays down, in effect, that children may only be hit by the teacher's hand on the child's hand or arm, or with one of two canes 'of the approved pattern' (and here it does not say where), and only by the head, or by certain assistants the head 'considers to be fit and proper persons to be so entrusted' (the head having set this delegation down in writing). It also says that any punishment so given must be written down immediately in the Punishment Book and signed by the teacher who gave it, further initialled by the head if it was not the head who gave it. This grotesque ritual – and all the rest of the rules – must have been a much-needed attempt to curb violence. One hopes at least it was meant to protect the children, not – discreetly – to shield the teachers. But you have only to talk to children (or to teachers or probation officers if you are on truthful terms with them) to know that the Punishment Book is scarcely used (like an uncongenial wedding present, it is kept out of sight unless the donor comes on a visit), that any teacher who simply feels like it hits the children, and that the teacher is likely to hit them with anything that comes to hand and would not dream of making an official journey to the head's study for 'a cane of the approved pattern'.

If a parent most unfairly manages to get hold of these confidential regulations which he is not supposed to see, and therefore becomes aware that they are being broken and that his child is being hit in a regrettably unofficial way, he can complain. Then the teacher may be rebuked.

But the assault on the child remains entirely lawful. For by

English law – which says one person may only hit another if the other is very much smaller – a parent has the 'right' to beat his child. And for some reason, the law 'presumes' parents have delegated this right to all teachers.

And as long as state-school classes are so large and the calibre of some we persuade to become teachers is so low that the implementation of our glorious 1944 Education Act depends on beaters (who, incidentally, make it very difficult indeed for non-beaters to teach), teachers in England will continue to use this 'right' – unless parents wish to take the trouble to say they have never delegated it.

*

Back now to the Islington children. Oddly, their incorrect grammar, their Cockney accents help one to be optimistic. If they told their wretched experiences in perfect English, you would feel they had been neatly filed away – 'Conformed to the approved pattern. Treatment successful' – and you would be depressed beyond bearing. But they grope for words, and then, trusting you, begin to tumble about in the unfamiliar paths of their own language; and you are aware that they are miraculously still alive, still holding on to their own identity.

They are not aware of the L.C.C. regulations, of course, since they are 'confidential'. So you ask questions, delicately.

They used to use two rulers. They felt just like the cane, you know, on your hands. And you used to come in, you know, being late or something, or been larking around in class, or just speaking in the class while he was teaching, and he used to call you out in front, and he used to use the ruler, you know, on your hand, on each, and about four times, three times, for talking. A load of them used to get it.

Another boy says:

They used to use a wooden spoon to hit you with. Fighting, having a muck about, all that – he used to whack you across the bum with it.

No, your name wasn't put in a book [said one]. You were just caned if you did something wrong. They didn't tell your mum or dad or anything.

I got caned more by the teacher than any of the others. I never had my name put in the book. The head didn't write in a book, either. He just seemed mad with us, you know, the head [said another].

We had to fetch the book sometimes. It depended on how the teacher felt [said another].

'When you have your first one, you don't get your name put down. You just get the cane. Only the second time. . . .' (The children at this school thought, and were intended to think – maybe even the teachers thought – that this was giving them another chance, doing them a favour. What it really meant was that there was no record that the child had been hit.)

But sometimes the child told Mum. Not always. Even the children who know Mum will support them do not always tell her. Some don't want Mum to be upset, for many of them are aware, in Islington, that Mum has a hard time of it. (Some of them see Mum as a different sex from contemporary girls.) And some don't want her to kick up a row at the school. Some accept it because violence is part of their lives, and they do not expect anything better; by the age of nine, some of these children no longer think in terms of justice, let alone kindness. Some don't want to isolate themselves from their fellows. Some have found from experience that, though the hitting stops, subtler cruelties take its place. Others think that if they told, Dad would probably hit them too, for good measure. Others are too ashamed, certainly not of the 'crime' that brought the punishment, but of the punishment itself – the humiliation is so shocking and degrading.

(Besides, children of primary-school age often keep home and school completely apart; and that is precisely why it is essential for parents and teachers to be able to trust one another, and to meet and talk informally and often.)

But sometimes a child trusted enough, or despaired enough, to tell Mum.

There was this little kid outside school, and he got the cane, you know, just for standing there. And his Mum went up the school and punched the teacher in the eye.

One boy said:

I was caned often . . . twice a week. For talking on the stairs. Well you see, they pushed from the back. And if you run, you'd still get it.

Two or three I used to get. Each time you go, every day it doubles. Once, like that, I got four on one hand. I told my mum, and she come up, and he just said he won't do it again, and after that I never got it any more.

Occasionally Dad turned up.

He used to hit you, you know. He used to get you down like that and he used to hit you across the head, with the edge of his hand, hit you across the side there. My dad come up and he hit the bloke, and he didn't do it after that.

So when this happens the teacher does not hit that particular child again. But he feels resentful and bitter, because he has been excluded from what he regarded as a free-for-all. Most teachers will say quickly, if you query their right to hit children, 'But their parents hit them!' Often they will put on a tone of extreme self-righteousness, and say 'Why, they *tell* us to hit them!' I have no doubt that many of them do, in classy suburban areas as much as in the slums. But some people think education was intended to help people out of the muck and misery of ignorance.

I could write much more of what these Islington children said. I am aware that children, particularly emotionally deprived children, do not always speak the *factual* truth. The actual number of times the boys were caned – the number of days or the number of strokes – may be inaccurate; I will not quibble about it – give or take a few strokes. That they *were* caned or hit in various ways I have not the slightest doubt. And that the atmosphere in their schools was such as they have so evocatively described I again have not the slightest doubt.

I have all their statements recorded on several tapes, and most of it – not all – neatly transcribed on to 150 typed pages, including all the names of the teachers and the schools (which I have disguised in these extracts). But there is enough set down here to show you what these children were like, what experience of school they had had, when in March 1960 they entered their new school, Risinghill Comprehensive, headmaster Michael Duane.

The head

A school which takes its responsibilities seriously will not just leave to chance the working out of its influence over its pupils. It will have a policy.

MAJOR W. M. DUANE [*extract*]   1946

Generally speaking I can only say that I hold the highest possible opinion of this officer and consider him to have been probably the best of my staff, and I am quite certain that he will make a success of any job he may undertake in civil life. He has a pleasant, cheerful character and is at all times an amusing and interesting companion – he has been most popular with all ranks at this H.Q. His many interests are reflected in considerable independence of opinion and character, but he gets on equally well with those who do not agree with them; though he enjoys putting over his views, he never rams them down other people's throats and is quite broad-minded enough to appreciate the point of view of other people.

His work has been uniformly of the highest quality – he is reliable and hardworking when hard work is required and is capable – though I do not think he likes it – of doing detailed work fast and accurately. He is most energetic both mentally and physically, and has plenty of common sense. He has undoubted organising ability and powers of leadership, while his independent character ensures the capacity for original thought and sound judgement.

On reading this testimonial through it sounds a bit too good to believe, and possibly it might bear more weight if there were some bad points included – I cannot however find any within my knowledge which are worth adding.

> (*Signed*) V. FitzGeorge-Balfour
> Brigadier,
> Chief of Staff,
> 8 Corps District.

When Mr Duane hit the headlines in January 1965, there must have been a vague feeling that he had been born that moment, or at least only a year or two earlier, fully girt for battle. In fact, as the extract above shows, he had attracted attention some years previously in a capacity that perhaps surprises some people.

Risinghill was his fourth headmastership, and he had had teaching experience at several other schools. When he was a student at London University Institute of Education, one of his practice schools was Owen's Grammar. The head there was impressed by his work and asked him to join the staff. He taught there for a while, then the war intervened; he went back afterwards to Owen's, and then the Institute asked him to come back as a full-time tutor.

At the Institute he had valuable experience lecturing to teaching students, training them, discussing work with them; he took part as lecturer in several new schemes, including the new Emergency Training Scheme for people released from the Forces and wanting to become teachers.

In 1948, when he was thirty, he decided he was ready to run his own school, using the ideas that he had now worked out. He was accepted as headmaster of a new school at Howe Dell, near Hatfield; the chairman of the governors who accepted him was a woman of progressive views, and the County Director of Education was Mr John Newsom (later to become known to the whole country as Sir John Newsom, champion of the 'average' child, and main author of the Newsom Report).

After a long discussion of the policy Mr Duane put forward, Mr Newsom asked him how long he thought he would need to set this new school on its feet. He said certainly not less than three years. Mr Newsom said 'You've got five. Five years with no questions asked.'

At the time of his appointment Howe Dell was not ready. Mr Newsom asked him if he would take over the headship of Beaumont Secondary Modern School, in St Albans, for one term in the meantime. He agreed to do this.

After this one term, he received a letter from John Newsom.

. . . If you can do what you have done at Beaumont's then there is no doubt that the Old Rectory at Hatfield will soon become one of the greatest jewels in our educational crown! We are all most indebted to you and encouraged for the future . . .

Some weeks later, a letter arrived from the divisional education officer.

Dear Mr. Duane,

The time is at hand when we are to lose your services in this Division, and the Governors and Committee have expressed a wish for me to thank you for the way in which you have helped us by controlling Beaumont Boys' School for a term.

This School is so very different from the one you took over in September that anyone connected with the former establishment would scarcely recognise it as the same School now.

There is an alertness among the boys and an eagerness which is a delight to watch. It is easy to notice a great difference in the Staff too, so that on all sides marked changes have taken place.

It is seriously contended that the day of miracles is past, but in the eyes of the Committee so great changes have been accomplished in so short a time that it would not be too extravagant to refer to the changes as miraculous.

In thanking you for your work here, may we express the hope that you will find joy and satisfaction in your new School at Howe Dell.

> Yours faithfully,
> F. Goacher,
> Divisional Education Officer

When he started at Howe Dell, he found that there were three difficulties that were set to clog his wheels permanently. The progressive chairman had been replaced, and he now had an authoritarian chairman of governors (who had not been on the interviewing Committee, and who, like most of the governors, was a Tory pundit used to exercising power in the district), a group of pupils from an authoritarian orphanage (which sent other groups of children to authoritarian day schools), and an authoritarian inspector.

Apart from this, there was a class of difficulty that was stupid and unnecessary and time-wasting, but that would eventually be cleared up, given patience. The seventeenth-century rectory building which was the school was extremely difficult to organize. Its numerous tiny rooms made nonsense of the teacher–pupil ratio since the classes couldn't fit into them. It was filthy and difficult to clean, but the cleaners' wages were fixed so low that Mr Duane found himself spending the weekends scrubbing floors, cleaning lavatories and stoking boilers, because no domestic staff, quite understandably, would take it on at the

rates of pay the authority refused to raise, and Mr Duane refused to allow the children to come to a filthy school. For a long
time he had to do the secretarial work as well.

Furthermore, when the school opened only the barest essen-
tials had arrived, so that the provisional timetable had to be constantly changed since there was no equipment to implement it;
the children quickly began to react to this chaos, and decided
that they had no purpose, that they were not taken seriously,
and could do as they liked. When the equipment finally did
arrive, an attitude had been set up which it took Mr Duane and
his staff considerable time to reverse (and which had, by then,
created a twisted picture of the school in the village).

All the other difficulties were stimulating ones to be met,
worked on and overcome. Many of the children, coming to him
at eleven and twelve from a dozen different villages and from all-
age village schools, could only read simple sentences, and that
with difficulty; some could not read or write at all. They arrived
mostly without any record of their previous education, and some,
being backward, could not give the name of their previous school.
Their homes were poverty-stricken, without any social graces or
interest in learning, and were often full of strong emotional
tension. Many had had very little social training – their table
manners were non-existent. The older ones had had no social
life or leisure entertainment. Mr Duane estimated that the work
they were having to do at Howe Dell was two years behind the
work children in a comparable urban school would be doing.

The teachers had to be helped to understand his aims; this,
he saw, was vital. One, for instance, thought that the head
'considered it desirable for children to do what they liked and
not to be held accountable for their actions'. A few, when things
were still difficult, thought the cane would solve all problems.
But gradually they began to understand, to respect, and to feel
warmly towards what he was trying to build up; as so often happens
when children are allowed to, it was the children themselves who
taught them.

During the first year, for instance, a boy climbed up a water-
pipe in the lavatory, and in doing so pulled down a cistern and
smashed it. Although he might fairly easily have escaped detec-

tion, he came to Mr Duane, white in the face, and told him. Mr Duane put the affair before the whole school for their consideration; he explained he saw it as thoughtless damage that it was not right to ask ratepayers to pay for; what then did the children suggest should be done? About half a dozen promptly suggested the cane. Mr Duane pointed out that the cane would not restore the cistern; nor was it needed to discourage the boy from doing it again – it was already clear he would not do it again. Some children then recommended that the boy should be made to pay for the cistern. He asked them to imagine what their own parents would say or do if a bill arrived for over ten pounds. Then a number of children proposed that everyone pay a small contribution towards the cost, but that the culprit pay more than anyone else. Within a few days two of the boys had, quite on their own account, taken round a small box and a notebook and made a collection of six shillings, and three girls had brought various articles to school to start a 'sale of work' to raise more.

By the first autumn the hostile gossip in the village, based mainly on the difficulties of the first term, the rejection of caning, and the children's pleasure in going to school, was beginning to melt away and the school was beginning to be accepted; the staff was happier, and able and keen to discuss, criticize and co-operate in a healthy way, in terms of '*our* school'.

It must have been about this time that Dr Cora Tenen, working with Professor James, arrived from the London Institute of Education to spend some months in the school. They were working on a UNESCO research project, aiming at finding out how far personal contact with a member of a particular people influenced a person's attitude towards that people as a whole – in this case, how far these backward village children would react to having a couple of African teachers. Their findings were published in a book called *The Teacher was Black* (Heinemann), which also contains two chapters by Dr Tenen describing the school.

Common as are out-of-school activities nowadays, the interviewer has never known a staff who so unquestioningly spent such long hours at school, out of genuine interest in and liking for children.

Relations between the headmaster and the children were clearly of the parent–child type. He was a very approachable man, with none of the awe-inspiring marks of the conventional headmaster: the sort of person to whom the children will readily talk. And they did. There was a back entrance to his room, reached by an old staircase, and up those at all hours there trooped a constant procession of boys and girls, singly or in little groups, to put some suggestion or to seek help in confiding some personal trouble. . . .

. . . The headmaster and his staff were enthusiastic believers in the new method of education. The Headmaster had previously been a lecturer in educational method, and had taken over this school in an attempt to translate principles into practice. . . .

They interpreted learning in this widest sense, so the emotional needs of the children as individuals were considered to be as important as the more conventional academic requirements. . . . The Headmaster and his staff made it their business to know as much as possible about the home life of each child, and to help each to understand and solve its personal problems. In his spare time the Headmaster visited the villages from which his children were drawn, and talked to the parents in their homes and at village meetings, explaining to them his aims in the school (no easy task, in view of their own educational and social background) and discussing with them problems connected with their children. . . .

In the daily life of the school the aim was self-discipline: not authoritarian, imposed from above by more powerful adults, but collective, and the few general rules there were had been arrived at after discussion with the children and evolved from their common experience, not without dust and heat.

There was no corporal punishment. . . . Because the aims of the Headmaster and staff were to free the children from the distortions caused by fear, and to help them to acquire self-confidence and the ability to live harmoniously, the treatment of misdemeanours aimed at being constructive rather than retributive. Relations between children and staff were very informal and friendly. . . .

In a society where schools are still largely authoritarian in discipline, the problems faced by teachers with ideals such as those held by the staff of this school are sufficiently formidable. But in the circumstances of this school the experiment raised problems from which the boldest and most idealistic might have been forgiven for flight. The sudden change to a school world so different from any previously experienced, so much freer, in surroundings so enticing and so much less circumscribed, among adults so surprisingly loath to use force to obtain obedience, occasioned in these children widespread re-adjustment in attitudes of behaviour. For a time, as might be expected, the behaviour of some of them was rowdy, aggressive and destructive, as long-standing inhibitions were worked out. But by the time the interviewer came to the school it had been in existence a year, and a more orderly community was emerging.

The children, incidentally, seem to have enjoyed having their African teachers very much.

In the summer holidays, Mr Newsom selected Mr Duane to represent English Modern School Education at an International Conference on Secondary Schools in Holland. They went together, and afterwards Mr Newsom said he was delighted with Mr Duane's contribution to the conference, which had drawn on the work at Howe Dell.

The chairman of the governors was Alderman G. Maynard, a man of considerable influence in the area, and convenor of the Conservative group on the county council. The vice-chairman of the governors was another Conservative county councillor. Three more of the governors were also Conservative councillors in a slightly smaller way (parish or rural district). The whole district seems to have been moulded by the Tories for a very long time; and after a brief period when the 1944 Education Act had led to bright visions, or at least glimmerings, in even the darkest areas (Mr Newsom himself described the district from which the Howe Dell children came as the worst in the county), the Tories were back once more.

Within less than two years from the start of the school ('Five years with no questions asked') there had been a special inquiry, a special visit by an H.M.I., a check by two inspectors and finally a full inspection in November 1950. Each one denounced Mr Duane's policy, the aim, that is, for which he had been appointed, but not, of course, by Alderman Maynard.

In October 1949, the orphanage launched the preliminary attack, complaining that the children were not being taught typing, book-keeping, shorthand or discipline. They made it clear that the group of their children who went to Howe Dell were beginning to take a different view of life from the groups who went to other schools, and that they would not permit this: they warned of 'really serious consequences'.

Almost simultaneously with this, someone – one would have expected it in the organizational way to have been the chairman of the governors, but he denied it; so who was it? – demanded an inspection, claiming certain teachers were spreading Communist propaganda among the children.

Meanwhile dark whispers of 'sexual orgies', such as often spring up around non-authoritarian schools and from which therefore state schools had been hitherto immune, had been growing insistent – though not apparently worrying Mr Duane, who on being told that a Howe Dell boy had 'had sexual intercourse with four girls on his way to the bus stop', roared with laughter and said 'I take off my hat to him.' (The story continued to be spread, now with the addition 'And Mr Duane publicly expressed approval!') Alderman Maynard himself announced that a 'sex film, with a black man and a white woman', had been shown at Howe Dell. This turned out to be a Cyril Bibby film strip on human physiology, in which the male figures were shaded more strongly than the female. Mr Duane's light-heartedness angered the authoritarians; and claiming that one of their girls had had her knickers pulled down, the orphanage withdrew their children and demanded an inquiry.

The county council appointed an Inquiry Committee – Alderman Maynard and Sir William Acland.

The Inquiry Committee found that there had been 'no evidence of indecent interest'. But they simultaneously stated that they were 'much impressed' by the orphanage matron's 'very proper concern' for the children, however mistaken her fears ('though possibly over-emphasizing the seriousness of this particular occasion'), and 'very disturbed' by Mr Duane's lack of it. They decided that 'the time, the place and the opportunity for undesirable horse-play of this kind ought not to be given', and ordered that a barn where the children played should be put out of bounds, and their outdoor playing-space curtailed.*

Gathering momentum, they went on to say 'Although no sub-committee of the Education Committee has yet received a report

*The children had been jumping on a pile of hay in the barn.

on Howe Dell since its inception, it is only fair to say that the
Senior Officers of the Education Department are extremely
disturbed by both the standard of scholastic attainment and
behaviour revealed when they and His Majesty's Inspectors have
visited the school.' They expatiated on this.

They also said that Mr Duane had mentioned various difficulties, but they were not relevant to the incident being investigated,
and would therefore not be gone into.

Finally they, in their capacity as Committee of Inquiry,
recommended that they, in their capacity as governors of the
school (together with the other governors), should discuss this
impartial report.

The school staff wrote to Alderman Maynard to ask if they
could be present at this next meeting, but their letter was not
answered.

Consequently, when the governors' meeting announced to Mr
Duane that 'a five year programme as envisaged by the Headmaster at the expense of the children could not be tolerated',
there was no opposition except from Mr Duane. Mr Duane
pointed out that this policy was the policy he had been appointed
for, but he was told 'whatever that policy might be, it must be
modified in view of the facts'. At this point, he seems to have
offered his resignation, but it must have been ignored in the
thunderstorm.

The governors had an exciting evening. They also discussed
the second visit by two inspectors, who had reported that the
children's manners were bad and their work was bad, and indeed
had not said one good word about the children or the staff.

Then they moved on to the matter of a questionnaire which
Mr Duane had sent out to all parents, asking such questions as
whether the child seemed to be happier at school, less happy, or
much the same – more interested in school work, less, or much
the same – more helpful at home, less, or much the same, and also
gave a space for parents to write whatever they felt to be of interest.
He had sent out 150, and had received back – from semi-literate
country village parents, hitherto hostile – 137. Seventy-two per
cent of the replies said the children were happier, sixty-two per
cent said the children were more interested in school work,

fifty-seven per cent said the children had more self-confidence.
The governors instructed him not to do such a thing again; it was
most 'ill-advised'. This was February 1950.

In September and November 1950, at the request of the
governors who 'had been disturbed by events of the previous
period', a full inspection took place. The conducting H.M.I. was
a man who had already at Beaumont's School told Mr Duane
he believed corporal punishment to be necessary for children.
   The inspector, it seems, questioned a class about their reading.
He asked how many belonged to a library. One boy, John, put his
hand up, then, not being sure what the inspector meant, put it
down again. The boy next to him whispered to him to put it up.
The inspector then spent two minutes castigating John in front
of the class for being 'insolent'.
   Another boy said 'Do you mean the school library, sir?' The
inspector replied: 'Don't be so damned cheeky, boy.'
   He must have been further irritated by encountering such
children as May and Bobby. May, on being asked by him where
she came from, said she did not know. He asked her the name of
her last school. She didn't know. She was eleven years nine
months old, but her reading age was seven years, her arithmetic
age was eight years, and her I.Q. (Cattell non-verbal) was eighty-
seven. Bobby, who was twelve years six months old, had a reading
age of seven, an arithmetic age of under seven, and an I.Q. of
sixty-seven. For the inspector had several times told Mr Duane
that children produce whatever standard of work you expect
them to, and that the Howe Dell children were not backward.
   Immediately after this inspection had taken place, the inspector
suggested to Mr Duane that he should reconsider his philosophy
and the direction in which he was moving. This was an unusual
thing to do, since no verbal report had yet been officially made,
and no printed report had yet been issued for discussion.
   When the inspector did verbally present his report to the
governors' meeting, it was to say that:

The Headmaster is largely concerned with providing an environment which will allow the children to adjust themselves more harmoniously to one another and to adults. The Inspectors have asked the

Headmaster to reconsider this point of view. They doubt whether the present Staff is capable of understanding and implementing the Headmaster's philosophy. If he continues to adhere to this point of view he will send out children who are not well-mannered, not interested in a wide range of subjects, and not competent in basic skills. . . . It might be legitimate in an Independent School to adopt his methods, but they could not be tolerated in a State school.

The inspector might have been expected to be a little incommoded by the fact that his colleagues had reported that in many of the subjects the work was 'good', even 'very good', and 'really remarkable'. One colleague, viewing art work, said 'It's a relief to see something gay and untidy and living, after the unconscionably dull and pretty things I have to wade through in Grammar Schools. I wish they would do something half as good as this. This has got guts!' But the inspector had the governors with him.

On 21 November the staff asked Mr Maynard once again to arrange a joint meeting of teachers and governors. They asked permission to discuss the inspector's verbal report and its implications. This time the meeting was granted. It was angry and sardonic.

Mr Maynard made such statements as 'There must be no risk of variations from the traditional.' When a teacher suggested that closer contact between the governors and the staff might be more constructive and friendly, he replied that the governors were far too busy to hold tea-parties.

Finally, after trying to explain their work, the staff gave up and left. The governors asked Mr Duane to leave the room, and wait till told to re-enter. During this period Mr Maynard insisted vehemently that Mr Duane must be made to use the cane.

Mr Duane was then called in and told that the staff should not have asked for a meeting with the governors (a meeting that is laid down by right in the Articles of Government); that the staff should not meet the governors – only the head should meet them; that the headmaster must get over the governors' requirements to his staff as *his own* policy; that in his reports to the governors he must make no attempt to shield his staff; that the school was not to be experimental in any way; and that he was on one last term's trial.

Some weeks later, as is the usual procedure, the report was issued in printed form. It contained more detail. It was somewhat scathing about the children's use of the library.

(It is worth noting here that the I.Q.s of these children ranged from 120 to fifty-one. Some of them could not read at all. And yet, an *average* of four books a term (that is, including the non-readers) were being taken out personally, by each child, each term, and taken back to homes that had never before encouraged education. Another inspector might possibly have seen something interesting in that. And this was quite separate from the very considerable use made of the library by the children in the course of their lessons – and not only their English lessons.)

It stated that the children's attitude to school property 'could be judged from the fact that the towel-rollers had had to be padlocked to their frames'. (In fact, they were padlocked because, through bad designing, the roller jumped out of its slot whenever the towel was pulled. They were padlocked in exactly the same way in many other schools where this same unsatisfactory fitting had to be used.)

It suggested that introduction of 'the family method' at dinnertime would help in the children's social training. Mr Duane had himself said this previously. He had asked for the equipment for this a considerable time before the inspection, and had been told it was not available. After the inspection he had asked again – and been given the same reply. Nevertheless the tables were laid by the children and decorated with flowers picked by the children; and at each little table sat a teacher, for the staff and any visitors always dined with the children; though limited by the official response to their needs, the school was getting in some very effective social education.

The month after the printed report was issued, a governors' meeting decided the school could manage without a music teacher, since, as one of the governors put it, 'music was one of the frills' for children like this, and it was preferable they should concentrate on 'basic subjects'; she herself held an L.R.A.M. diploma.

In the same month, Mr Duane, who was by now becoming respected and popular in the district, was appointed a J.P.

On 23 April, another two months later, he sat on the same

bench as Alderman Maynard (who was there in his capacity of chairman of magistrates).

On 24 April, Sir William Acland and Mr Simmons, the District Education Officer, visited the school. They did not raise with Mr Duane one point that had appeared in the report, nor check with him that the governors' recommendations were being carried out. No hostility was expressed. Mr Simmons even stayed for a cup of tea.

On 30 April, Mr Duane was nominated as Labour candidate for a seat that had been held for a very long time indeed by a Conservative, the husband of a governor.

On 1 May, John Newsom wrote to Mr Duane asking him to consider whether it was discreet to take on public duties when his school was not yet well established, and warning him that he had had to listen to a lot of comment on this subject lately. Mr Duane then tried to cancel his candidature but it was too late.

On 8 May, Alderman Maynard, in his capacity as chairman of the county council Urgency and Staffing Sub-Committee, passed on to him a decision by that committee forbidding him to sit on the bench during school hours.

On 15 May, Mr Duane wrote to the local newspaper, which had asked all R.D.C. candidates to supply 'local and political details' about themselves to help electors in making their choice, and emphasized that, if elected, he would be unable to attend any daytime meetings, or to do any Council business in the daytime during term.

On 19 May, he took part in the Rural District Council election and was not elected.

On 22 May, a governors' meeting was held. Ostensibly it was to discuss school progress, as usual. Alderman Maynard asked angrily why five boys and girls had chosen to stay on instead of leaving. He asked if they had done so 'because they liked playing about at school.' Mr Duane said they had stayed on because they were doing advanced work which they found satisfying.

Alderman Maynard asked why Mr Duane had not told the governors of any out-of-school activities. Mr Duane said simply because he had taken them for granted. He then listed some of them, including a visit to *Swan Lake*. Alderman Maynard then

asked whether Mr Duane thought *Swan Lake* was more educational than picking potatoes? Mr Duane replied that potato-
picking was educational only if it was part of the series of
processes – preparation of the ground, planting, and so on. Alderman Maynard then asked him to leave the room.

Nearly an hour later, Alderman Maynard said he could return,
and that the governors had decided unanimously they had no
confidence in him. It seemed a long time for a unanimous decision
to be taken.

The next month, June, the governors reaffirmed a formal
resolution of no confidence, and asked the education authority
to terminate Mr Duane's employment. Petitions from the parents
and the staff were ignored.

By now, Mr Duane was fighting a legal battle with the help of
his union and with Mr Arthur Skeffington as his Counsel.

The governors' resolution should have gone to the divisional
executive, and if upheld by them to the county council. Mr Maynard, however, seems to have regarded the divisional executive
stage as unimportant – in the sense that since many of the
governors were also on the divisional executive, he considered
this stage to be time-wasting. But there were some people on the
divisional executive who were not governors of Howe Dell and
who claimed the resolution in some anger, and – their attention
having been drawn to this point by Mr Skeffington – waited
formally for the governors to withdraw from the meeting before
voting. They stated that there was not sufficient evidence to
make a recommendation concerning dismissal and by eleven
votes to two recommended that no action be taken against Mr
Duane pending an early full inspection of the school by the
Ministry. This, oddly, seemed to have constituted no obstacle
to the governors' resolution demanding Mr Duane's dismissal
still coming up at the disciplinary committee of the county
council. (Mr Maynard was, of course, a member of the county
council.) Only John Newsom's personal intervention saved the
situation from becoming not merely unpleasant but public.

Mr Duane considered taking legal action. But a headmaster
who appears in a court case, even if he wins, would find it difficult
to get another job; and if he stayed at the school, he would still

have to work with the same governors and be tied hand and foot. Mr Newsom advised him to resign.

He resigned – and was immediately suspended with pay, for Alderman Maynard, in his capacity as chairman of the governors, did not want to wait for the end of term. Ironically, some weeks later, the Tories lost control of the Rural District Council.

Mr Duane left Howe Dell with a testimonial from Mr Bowmer.

I was a member of the interviewing committee at the time Mr Duane was appointed Headmaster of Howe Dell School, and was very much impressed by his personality.

Since then I have been very much interested in the way he tackled a difficult problem. This school was an educational experiment involving the bringing of children from a scattered rural area into a central town. The effect on both children and parents was even better than our wildest hopes. Apart from his exceptional educational ability and experience, Mr Duane has a quality of leadership which is rare even among headmasters.

He is thoroughly honest, reliable and sincere. I am sure that his pupils will gain strength of character as well as a keenness and zest for life. Mr Duane is convinced that in secondary schools lie the fundamental problems, educationally, of today, and the opportunity of doing worthwhile work. I entirely agree with him, and I shall watch his future career with great interest.

If Mr Bowmer was a representative member, it is evident that the aims and attitudes of the committee that originally interviewed and appointed Mr Duane were very different from the governors'. Mr Bowmer was evidently sincere, and it is a pity that his personal work with the education authority had not enabled him to have more frequent contact with Mr Duane. He was a member of the divisional executive and what might be called the Hatfield by-pass.

In Howe Dell, Mr Duane's dealings with governors and officials had been infuriating and frustrating, and the report on the school had been bad, yet his work with the staff, the children and the parents had been rich, satisfying and creative.

At Alderman Woodrow School, Lowestoft, his next headship, he had an excellent report; yet the richness and vitality were missing. He had hoped to get his teeth into something again and seems to have felt he was being fobbed off with blancmange. The inspector was friendly, the education officer was sympathetic, the chairman of the governors was disposed to be as agreeable towards him as towards his opponents; yet everything stayed on the surface. Discussions and arguments were about trivialities, with no echoes except those of querulousness, and manoeuvrings within the hierarchy were less flamboyant and less meaningful than at Howe Dell.

People say you have to live forty years in Lowestoft before you can talk to the people. It was a town where things moved slowly and without fervour. Fishing and ship-building were both low at that time; some people were poor and more than that number were out of jobs. But there was none of the violence, the problems that cry out to heaven, that he had met first in the country villages and then in the London school where he had taught for a little while after hurtling out of Howe Dell.

It was a Labour town in the middle of a vast Tory district, but it had no vision in it beyond next Friday's pay packet. The teachers and the educational hierarchy were still chuntering out a feud that went back to the days immediately after the Great War, when teachers had come out on strike and run their own schools in church halls. In 1944, after the Education Act, they had fought again, refusing to allow the county council to control its schools, and so Lowestoft was made an 'excepted district'. (It was an excepted district in another sense too – the education authority did not recognize the National Union of Teachers. How 'awkward' – authority's frequent word for Michael Duane – that Mr Duane became secretary of the local branch.)

It was a long-established school, the education officer told him confidentially, and he would need to go slow. In fact, people believe that he would never have got this headship at all, if Mr John Newsom had not thought he was the sort of head our schools needed, and said so.

At this school he inherited corporal punishment. That is to say, the previous head said to him, 'Of course, we don't use corporal punishment. We have a Punishment Book, but I can't remember the last time we used it.' Mr Duane had not met this gambit before and did not laugh.*

Once he started at the school, he found that boys were being caned in the classrooms, frequently, by practically every teacher, except the ones who had already caned so much that now their scowl was sufficient. They were not entering it in the book.

Mr Duane held a staff meeting. He said that he personally disapproved very much of corporal punishment, but wasn't going to make things difficult for the staff before they supported his ideas. All that he intended to do now was to make sure that all caning conformed to the Ministry regulations; that is to say, from now on he would take the responsibility for it.

This was received very coldly indeed. Some teachers ignored it. Once he heard a boy cry out in pain, and walked into the classroom and found a master beating a boy with the blackboard ruler; he took the boy straight out of the class and into his own study.

Later he discovered that this particular teacher, when Mr Duane had addressed the school at assembly, would take his class into his room, shut the door, and say, 'Well, you can put all that right out of your minds. He thinks he runs the school but he doesn't. He's only been here a year and he doesn't know what he's talking about. I'll deal with you the way *I* like, not the way *he* likes, and I want that understood!'

Others, less confident but equally belligerent, began storming into his study, hauling boys behind them for punishment according to Ministry rules. When Mr Duane asked them both to sit

* Michael Pollard in *The Teacher* (14 May 1965) wrote: 'I remember being taken along to one new junior school, where the headmaster much impressed my mother with his views on discipline. He had a cane, he said, but he couldn't remember the last time he'd used it. It must be at the back of his cupboard somewhere. This was a great relief to me, because the class teacher at my previous school had wielded rough justice with a leather strap which looked suspiciously like the property of the Southern Railway. I had been in the new school only two days when the head miraculously found his cane and began, perhaps with the abandon born of years of deprivation, to lay about him in all directions, a practice he continued with unabated fervour during the two years I was there. I had forgotten this incident, until not long ago I went to look at a school where I'd thought of taking a job. "I can't remember the last time I used the cane," said the Head. "I've got one somewhere, but by the time I found it I'd have forgotten who I wanted it for." I can almost swear that it wasn't the same man.'

down, and then, having heard the teacher's story, asked also to hear the boy's, the teachers considered themselves insulted. (The boy's story was referred to in advance by the teachers as 'a pack of lies'.)

But there were some teachers, mainly the younger ones, who found that sitting down in an armchair made them feel less angry, and even that listening to the boy's version made them realize they had made a mistake. They had the intelligence and the grace to say so. Several of these were Emergency Training Scheme teachers, who had experienced life and people outside the classroom; from teachers like these he began to get an understanding co-operation. But it was slow and frustrating. Once he asked the chairman of the governors to take action against a teacher who hurled hammers at boys in the workroom; but the chairman begged to be excused.

Alderman Woodrow Secondary Modern School was a boys' school only, but a girls' school shared the building. At one point in the corridor was a swing door which marked the barricade, and the door was continued on the other side of the wall, in imagination, across the playground. This invisible barrier, a peremptory slash through the air, was visible and even vociferous to all teachers.

To Michael Duane this seemed nonsensical, unnecessary and retrograde. Furthermore, it made for considerable practical difficulties, since the boys and girls were never supposed to meet within the joint building either. But even with the H.M.I.'s support he could not carry the day, and his suggestions that the two schools should combine were described as empire-building.

On one occasion the girls' headmistress insisted meaningfully that boys and girls had been playing together in the furze bushes at one side of the playground. It seemed a most masochistic place to choose, said Mr Duane incredulously. She said he was disgusting and vulgar, and had all the furze bushes cut down.

He managed to get G.C.E. work going for the first time in the school. And then he was struck by the odd fact that when 1,020 Lowestoft children, for example, would like to get into grammar schools, and there are only 120 places, it just so happens, miraculously, that there are exactly 120 children and no more who are academically suitable that year; and he wrote to the local press, the *Lowestoft Journal*, about it, a little sardonically.

The editor rang him back, and said 'Do you really want to sign this letter?'

Mr Duane said, 'Of course. What value is it unsigned?'

The editor said, 'All right. On your own head be it.'

It was indeed. The chairman of the Committee for Education denounced him for 'questioning my authority in public!' And the School Management Sub-Committee, in a report to the Committee, 'deplored his action in writing a letter which appears to question the accuracy of and to criticise a statement by the chairman'.

Whereas in Howe Dell the Tory technique had been to slash out metaphorically with a horse whip, in Lowestoft he was introduced to the new-style Labour technique of building an attractive 'image' in front of the facts. Mr Duane was depressed by the way adult prestige was considered more important than the children.

Two years later, the school had its inspection.

This is a good school. . . . The Headmaster and staff are to be commended for what they have achieved. . . . Throughout his term of office the Headmaster has had many difficulties to contend with, not the least of these being staffing problems. In spite of this, he has developed a good organisation. He is hardworking, able and thoughtful, and has high standards in many directions. With improved staffing, he has gradually, but surely, gained the confidence of the staff. The schemes of work, with their accompanying comments and guidance by the Headmaster, are remarkably comprehensive and helpful, and it is clear that his ideas have had a strong influence on the staff. The Headmaster undoubtedly knows his school and there is a good spirit in it.

It could scarcely have been better. John Newsom congratulated him on it. But Mr Duane felt it was time for him to go. Like the old man in the White Knight's song, he was beginning to feel he had put his fingers into glue. The friendly inspector said, rather regretfully, he was not at all surprised.

The place

The social challenge they have to meet comes from the whole neighbourhood.

Islington, as I said earlier, is not a district of delight – though, after the fashion of London, dream names may be given to nightmares. Who except a Londoner would expect Half Moon Street, a romantic reference to the beautiful curve of the pavement, to be made up of rotting gutted houses with rotting gutted cars outside? You stand there and stare at the shell of a house, and a neatly-dressed intelligent-looking young woman leans out of an upstairs window next door, in a piece of the terrace that holds together, and her face is silent and hostile. 'Live like pigs, don't we! Disgusts you, doesn't it! Go on, look! Look a bit more!' says her cold stare. So you move on.

And now you stand on a front doorstep, crowded in by two overflowing, stinking dustbins. On your left is the 'area' of the house next door, filled from basement to ground-floor level with rubbish and old iron – another gutted house, burnt out or bombed out, anyway a rotting crumbling shell, propped up only by a horizontal tree trunk along which an alley cat is delicately walking like a wild cat in a wild desolation.

But there are not only these decaying dumps in Islington. Very occasionally, round Highbury or Canonbury, in a sudden secluded square that you come on with a start in this district of murder, violence and prostitution, are cool, graceful, charming houses that might have been transported in a Heal's van from Hampstead or Highgate, St John's Wood or Chelsea, houses that have been bought up and given new and elegant life by writers, artists and actors with money to spend on them, houses that bizarrely have led to two restaurants in the antique market featuring in the *Good Food Guide*.

And in between there are respectable council flats, very good those that I have seen, but with rents that sometimes bring the grandmothers in to share, and drive the mothers out to work; yet the people who live in the council flats are probably happy with their mothers living with them, for it is part of their tradition. Perhaps it is Nan's importance in Islington that not only gives warmth and security to grandchildren who might otherwise have none, but also holds off new ideas.

But in Risinghill Street itself – another enchanting name – there are no glammed-up places. Coming from Chapel Street market, with the stained newspapers snarling like quarrelling dogs on your heels and the gutters running with the smell of fish, you would face Risinghill School.

On the right is the church on the corner, where the old men on assistance sat on benches, facing the pub, and watched the continuous deafening mind-blasting traffic go by; and in the bit of space left on that side is a large scattered ugly warehouse with dozens of smashed windows, empty and disused for years, until one year, 1964 or so, it began to tick over secretively again.

On the left is a soot-blackened wall with dead windows wired over, barred over, boarded over, iron-plated over; and adjoining that a four-storey block of stinking rat-ridden houses.

The best introduction to these houses is from someone who lives in one.

At the Town Hall they say 'You've got a roof over your head. You should be grateful.' I was born in this street. Do I have to die in it? I've looked at that church for twenty-three years and it doesn't get any better. Nobody knows what's happening. It's been going on for years. They don't even know we're living here.

Last year I had a miscarriage. I've had psychological treatment. The doctor told the Housing it was the way I was having to live. I do my washing in the sink, hang it up on the stairs. We live out of cases; there's nowhere to put up chests or cupboards.

We used to have this room [the front room] as the bedroom. We slept all together in one bed; there was no room for another. I had five sheets of brown paper and six plastic tablecloths pinned across the ceiling to keep the rain out. There were holes you could put your head through. One day I lost my temper and moved all the furniture round into the other room. I don't know how I managed it – I was so angry, I suppose.

Now we can have two beds. But what's it like between husband and wife when the children are in the bedroom with you, watching? You feel like animals.

The kids know everything that goes on; we can't keep anything private.

My little girl is six and she hasn't ever been able to play. She can't play downstairs because every car from the market parks in the street. I can't spend my life sitting on the doorstep watching they don't get killed. They play here on the stairs.

When I was little I played with other children. I had children in the house. These two can't.

They don't talk like children. The only way I got them in the nursery school was the doctor said they were so nervous because they never saw anyone. Now they're better – not frightened of people.

My husband goes out fishing every Sunday because he can't stand sitting in this place. He comes from a nice family. He was educated till he was twenty-one. We can never have relatives here – how can you sit people down to tea here? Four of us can hardly get round the table. Only animals live like this.

This time last year I couldn't stand it and I walked out. Fifteen days I was out; my husband was almost putting the children in a home. I lay paralysed on that bed for nine days; I couldn't move from the waist down. The doctor said I just couldn't stand living this way.

I've lost five stone in the last few years. The only places you can get in if you have children are places like this, or worse than this.

I don't know what we shall do this winter, with this as the living room. There's no room for a fire, no light.

The doctor wouldn't come up to see my daughter when she had quinsy; he said he wasn't risking his life. The old lady downstairs, smaller than me, the banisters broke and she fell down the stairs and broke her leg. She's been on the housing list twenty-five years.

We went on holiday. We had a brand new chalet – separate bathroom, running hot water, gardens, everything! My children went mad. They didn't want to go down to the beach, the sand, the sea, anything like that. The house and the garden were so marvellous to them. They never saw the sea – didn't want to.

You have to make four journeys to have one meal.

Before Christmas I went down to the Sanitary Department, and said the dustbins hadn't been emptied for five weeks. My sister's husband took a day off from work to clear out the basement; it was full of rubbish, and rats; it's condemned. My sister's toilet has never worked to my knowledge, but they use one in the yard. There's a broken sewer runs under the house – there's rats there.

There was mildew on the landing walls. Eventually the landlord started to clear it, but he never finished the job.

We've just cold water . . . and gas. I'd had an electric cooker, a washing machine, a Hoover, a Kenwood press. I can't use any of them. We had a carpet in the house when we moved in. After a year it was mouldy and we had to throw it away.

Whenever there's a gust of wind, the inside trap-door above the stove on the landing blows away and mice fall in from the rafters. And then the outside trap-door blows away, and the dirt and the rain pour in. I push it back with a broom. I keep plenty of Polyfilla to fill up the holes where the rats and mice come through.

The new ceiling the landlord has put in isn't even joined properly to the wall. And he didn't even pull the paper patch away and do the hole in the wall. He had a man five hours to do it, and my dad's been in the building trade over fifteen years and he said they needed two men for a fortnight on this job. He left plaster all over the walls for me to get off, and to redecorate. I've had rolls of lino standing in the toilet for two years and my husband says 'Why should I lay it? What's the use of it?'

I just want somewhere where I can have my own bedroom, where I can have a bath or go to the toilet without everyone knowing. I don't have to have something new. A seventy-year-old flat, anything, will do me. But they say I haven't got the right number of points. There are flats standing empty, but I haven't got the right number of points.

Where I lived before, they wouldn't deliver my baby at home because the place was so bad; we lived in the basement; and they wouldn't take me in the hospital. But apart from the basement those houses were fine. And now they're going to pull them down. We could be living in them. I wouldn't mind going back to that house – just not in the basement. But we haven't got the points.

She pays £3 10s. for this. She was unlucky – she came in a few weeks after the other tenants, who are paying about 14s. For this she is supposed to have two rooms and a kitchen and lavatory.

The stove is on the landing. On the half-landing below is a tiny room containing a sink, a small refrigerator, and, partially partitioned, a lavatory; a tin bath stands against the wall. There is no room for anything else there whatever. She fills the tin bath with cold water at the sink, carries it up the stairs to the stove on the landing, somehow gets it on to the stove, heats it, and somehow carries it into the living-room where someone can have a bath. She has an electric light bulb on the end of a long wire that she has run up from her sister's flat at the bottom of the house where, grotesquely, they have electricity; they lay it on the table. This is the room where the ceiling fell down. It's the room where the bed used to be. But one day she bent down to make it, and her head went right through the wall. She covered the hole over with a piece of paper to keep the draught out, so the man the owner sent ignored it.

You can put your fingers through the wall anywhere in the house. The tenants tie the loose gas-pipes to the wall with string.

The staircase is pitch-dark and crumbling (it took me a long time to go up and down it – I had to feel my way) and it is festooned with washing. This is the only place to hang the washing. But the children run up and down it like cats. This is where they play.

The condemned basement – a continuation of the six pitch-dark flights of stairs – stinks to heaven. There is no way of stopping children getting there, though her sister at the bottom has piled up anything she can lay hands on to block the way. The whole house stinks when it rains, like a fetid animal breathing. When I went there it was pouring, and the 'area' next to her house – it is in a terrace of four or five – was flooded deep in water, and five children were at the window gazing out on the stinking moat.

This young woman, despite everything, was intelligent, lively-minded, kind, not yet beaten down; but how long can you go on doing salvage operations on human beings, dragging them out, only knowing they will be drowning again any minute? Perhaps she is only all the things I have said because her doctor is giving her tranquillizers?

Only a minute's walk away, they built the new Risinghill School. I heard from some architects, friends of mine, about a new council estate that had a piece of modern sculpture set in front. The tenants, it seemed, complained; they didn't like it. The architect went down to talk to them, and because he was a genuinely progressive man he took the artist with him to explain to the people what the sculpture was all about. They both sincerely wanted to communicate with ordinary people, and they were happy to find themselves in jeans and big boots, covered with mud. When they had both finished speaking, one of the tenants said 'That's all right – we like modern sculpture. We understand very well the satisfaction of using everyday materials that belong to the area as a statement of art. What we're annoyed about is being stuck with a rotten piece like that when the estate up the road has got one that's really good.'

There are many people, and some of them are pleasant people, who are startled to find that the people they are explaining to have standards or opinions. It never occurred to the L.C.C. politicians (whose educationists, many of them, send their own children to public schools) that Islington people might not croon with pleasure at having their new school set in Risinghill Street.

They never considered the possibility that to working-class people in a country that is just beginning to move, socially, from feudalism, for whom social value and position has hitherto appeared to be ordained by God, a neighbourhood comprehensive school can look like a threat, that it can seem to be a cunning scheme to hold them back, a new way of trapping those who at last see a chance of getting out, the barbed wire beyond the cage.

They never thought that people do not really enjoy living among rats and broken sewers in semi-darkness, like modern cave-dwellers in the great metropolis, however much it may suit politicians – who themselves live more elegantly and have different worries – to feel sentimental about them.

This does not necessarily mean that such people want to move fifty miles away. But it does mean that they may want to move into a better street. At its most humble and despairing, it means 'I'd like to move into Barwood Street. I know the basements are condemned, but the upper parts are solid.'

I do not think that London working-class people of my generation – if I can presume to group any people together and give them one identity, which I know is spurious – like to move very far from the street where their parents lived and where they went to school themselves. For this is their only security – to go on living in the same street, till it crumbles around them, and the white buggy plaster dribbles incessantly into their food, and the gas-pipes hang loose from the wall.

Their children have begun to believe in themselves, and this, since it is the greatest, perhaps the only worthwhile, security of all, enables them to see all the others as unimportant; they – some of them – may begin to move away. And when they do, this bewilders and distresses their parents. (But fortunately many of the younger ones are not obedient enough, docile enough, or conscience-stricken enough to stay; and sometimes these set out thumbing rides to the ends of England, and across the sea, and to little islands off Spain and off Greece, where the sky and the sea are brilliantly blue.)

But the older ones stay in the same district with its 'slow decay' (a governor's words) and only think wistfully of moving into a better street where *part* of the house would be safe, or, if luck, in the form of the entirely magic and incomprehensible accumulation of 'points', allows it, into a council flat.

So our comprehensive schools, if they are to succeed, must be in one of the better streets. They must patently offer hope. (And this is more obvious, surely, while the public and the private schools continue in existence, emphasizing that for people with money there is no educational cage.)

But politicians of all colours tend to see people not as fellow human beings but as pawns in a chess game. And so in the cul-de-sac formed by the dead warehouse and the dead-alive houses, filled with cars and carts and barrows from the market, and sometimes with cars awaiting violent demolition or a slow passive dissolution, forming the dead end of it was the new Risinghill School.

It was intended perhaps to be dramatic, to show the New Jerusalem rising in the middle of squalor; but from the road it looked for all the world, when it was built, like an unwanted railway carriage abandoned for ever on a derelict industrial siding.

Some people have told me that the administrative side of the education service advised flatly against putting the new school in Risinghill Street, but the Labour politicians, enthusiastic for the glory they meant to win, beat them down; and that this division continued when the administrators saw the plans of the building and said it was 'unworkable' and again were beaten down. If this is true it would explain why the administrators (who controlled finance and labour) were so antagonistic to the school, so reluctant to give any help or make any adjustments asked for by Mr Duane; why should they work to prove themselves wrong? It would also explain why the politicians said bitterly not that Mr Duane had not built up a good comprehensive school but that he had not built up a 'good image' of a comprehensive school, not that he was no good as a headmaster but that he did not have 'the right aura for a headmaster', and that they were very very disappointed.

I have also been told that a meeting of H.M.I.s to discuss the building of schools in this area was so angry and disunited that two H.M.I.s walked out.

I have further been told that when Michael Duane's name went before the L.C.C. Education Committee as the choice of the governors (at that preliminary stage, 'the Advisory Board') of the new school, it was received with something of a clamour. The very discreet phrase someone used to me (a Labour politician speaking sadly of other Labour politicians) was that their objections were 'not very admirable, I am afraid'. It is likely and reasonable that the Lowestoft Education Officer in his confidential report should present Mr Duane – despite his fine inspection record – as awkward. But did people in London, weighing up this confidential report, know that many of the meetings of these two men were confrontations over union recognition?

I think indeed he was quite the wrong man for the purposes of both the administrators and the politicians (though the right man for English education). The administrators wanted someone who would keep a school quiet and orderly, a man who would only have to stroll through the playground and you could hear a pin drop; and the politicians wanted someone who could be manipulated or who at least would show he was grateful to be chosen. But long before the school opened, he had made it clear he was no manipulatee.

One of the schools that was to be incorporated in the new school, Gifford Secondary School, had been without a head for some time. Michael Duane had been given twelve months for working out the organization of Risinghill before it actually opened.* The L.C.C. then decided he could be head of Gifford at the same time. It did not seem to enter their minds he might simply decline, pointing out that he had been appointed head of Risinghill and that no mention of another concurrent headship had been made in the original advertisement, and that he would not think of doing anything but concentrate on making a success of Risinghill. They asked him several times, but he still said no, and went on with his organizing. So they angrily doubled the allowance of the deputy headmistress, and said she would be responsible for the day-to-day running.

The H.M.I. in the district, Inspector Clark, expressed considerable anger with Mr Duane at the time; he was to meet Mr Duane again at a critical moment four years later, with the same emotion but with better success.

As for the L.C.C., their anger simmered so unremittingly underground that five years later, when I asked at County Hall why Mr Duane had not been given another headship, and happened innocently to say that the amalgamation of four unwilling schools into the new Risinghill had made difficulties from the start, particularly as the toughest and roughest one had been without a head for so long, Mr Turner, the Assistant Education Officer, said furiously, 'Gifford did have a head! You're surprised at that, aren't you! He didn't tell you that, did he! Do you know who it was? It was Mr Duane!' He was supported in this statement by Mrs Leila Campbell and the Reverend H. W. Hinds, who were both new to this Department; the three of them made a little play of not being able to agree whether he was headmaster of Gifford for nine months or twelve. In fact he was not head of Gifford at all (I checked on this later) but the L.C.C. had intended he should be; and furthermore, if I had reported what they had told me, at this time when there was a lot of public sympathy for Mr Duane, it would no doubt have served to discredit him (for

*His headship officially began on 1 March 1959 (Risinghill opened in March 1960) and the L.C.C. specified that from that date he was to give full-time service as head, and 'would not be required to undertake any duties not connected with the work of the school'. They gave him a room at Gifford School to use as a base; in fact, he was not often there, spending his time at County Hall discussing and working out equipment, at all four schools interviewing all the staff, and at other comprehensive schools where he thought he could learn something.

they believed, incorrectly, when they spoke to me, that I was the regular correspondent of a national paper). But I am jumping ahead.

In 1960 then, four small schools came together, reluctantly, Gifford Mixed Secondary School, Ritchie Secondary School for Girls, Northampton Technical Secondary School for Boys, and Bloomsbury Technical School for Girls, joining a batch of eleven-year-olds coming from the primary schools. Apart from Gifford School which had had no head for three years, they had all had different heads and different staffs and different governors with different ideas, contexts, loyalties and traditions. Furthermore, the teachers of each school – and because of this the children of each school – had strong ideas about the status of their school as against the other three; and the head in each case had striven hard to gain that competitive status. Even the L.C.C. themselves called them 'disparate elements'.

Of the three heads, two came to the new school, which was unlike anything they had ever known, both philosophically and architecturally, for it offered freedom where they had thought always in terms of 'control', 'discipline', of locks and high walls. They came to positions which were both subservient to another head to whose philosophies they did not subscribe and yet of considerable importance. One of them certainly, both of them probably, came extremely unwillingly and unhappily. The authority appointed them to positions of importance before they appointed Mìchael Duane. Not only were they teachers whom Mr Duane would never have chosen to carry out his policy: they came to the school with no idea that they would have a head with a policy different from theirs, and who would need them to support such a policy, and even initiate it. They were probably told by the authority that the new head would need the help of their long experience, that the authorities were relying on them to keep the school firmly based, that they were the cornerstones of Risinghill. When, later, Michael Duane got the headship, I believe against considerable opposition, his opposers, perhaps even some of his supporters, must have thought the old heads would act as a brake. That this would mean that the school right from the start would be locked in an insoluble conflict, practically and psychologically, does not seem to have occurred to them.

And many of the teachers from the four staffs came too; in fact they formed nearly a half of the Risinghill staff, and, if County Hall had had its way, would have formed all of it. Some teachers were encouraged and promoted by Mr Duane and became, in many ways, more powerful than their ex-heads who were still with them; and such teachers would naturally tend to be ones whom their ex-heads had firmly and perhaps disapprovingly held down, with the support of the rest of the staff (who had also come to Risinghill).

Very many of them were not accustomed to working with adults, let alone children, of the opposite sex, and had not chosen to – and now had difficulty in doing so. In the Risinghill staff room, a teacher there told me, 'it was men at one end, and women at the other'.

The situation even before the rivalries and anxieties and difficulties of the children had been added was already very strained. It is not surprising that I was told that a good half of these transferred teachers were 'not easy' at Risinghill.

Although the L.C.C. firmly, even angrily, maintained to me that there is nothing at all unusual in putting four schools together to found a new one, and that there was nothing exceptional about Risinghill's start, I have not been able to find any other instance of it. Sometimes two schools have been put together, one large school that is moved into the building first, and then a small one which is absorbed. More rarely three schools have been combined. Teachers, hearing that Risinghill had been formed from four schools, rolled their eyes. One said to me 'How could anyone expect it to work!'

Another head told me that at one school where two previous headmasters had been brought in as 'underlings', the two of them had soon walked out of the school; and that after this the L.C.C. had decided to give 'displaced' heads new headships elsewhere. It was in a way quite an achievement that Risinghill's subservient heads did not walk out. Was it because women are more amenable than men? Was it due to Michael Duane's personality? Or was it because they were nearing retirement and in no position to be awkward to the pension-granters, and did this very fact bring its own resentments and calamities? Or was it because they had had certain calming assurances from educational officials?

The boys and girls came en bloc, that is to say at all ages and stages of development, each with his own previous personal experiences and his own personal brushes with authority and his own solutions, and with his own evaluation of adults and of himself. (But it is now generally recognized that new schools are best formed by taking a first-year group only, each year, and building up steadily into the new school's tradition. You can therefore go to new schools, and find in the first or second year that they are still, deliberately, half empty.) These children were the battered primary school children of my first chapter.

Many of them had been beaten at home, and many of those who were not beaten were neglected; so that many indeed had grown to think beating and violence were love. They had been shown over and over again that they were of no account; and hitherto education, which continued the beating, had also continued this grinding-down process, giving both however a high moral tone which their homes had spared them; the teachers in the district made grave absolute statements like 'Life is going to be hard and unpleasant for these children and the sooner they learn to accept this the better it will be for them'.

Ninety of them were already on probation for various offences, mostly 'breaking into and entering'. Many of them were in families that were being helped by Care Committees, by the N.S.P.C.C., by the Family Service Unit. (In 1963, a question in their English examination was 'What do you call a person who never eats meat?' One child wrote 'An old-age pensioner'.) A large number of them were badly disturbed.

No one had asked them if they wanted to come to Risinghill, or, one realized later, would have paid attention to their answer. Many of them had been uprooted once, years ago, when Risinghill primary school (now extinct) had been closed down and they had been sent to other primary schools. Now they had been uprooted again and brought back to one of the worst streets in the district. (Five years later, they were to be uprooted again, against their expressed pleas.)

The new school opened in May, and some of the children had only one term to go before leaving school; they were not likely to want to make any bonds from which, once more, they would only be torn away.

About a quarter of the children were not English. They covered in fact nineteen nationalities. Many of their families did not speak English, and were afraid of their children picking up immoral ways from English children. Many of the three quarters of the children who were English were not very enthusiastic about education.

A comprehensive school is supposed to have twenty per cent of its children in each of five different grades of intelligence. About half of Risinghill's children were in the lowest grade of all, and less than one per cent was in the top group. Within the neighbourhood the two Owen's Grammar Schools (with their 'top' reputation), the two Barnsbury Schools (old-established schools with 'tone', developed from the old central schools, which creamed off many children because they were both known as 'good' and yet were familiar to the parents), Holloway Comprehensive (which was based on a grammar school), Woodberry Down (set in an ambitious, intelligent neighbourhood and with enough Jewish children to run a separate assembly, one of the half-dozen or so comprehensives in London that are able to draw a full ability range), Giffard School (formed by Catholics, to use the old Gifford School premises with a slight change of name, and naturally drawing the Catholics), Starcross (a single-sex school with neat, uniformed pupils), and Highbury (which later, about the time of the Risinghill closure, was ordered to be amalgamated with Barnsbury, against the wishes of the parents who claimed they had been 'tricked' by the Education Authority) would inevitably draw the more intelligent children of ambitious parents away from Risinghill.

So most of the children were already outcasts, rejects, from all the microcosms of our society – whatever the impression given to readers of the *Daily Telegraph* on 5 March 1960 by a photograph of an impeccable-looking group of uniformed girls ranged round Michael Duane, the respectable 'right image' if ever there was one.

Since the L.C.C. had stated that the ratio of children in each ability group would be the usual twenty per cent, teachers for academic subjects had been engaged. When the position was found to be different, the staff could have been changed, but certain governors insisted on holding on to the academic staff as long as possible – useless, even perhaps unintentionally destructive, to the children. So these teachers found they had children of well below average ability in their A classes; understandably, they were bewildered, resentful, and frustrated.

Many of the staff were not interested in children like this; very few of them understood, or sympathized with, their background. Many of them in fact were not secure enough themselves to be of any use to such children, or to stand the strain of such an insecure environment. A district like this needed teachers who were mature* and well-balanced and who enjoyed life, rather than academic specialists.

It needed teachers who *enjoyed* the children, who knew they had grace, capability and tenderness, who saw them in their wholeness as young fellow human beings, not as lagging academic fragments. I believe every district, every school, needs teachers like this (but does our society supply them?).

A district like Islington can be locked in self-disgust. Before the war it was an appalling unemployment area, and parents who spent seventeen years on the dole (and I have heard of one who did) will talk about almost nothing else to their children; how else can they justify themselves, and in any case what else have they got? Parents talk to their children about the past, and their past is often the dole. The talk will be full of warnings; and their children may pity them but will often despise them . . . and despise themselves, for they were born from something despicable. These children in turn, when they grow up, often want the state to look after their children, for they do not believe that parents can. They need people who believe in them – not in the sense that they believe they can make them over into an approved

*Professor Carstairs, in his Reith Lectures in 1962, defined the mature person as someone who has: a realistic grasp of his environment, a sense of conviction about his own identity, an ability to cope with practical tasks, and an ability to establish deep mutual relationships with other people. Ernest Jones's definition was: someone who is able to give out love in greater measure than the need to receive it.

pattern, but in the sense, quite simply, that they *like* them. Academic teachers tend to like only children who are good at their subject.

Some of the teachers did like the children, and then they had a chance of doing their job well and even of being excellent teachers, but I believe they were in the minority; and although the staff were continually changing, this remained the position throughout the life of the school.

The building was a dismal failure. I had assumed that, since the architect had good intentions, what he was trying unsuccessfully to do with his numerous playgrounds and scattered buildings was to make small cosy units out of something overwhelming; but I have been told that mainly the awkwardness of the place was due to the struggle to build on a sloping water-logged site, and the insistence on doing all minor things cheaply. What the architect had produced was seven playgrounds with four (official) exits, and dismally drab buildings which incorporated six (originally eight!) dining rooms, for which meal tickets were to be issued separately in the assembly hall. Not only was the school graceless and stark; it was also impractical.

The entrance itself, from Risinghill Street, was almost indescribable. You could not believe it had been finished, that it was intentional. In perspective, it was a railway siding; from close to, a tradesmen's entrance. Mr Duane and the governors asked the L.C.C. at least three times, beginning over a year before the school opened, to buy the decrepit property in Risinghill Street, so as to put some spirit and joy and positive definition into the school entrance, but they did not. (Six years later, when they did this instantly for Starcross School, they flatly denied to me that Risinghill had ever asked them, and, by implication, that they had ever lacked enthusiasm.)

Despite all the exits, there was no gate large enough to bring in a vehicle. When a diesel roller had to be brought in to re-lay the playground surface, a twelve-foot hole had to be knocked in the wall. The men re-laid the surface, took out the roller – and remade the wall as it was.

There were scarcely any covered ways outside the school, and no covered playing space. The architect had forgotten it tends to rain in England. Water, water everywhere, nor any drop to drink. There was not one drinking fountain outside.

The cloakrooms were inaccessible from most of the teaching blocks, and were also insecure; for some time after the school opened, when workmen were still on the premises, unidentifiable people were coming in and out constantly; anyone could wander in. Things disappeared.

In these circumstances the children, who may not have had high marks academically but reacted sensibly to experience, began to carry their coats about with them or else wore them all the time. This angered many of the staff and inspectors; but it is worth observing that Dr Freeman, Islington's Medical Officer of Health, remarked in another context on the common practice among old people in Islington of wearing their coats indoors. The staff and the inspectors had not been brought up in districts where coats were stolen nor in houses where people died of cold, but these children had, and wearing coats indoors did not seem strange to them; it was very familiar. (Besides, anyone who knows slum children knows they wear their coats, necklaces, or caps, if they have them, like lifebelts – or like much smaller children everywhere will carry bits of old blanket around with them – desperately, as evidence of past or potential love or strength that might still tide them over . . . a private magic.)

The space at the top of the teaching block staircase, where any number up to 120 children might be milling round trying to change rooms, was less than 150 square feet, and even a saintly child if there was one would find himself shoving there. There was no soundproofing in the building; you could hear even conversations with startling clarity through the walls.

On a windy day the clock above every door was almost bound to fall off when the door was slammed; if it didn't, it stopped. (In 1965 I was in the school several times, and I never once saw a clock right.)

The glass panels were so large that if a window was broken twenty square feet of glass had to be replaced. (Nine tenths of the windows broken were broken out of school hours, sometimes by stones thrown by adults.) The L.C.C. refused to protect them with wire, and told Mr Duane to restrict the children's playing space. He refused, saying they had too little as it was. The glass in the doors too, as he pointed out, should have been wired; the regulations required them to be, but in fact they were plain glass; eventually a child put his hand through one and had to have twelve stitches in it. The place was like an oven in summer, a refrigerator in winter. But the most appalling thing was that the windows were made to slide open, leaving an open space of twenty square feet at waist height from the floor. They terrified the staff and fascinated the children.

Mr Duane asked for these windows to be altered in 1960, 1961, 1962 and 1963. By the autumn of 1961, he was asking the National Union of Teachers to help. He asked on the children's behalf and on the teachers' behalf. Eventually the L.C.C. made a half-hearted and useless attempt to do something as cheap as possible. Then, in 1964, a child fell fifteen feet to the ground. Several children saw him fall, or heard him scream. His father came to the school. The L.C.C. saw to the windows at last.

A lot of mistakes had been made, and not only architectural ones, some doubtless with the best of intentions. But authorities, while they like experiments which bring prestige, do not like experiments that really *are* experiments; they like them to be sure-fire. After all, they have spent money on them, and staked votes on them. For all these mistakes, made before the school opened, Michael Duane was going to have to carry the can. Unfortunately for the authoritarians he was not a man to carry a can quietly and respectfully, touching his forelock on the way.

The teachers

Both boys and girls will be faced with evolving a new concept of partnership in their personal relations.

Risinghill, like every school, has a Punishment Book. Risinghill's has one entry only:

Date	Name of child	Age	Form	Offence	Details of Punishment	Signature of master or mistress who inflicted the punishment	Initials of headmaster or mistress
18.5.60	John Roderick	13	D2	Theft	2 on seat	Andrew Thorpe	M.D.

This incident took place within a short time of the school opening, and was discussed at a staff meeting. Johnny Roderick came from Gifford School; the school faces Pentonville Prison, and while Johnny was in school, his father was frequently opposite – in prison for theft. He was there, in fact, when Mr Thorpe caned Johnny for theft.

The staff meeting decided it was wrong to cane a boy who was imitating his father; and that not only was corporal punishment wrong in this specific case – it was unnecessary, always. Mr Duane was not present at this meeting and he knew nothing about it, but when the decision was passed to him he was pleased. The next day, he announced to the assembled children that there would be no more caning.

Educated people today tend to see words as a shield against action. Many of the teachers had probably never thought of translating what they said into fact; they had merely been entertaining themselves with indulgent philosophy. When Michael Duane made his announcement, these teachers were angry, because they were frightened and because their ordeal had been decreed by themselves. They said nothing at the time, but much later they said 'We didn't mean you to tell the children', and

Michael Duane said, simply, 'But you are not doing away with corporal punishment unless you tell the children.'

The children were incredulous. To them the point of being big was that you could hit littler ones; adults at home and at school had always taught them that; it was the whole basis for growing up.

Michael Duane himself had no illusions about what would happen. He did not imagine that these children would instantly become grateful and angelic. If he had ever thought so in theory, he had all the experience of Howe Dell to teach him otherwise. But he believed that if we were to set human beings free we would have to put up for a while with all the scars of their slavery.

But not only the children, the adults too had to cope with freedom. How many of them could stand it? Most of the teachers had gone from school straight into training college, from training college straight back into school. Nothing in the imposed pattern of life had ever changed for them; they had only taken a step up the authoritarian ladder, so that when decisions were handed down they would not now be the lowest rank to receive them.

When Risinghill opened, a third of the staff vacancies were still not filled; this third had to be filled up with constantly changing supply teachers, and this situation continued pretty well throughout the life of the school. Getting a good staff was the central problem, and remained the central problem. Cyril Ray, the writer, who was one of the governors and took a very affectionate interest in the school, told me 'We had to accept people we knew were second-raters on to the staff – second-raters academically as well as personally', and, on another occasion, Mr Duane said 'All our problems of discipline and organization stemmed from this. They did not know how to deal with children who are uninhibited and therefore a threat to the authoritarian standard . . . and they were not trained for a big school where the head is not present as a perpetual father figure and continually within reach to sort everything out for them.'

When I went to the school, it was very evident that many of the teachers resented very much that he was a father figure to the children but not to them. Such a remark may come as a shock to people who do not accept that teachers are as neurotic as the rest of us today. On that occasion the staff of Risinghill seemed to me to divide into three; and I suspect they always did.

Some were very good, generous and imaginative. But they were in the minority, and were being fought by other staff as well as by the environment (though the environment was not the deliberate enemy that some of the staff were, but rather a material that they had to learn to work creatively with). Because of this, and because they were creative people, they were frequently exhausted. They brought to the school their own individual ideas, and their own appreciation of, and pleasure in, the children. They were mature human beings. They would have been an asset anywhere. At Risinghill they were gold, because they gave equal friendship to children who had known very little of it and only knew adults as enemies. They could walk alongside the children; they knew, as so many teachers do not know, that children do not have to be battered and badgered and hectored and moulded, but that they simply have to be helped to grow by people who have faith and delight in their growing. I have called them child-centred teachers.

Some teachers did not want freedom at all. Some of these were old and some were not; but they had long ago surrendered their personality, the wishes and beliefs of their own personal life. If anyone were to question the validity of this sacrifice they could not have borne it, for it would have meant their whole life had been wasted; and who can bear to think of the waste of what will never come again? So they could not stand seeing children saying and doing things that they were never allowed to say or do, or watch them beginning to frame possibilities that for them were crushed in childhood, and not always (eventually) by other people; and there was not only resentment and jealousy in this, but a hopeless sense of waste which they could never face. So they told themselves that children should be quiet, that they should be so afraid of you that you should be able to hear a pin drop when you crossed the playground, that children were naturally bad and needed the badness beaten out of them, that individuality must be crushed down by will-power, and that there was satisfaction in this, and that God would reward people who kept their desks tidy, their lines straight, and never splashed outside the lavatory bowl. Such teachers do not make schools into joyous places bubbling over with vitality, and do not intend to; and in fact if you hint at such possibilities they will say contemptuously 'Well, of course, if you think that a school is a place where you *enjoy* yourself . . . !'

Everything and everyone had its one proper place for people like this. They said things like ' I've never taken work home before and I'm not going to start now.' They were astounded at the mild suggestion that they might be friendly with the children's parents.

In fact, informality altogether was to them a very suspect quality indeed. So you would later get Inspector Macgowan condemning Mr Duane's familiarity to the children, and his familiarity to his staff. So you would get Mr Carr accusing Mr Blaize of 'immoral purposes' because he was taking some boys on a camping weekend.* Such teachers had never seen their pupils as fellow human beings before, as Martin Buber's ' I ' and ' Thou ', and the very suggestion of it unnerved them as much as if they were Southern whites and the children were Negroes; and in the same way many of them translated it sexually.

They were used to a system where you were *told* by the person above you, and then you *told* the person below you. (A teacher told me that he went to a weekend conference where teachers, Institute of Education lecturers, and training college lecturers led discussions; but that the training college lecturers took it as a personal insult when students in the body of the hall questioned what they had said, so that discussion was impossible.)

Such teachers went their own way. Since Michael Duane had, in their sort of language, ' demoted ' himself by being friendly to them, and friendly to the children, and friendly to the parents, they ignored him. At least one of them (several of them, according to the children) went on caning; and at least one of them 'shut the classroom door firmly' every day on all that rubbish. (Mr Carr used to say to his class 'Don't worry, I'll cane you before Mr Duane gets to you'.) But though they tried to ignore him, the fact that their new head did not approve of the outlook that had hitherto brought them full marks, was emotionally exhausting.

---

* See the example the teaching student contributes in 'Last words – for the moment' (p. 273).

I have called them the traditionalists, disciplinarians, authoritarians.

But a third section had first been bewildered, and then, under the influence of Michael Duane's personality, decided of their own accord to try to do what *he* wanted – to help him to accomplish *his* aim. These teachers took Michael Duane's warm spontaneity personally, so that they felt their work was a symbol of a special relationship between them; and when he merely took their work with a quick 'Thanks', or 'Right you are', they felt rejected. Simply because he did so much, they assumed he meant them to lean on him; and when he showed that on the contrary he expected them to stand on their own feet and make their own decisions, again they felt humiliated. So then they began to say things like 'He takes us for granted', and 'He cares more for the children than for us', and – astoundingly – 'We have the right to be led' (each of which statements has been made to me, the first two by several teachers).

In their immaturity and their sudden freedom from the chains – and the certainties – of authoritarianism, these teachers found it very difficult to accept that he expected more strength from them than from the children. They were in a continual state of conflict. You would find such a teacher flaring off in an appalling outburst against coloured children, and, reprimanded for hitting a coloured child, saying 'Well it doesn't hurt them like it does white children!' . . . and then taking some children away on a trip entirely in his own time and at his own suggestion. Children would tell you of another, 'He has no control over his class. They just walk out of his class and he spends all his time trying to find them. We just laugh at him' – and you would find that sometimes this man would speak with sentimental philosophy of the needs of the children, that at other times he would attack the children in front of the press . . . You would find another treating the children with contempt, cutting destructively through their intimate, troubled conversations – then inviting a group of them home to tea. Such teachers thought of themselves as quite different people from the people they really were. They would describe their philosophic ideas glowingly, so that when you saw what they really did you were shocked; yet occasionally they actually *did* what they thought they were doing all the time, like a clumsy child who for a second manages to fit his tracing over the first colourful picture; these moments must have been very satisfying for them, for the children loved them at such times and, generously, forgave and understood a great deal.

But they would do destructive things and constructive things quite unpredictably. And since their conduct was based on the unconscious treasuring of Michael Duane as an adult's father figure, and since he refused, with some amusement, to be an adult's father figure, they too were exhausted, filled from day to day with frustrations, resentments and anxieties, which they took out on the other teachers, on the children, and at critical times on Michael Duane. Personally, in the particular context of Risinghill, this group alarmed me. For such people, being anxious, often lean a great deal on authority, and can therefore be easily made use of and manipulated by an authority which despises them. Such people can do a great deal of damage without ever intending to, or even being aware that they are doing it; and when it is done they are appalled.

One of the Risinghill staff said later to me:

In such a building, and with such a background, the children would only behave well if they *supported* the staff; the staff who believed they could rely on force were relying on a fallacy. But it was so difficult for Michael Duane to convince them, because this was so new; there was no research to support him.

And also, at the beginning of Risinghill, the staff knew nothing of the difficulties other comprehensive schools had had. After the Kidbrooke affair, the L.C.C. invited reporters to go into selected comprehensive schools; and it was only then that one heard of difficulties that had had to be met elsewhere in the first year, and knew that Risinghill was not unique. We should have had this explained beforehand, by the inspectors – or else, as they knew this, the inspectors shouldn't have given us such a bad start.

I knew they were children who would not normally be interested in reading. But I had the idea, as so many do, that if you are simply pleasant, the children will instantly respond. But in that first year, the children didn't; they were very hostile to anyone in authority. And teachers from grammar schools – and people like me – were very hurt that their desire to help should be rebuffed in this way. We didn't realize then that their previous schools had been broken up in the same way; now we know ourselves how they must have felt twice over. I suppose the hostility extends to their homes as well as their schools. It seems to me fantastic that the authorities should not have realized the resentments and difficulties when they first uprooted these four schools and put them together.

The teachers felt inadequate, and looked for someone to cope with their problems for them, and when this wasn't done looked for a scapegoat. Some of the *most experienced* teachers told me they expected things to be sorted out for them. I even sometimes felt this myself though I didn't say so.

I don't think we were able, most of us, to identify with the children's future, and to know what their adult life was going to be like. We were terribly in the dark. We had to keep going back in our minds and trying to think what life should be like, and how different the life we were thinking of was from the life the children were thinking of.

The teachers who wanted only to teach specific subjects were very hurt because what they felt they had to give seemed often so inappropriate. What the children needed one often did not know. What one had to give did not fit – it was often what one had wanted oneself, but one's life had been so very different from these children's.

Why should teachers expect every child immediately to respond to them and be attentive? When the child doesn't, the teacher becomes so hostile that caning follows.

Some teachers knew they couldn't play the 'family' part demanded of them. Others tried, and went to the extreme and became too emotionally involved. It would have been much easier with children from good homes. But do we then intend to give good education only to children from good homes?

In fact, the children from good homes responded well, and became very co-operative, and wonderfully tolerant of the difficult children – it amazed me. I felt that many children had *benefited* by the responsibility they had taken for other children. Ben Andrews, for instance – during his holidays he worked with a playgroup, and was appointed over the heads of grammar-school children because his attitude to younger children was so good. An inspector coming to a school wouldn't see this, and wouldn't talk to the children; I think he might think it unethical.

I think perhaps Mr Duane felt his duty was more to his pupils than to his staff. Sometimes a teacher became upset, and wanted to be put first; then the teacher didn't want impartial fairness, but comfort. I know this is irrational, but in a place with such emotional pressure it tended to happen.

It would be unreasonable to expect teachers to be less neurotic, less unstable, less psychotic than the rest of the population of London today, and I do not do so. We are all suffering from the strain of contemporary society. But it may possibly be that teaching attracts more than its fair share or having attracted just a fair share gives power and approval to their neuroses. . . . And besides one needs to be well balanced to keep one's optimism in an area like Islington (though one must remember that areas like Islington are where most of London's citizens live).

Yet if we looked for teachers among those who loved their fellow men as well as pensions, and among those who were adventurous as well as afraid, the quality would improve. But we would then have to face the fact that un-neurotic teachers might want to carry out un-neurotic education, and that would make a deep upheaval.

I asked several of the child-centred teachers what proportion of the staff they thought any use at Risinghill. Estimates varied from a generous 'less than fifty per cent', through 'twenty per cent', down to 'six out of seventy'.

Apart from keeping his day as clear of paper-work as possible, so that he always had time to discuss difficulties and successes with his teachers, Mr Duane organized very frequent staff discussion meetings – two a week to start with, so that everyone would be free to come at some time. At first sixty teachers used to turn up to each discussion. One teacher said she went over to the lavatories and found some girls there smoking, and when she told them off they said . . . something . . . well, she couldn't repeat it. 'But what was it?' he asked. She said 'No, I couldn't possibly tell you.' He sensed it was really something *she* wanted to say through their mouth, and he said 'Was it something about me? If it was, say it – I'm used to hearing rude comments.' So she said 'They said "That silly old bugger won't mind!"' He laughed; he was genuinely pleased because he was getting some truth, and because the teacher had found a way to release some hostility undangerously.

But one of the senior members of staff became very distressed and anxious, and would not stay at meetings where junior members of the staff were permitted to say whatever they liked, and this teacher gave very emotional reports on such meetings to County Hall, who didn't like it either.

County Hall did not have to worry. The discussions were broken up by the teachers themselves. A group of men teachers from one of the four original schools pushed corporal punishment as the solution to every problem, at every meeting; and after weeks of this incessant drumming, the rest of the staff was bored and angry, and refused to come any more. The discussions had been broken up by imposed force, of which corporal punishment is, after all, merely another facet. From then on, the only discussions that could ever be held were casual, spontaneous ones in the head's study, and in these, naturally, only already sympathetic teachers were participating: the others were so embarrassed and disturbed by informality in surroundings that they felt should be august (people actually drank wine as they talked!) that they kept as far away as possible.

Later, I was very puzzled to hear his staff complain Mr Duane did not give them leadership. I had never come across a school where the head initiated, or tried to initiate, both spontaneously and with specially duplicated papers (of a standard incidentally so thoughtful that I fancy this too rather narked some important people), so much discussion about policy and methods. Afterwards I realized that many of the staff did not want discussion – they wanted to be 'told'; and secondly that they wanted to be led in a completely different direction from the way Mr Duane was going. This is what 'no power of leadership' meant, a phrase which later on the L.C.C., pulling determinedly in the opposite way to him, was to use too.

Furthermore, Mr Duane himself, like all or almost all the adults around him, had also been brought up by authoritarians. But unlike most of them he had not succumbed, and had preserved his honesty. He was resolved that no child should experience the humiliations, the violence, the undermining of integrity that he had experienced, but should instead be allowed and encouraged to grow from his own inner source. All this made him a person of tremendous value to growing children, and to education in practice. But from his own fight with authoritarianism, he still retained, at this stage, a weakness. He was over-concerned that all adults should understand what he was doing and concede that it was good. And this made him try over and over again to win over those teachers who were against him, rather than face up to the fact that they were incompatible, and he must make them go. It was this quality that was to vaguely irritate Inspector Macgowan, so that he complained in his 1962 report that Mr Duane 'esteems cordiality among the major virtues'. But the inspector thought that if Mr Duane could demolish this 'cordiality' in himself he would treat the children differently; in fact, he would have treated the staff differently, those who opposed his creative approach, and *just possibly* this might have saved Risinghill.

This was a wild time. The children found it difficult to believe that Mr Duane had meant what he said. They tested him, they tested the other teachers. Some of the teachers felt they had been cheated anyway, tripped up by their own willingness to give an opinion which their training and service had taught them was a dangerous thing to do. Several went on caning, and the L.C.C. Inspector, apprised of this by Mr Duane who asked for disciplinary action, would do nothing about it. Every time a teacher did cane, the testing time was made a little longer.

The teachers who were frightened of children either caned them or fawned on them. The children used the word 'soft' for both these types of teacher; they were unerring in this summing up. But Michael Duane (at any rate in my experience, though one good child-centred teacher who warmly supported Mr Duane queried this) they did not consider 'soft'. One boy said to me 'Some of them come from schools where they used the cane, and they reckon you can't manage without it. Trouble is they don't get trained for this kind of school. They're too soft. If they were all like Mr Duane, this would be a terrific school.' And another told me 'Mr Duane has proved that if you don't use the cane, people respect you. The pupils respect him. It's the *teachers* who think he's soft not to use the cane – not the pupils. Things are much better here now – people behave better.'

Cyril Ray said to me 'Mr Duane told me how a boy waiting

outside his room to see him was beaten up to teach him not to
crawl to the head; and a man who, in the circumstances, decided
to face violence with deliberate non-violence, since to face it with
violence merely demonstrated that violence pays, was in my
view absolutely magnificent.'

Boys were indeed often beaten up, at the beginning, for telling
Mr Duane things, and he was much aware of this danger, and
concerned for them. Children would come to him, obviously
under a great emotional strain, saying they wanted to tell him
something, 'but please *please* don't let anyone know it was me
that told.' He always assured them that he wouldn't, and would
go to great trouble to find an alternative source for the same
information, so that if it was necessary to back it up he could do
so without bringing the child in. As for the children who did the
beating up, he would talk to them, talk and talk; 'What else can
you do? What is the sense of you beating *them* up? Then there
is no end to it. You must simply talk and talk and talk without
ever getting tired.'

One day a boy came to school feeling murderous. It had begun
the previous day, after school. The events of these children's lives
were the events that have made blues and folk-songs and ballads,
and at this safe move from reality middle-class adults will view
them with equanimity, nostalgia and a sense of beauty. So I
jotted down a somewhat altered version of this incident to be
sung to the tune of 'If I had the wings of an angel'.

> My friend, oh my friend he is Joey,
> And my girl she is Mary Malone,
> Oh it's women who cause all the trouble
> Because they won't let you alone.

> We walked after school through the market,
> And we lingered and lingered outside,
> With the barrows piled up in the middle
> And the homes falling down at the side.

> We climbed in a big empty barrow,
> And the cider was golden and cool,
> And drinking three bottles of cider
> Is something to do after school.

Oh my mother she works as a cleaner,
My dad is a betting man,
My sister's a slag* in the market,
And I do the best that I can.

My mother's a couple of husbands,
My sister has any lad,
The baby belongs to my sister,
But I know my own true dad.

It was cold, so I lay down on Mary,
It was cold in the barrow that day,
So I started to love up my Mary,
And Joey he pulled me away.

He shouldn't have treated me roughly,
He shouldn't have handed me blame,
He shouldn't have pulled me off Mary
And called me a dirty old name.

The church struck ten when we parted,
And Mary she cut round the stall,
And Joe walked the stinking alley,
And I climbed the gap in the wall.

The chopper I took in the morning,
It was one of my father's own tools,
I took it from under my jacket
And I followed my Joe round the school.

Poor Joe he was scared of the chopper,
He ran like a whippet, and cried.
He ran through the door of the classroom
And the blade split the door outside.

Oh Joey, oh Joey, why did you?
Why were you so unkind?
You knew I was drunk on the cider,
You shouldn't hit a friend when he's blind.

Oh Joey my friend, how could you?
You made my blood run cold,
I was only loving up someone
Who scarcely is twelve years old.

*A prostitute.

It's women who cause all the trouble,
It's them get you caned at school,
And when you get sent off to borstal
They've a new boy to make look a fool.

And when you're grown up and you're married,
They take the whole of your pay,
And you slave out your guts in the market
While they lie in bed all the day.

I emphasize that I have changed the details; they are not a description of the family involved. I have even altered some of the details of the actual events – the boy in fact did not follow his friend into the classroom. But I think I got down the attitude accurately, and I came on this attitude a good deal in Islington. In actuality, 'Joey' came to Mr Duane, very distressed, and said 'Robert's after me with a chopper.' Mr Duane left Joey in his study, found Robert and said 'Robert, give me that chopper.' To his huge relief, Robert went instantly to his locker, and took out the chopper – a very competent-looking hatchet – which he laid silently in Mr Duane's grip.

Not wanting to leave the two boys together in the school in his absence – he was due at the juvenile court where another of his boys was appearing (he always attended and did his best to explain what they had done and why) – Mr Duane told them to jump in the car, and they talked the matter out as they went along. When he got to the court, he gave them a pound note, and said 'Spend the day out. Take a boat on the river, or go to some museums – do something you've always wanted to do and enjoy yourselves. See you at school tomorrow.' When he got back to school a little while later, to his surprise he found the boys there. They were cheerfully and amiably friendly, and have remained so ever since ... though 'Joey' when I last saw him was still anti-girl and told me that it was a girl who had knocked out 'Robert's' front teeth.

That first year was the year of the gang fights. The boys of Risinghill came from Northampton, a boys' small technical school, and Gifford, a large mixed. Because the Northampton boys were older – they tended to stay on at school a year or two past the school-leaving age – they were chosen as prefects at

Risinghill. Furthermore, they were well-spoken, and had always worn uniform, which meant they were different from the Gifford boys, readily identifiable, and an easy focus for anger.

The Gifford boys brought their own leaders with them – Tom, a neat, carefully dressed boy, and Sam his lieutenant, more dishevelled and hoarse, together with a close guard of four or five, and a very large and more fluctuating crowd of supporters. They must have resented going from a school where their authority was undisputed to a school where, judged most fairly, everyone was starting again equally from scratch and, judged at the worst, where other boys, prissy uniformed strangers, were given control of them. Furthermore it seems to me this group of prefects, cohering, acting together, and powerful, must have seemed to them only a rival gang, and what is more a gang unfairly and arbitrarily backed by higher powers.

The Gifford gang began to demonstrate that they were not to be treated as kids, by dropping out of lessons and, soon, out of school. There were four exits apart from unofficial ones, so disappearing, in the early days when people wanted to disappear, was always easy; at Gifford, an older building, this could never have been done. The possibilities must have appealed at once to their resentment. This demonstration went on through the first term of the school.

In the second term, things got more dangerous. The prefects, coming back to school after the summer holidays (the school actually opened in May), felt more self-confident and ready to govern. Within one day, two events twisted the tension unbearably tighter (apparently set going by 'a row over a couple of girls', though this was only mentioned once, very unwillingly, to Mr Duane by Tom). The prefects had taken over a room for themselves, which had infuriated the Gifford gang. That particular day, wielding a bicycle chain, Tom drove Mike, one of the prefects, back into the Prefects' Room and virtually kept him prisoner. The same day, a group of prefects harangued Tom and Sam threateningly, in front of a crowd of about two hundred in the school playground, telling them plainly they'd 'do 'em'.

This day began a series of furious incidents, which nevertheless never resulted in any *person* being seriously hurt. Bulbs were stolen, door handles unscrewed, roller towels set on fire, mirrors smashed. (Not all of this was done by the gang, and not all deliberately; some was done absent-mindedly, by adults as well as children. Mr Duane reported seeing a fifteen-year-old talking earnestly and simultaneously cutting the paint off a pillar so that it formed a pattern, and seeing an adult, similarly talking intently, picking out the putty from the window-frames. The gang was not responsible for all the damage that occurred at this time, but they were responsible for most of it.) Yet no human being was badly harmed . . . even though these were children set against authority, who were even, some of them, trained for crime by their parents (some of the Gifford gang were on probation because they had been organized to do a job by one of the fathers who landed himself in jail), even though their groupings included Cypriot refugee children whose parents, brothers and sisters had sometimes been killed before their eyes and for whom fighting was therefore murderous, even though in the neighbouring district bloody racial riots were taking place and in their own streets swastikas were chalked on the walls. . . . Yet these children who were constantly working themselves into white-hot feuds never in fact hurt anyone really badly. The worst that happened was that a boy's face was scratched – only scratched – by a *safety* razor; and that happened one evening after school.

Going over records of these events I have wondered and been intrigued over the way everything constantly petered out. And it seemed to me it was because the inflammable ingredient which would normally be present – adult provocation – was here lacking. Children are very easily provoked into doing silly, sometimes dreadful things, and adults – teachers, parents – very frequently provoke them. But all the usual adult provocations – caning, calling in the police, shouting, threatening, forcing into corners – was not supposed to take place at Risinghill, and, as far as Mr Duane was able to control or choose his teachers, did not take place. (I remember that during the period of the gang fights some of the boys of the Gifford gang maintained with white-faced sincerity that not only did the prefects threaten to beat them up, but that a particular teacher egged on the prefects; Mr Duane called a special brief staff meeting and emphasized that, however furious the teachers might find themselves growing, 'any breath of a suggestion that we contemplated or sanctioned violence, however well-intentioned, would simply undo in a moment everything we were trying to build up.' Of course to some people this merely showed 'he did not back up his teachers'.)

When Tom, some time afterwards when he had left school, was asked what broke up the gang feuds – particularly the racial fighting – he said simply 'We needed them, to make up our football side.' At one time during this period, if asked the same question Mr Duane would probably have said it was the School Council that did it, for at this time the spluttering flame of the School Council suddenly flared up candidly (the majority of the staff quickly decided they preferred darkness and smothered it; but that comes later). At the School Council, the gang fighting was discussed, and it was here that the groups pledged themselves not to fight any more but to bring all disputes to the Council. Even Sam, who was reluctant, saying disarmingly when amiably questioned, 'Well, I like a punch-up!', decided finally, without pressure, to give his word. For the first time the School Council, an entirely new and alien element to these children of violence and no account, had a real issue to deal with, and it thrived on it.

But all these possible reasons for the disappearance of violence mean only one thing. The pupils had creative relationships *demonstrated* to them; they saw the value of them in action, and it made sense.

After the Council meeting, Tom exchanged his power to bring crackling chaos in an instant for the slow pleasure of affectionate co-operation. A word from him stopped a racial fight that was teetering on the edge. One day he came to Mr Duane with a couple of hammers which he had taken from two boys who were beginning to smash up the wash-basins. Tom brought them doubtfully, worriedly, almost furtively. But Mr Duane never trumpeted abroad his new virtue, as another headmaster might easily have done, setting all nerves jangling again. He received the hammers as one receives a small gift or small service from a friend.

When Tom left school, after his one year at Risinghill, he sent his kid sister away on her school journey to Spain. The £27 she needed had been saved entirely by Tom.

One day, a woman who did domestic work in the school came to Mr Duane, very distressed. Her basket, filled to the top with shopping, had disappeared. He instantly made an emergency announcement to the school. He explained to the children that the shopping was for her family, that she had spent all her money on it, and now her family would have to go hungry – for days, maybe – if it wasn't returned.

Two boys came to him, shamefaced, and said they had taken it.

'Where is it? We must give it her back.'

'Well, we can't; we've eaten most of it.'

'All right. Take this pound note. Go to the market, try and remember every single thing that was in the basket, and fill it up again. Let her have it all back as quickly as you can – she's upset. Then come back here and we'll discuss how you're to refund me.'

They took three weeks to pay him back from their pocket money.

There was no anger, no contempt, no moral pressure in this solution, but only a desire to make the concern of everyone for everyone manifest, and to help children instantly to right the wrong they have done so that they can feel at one with the world. (What price the cane? One might compare this episode with an episode I heard today of a boy who was thoroughly thrashed by his headmaster, got up and said coolly, 'And do you expect me to behave differently now?')

At Risinghill one began to see a developing back to the concern of one person for another that so often adults, who themselves have been warped, will over and over again warp in children. Mr Blaize told me how once, faced with a difficult child in his class, a girl who endlessly caused trouble, he eventually threw her out. (She was a child who should have gone to a special school. A large number of children at Risinghill were waiting for places in special schools that were never forthcoming.) Then when he became calmly and fully aware of what had happened, he realized it was not the girl's behaviour that had upset the class, but his own; that the class had reacted hostilely against his own rejection of the girl, and that he would have done better to have worked with the class to help the girl.

This concern of children for each other is a wonderful power for growth; I have often wondered if teaching students are taught in training colleges to build on this natural humanity; I doubt it very much.

(Authoritarians who hate any action to be made 'outside the usual channels', who hate children to move out of their desks, or – if out of doors – out of an orderly file, who hate adolescents to be 'unattached', that is, not on the membership of some named club, often however do not at all like people to be genuinely *attached*, attached to each other that is, because this, they feel, takes them instantly out of the control of authoritarians. It is a very sad business.)

I remember once, when I was with about ten two- to four-year-olds, one of the little girls, Susan, started screaming. Children of this age do have fits of temper and screaming, and adults generally hit them for it. In Susan it reached an intensity of passion that I had never seen before. She was beside herself, quite out of her own control, and was screaming no longer in fury but in terror, screaming to be saved from herself; when I looked at her, I knew at once what the Bible meant when it said someone was possessed. She would do this when she was frustrated – by her own weakness, or by someone, out of friendliness, helping her. Joe, a child who loved her and whom she loved back, had done some service for her; and it was something she had intended to do herself. Her screams paralysed the whole room.

I scooped her up in my arms – very difficult to do, for she was thrashing about violently and convulsively – and managed to sit down and clutch her on my lap. 'Susan is upset,' I said to the amazed silent children. 'We'll sing to her until she feels better.' And the children gathered round and sang.

They put down everything they had been absorbed in, and came and stood by Susan. Now and then they would put out a hand and touch her back, delicately and reassuringly. At first, she would stiffen against it hysterically and the screams would get louder, and I would wonder if it was wise; but the children knew best, and they would gently do it again, singing sweetly all the time; and after a while she began to enjoy their friendship and to bask in it as if she were lying in the sunshine.

Just for a few seconds she lay on my lap, quite tranquil and quiet, and I put my cheek against hers. 'There!' I said. 'We've helped her feel better.'

She jumped up, flashed a radiant and very shy smile at everyone, and went back to her game, humming to herself; and everybody else did the same; nothing was ever said about it. I learned a great deal from those children, not only that day but every day; and if I were running a school I would not have any adult in it who was not open to learning constantly from children.

Such growing concern for others was evident to anyone who visited Risinghill and who was open to it. Unfortunately many of the teachers and other people in positions of power were not open to it. One of the inspectors, who maintained that six of the best would cure almost anything, seeing a nuclear disarmament symbol chalked on a playground wall, was heard to exclaim furiously 'I'd sooner see four-letter words [chalked on the wall] than that!' That was his angle.

A traditionalist teacher at the school was amazed to hear how friendly and helpful I found the children, later on. She despised me for it – thought I was unbalanced perhaps; she herself thought they were dreadful, but did not expect them to be anything else; she handed them religious exhortations, but she had no faith in them and did not see the grace they had. 'For children like this, the world is a hard place,' she said, 'and the sooner they learn it the better.' When I said 'But the world is not static. The world is what we make it. And these children are some of those who are going to make the world, surely, who are going to change it,' she looked at me for a moment; 'Yes,' she conceded eventually, 'the world does sometimes change.' And on this note of complete passivity, we parted. Not 'Yes, children do change the world.' But 'Yes, the world does sometimes change. . . .' Why do not religious people feel that to stamp on any of God's work, to neglect deliberately to bring it to full flowering, is blasphemy?

Some of the political governors too saw the devil in the children constantly. Partly of course they were influenced by the open site of the school, which spread out all deviations from conformity before everyone's eyes; they were public relations people, as so many politicians are nowadays; they saw votes being lost on all sides. Such governors would speak bitterly of untidy playgrounds, full bins, and running shouting children. One of them, coming into school after hours, when the cleaners were sweeping out the rubbish and putting it into boxes, looked at the boxes – empty cardboard cartons – and said sternly to the astonished women 'This is what gets the school a bad name!' I cannot remember now whether it was the same one, or another, who once stood beside Mr Duane, looking out into the playground, and was enraged. Though Mr Duane stared, he could not see anything dreadful happening, though the governor kept urging him to see to the matter at once. Eventually, the governor dashed into the playground, and hauled two boys out of it and into the study. 'There!' It seemed that one of the boys had been swinging the other one round, helping him on his way with a foot. Mr Duane stared at them, thinking the boys must believe he had gone out of his mind, and wondering what on earth he was supposed to do to 'discipline' two children who were obviously, judging by their giggles, amiably and cheerfully disposed towards one another. 'Well, Christos,' he said at last, groping for words, 'why were you kicking Petros?' The two boys looked at each other and laughed warmly into each other's face. 'He threw clay at me in the art room,' said Christos; and they poked each other in the ribs. Mr Duane rumpled their hair and pushed them out; 'All right,' he said, 'just see you don't hurt one another.' The governor was scandalized at such laxity, and raised the matter at the next governors' meeting, exclaiming 'Why, for heaven's sake, can't they behave like children in Hampstead!'* (This cry, slightly varied, was to be passed like a sad bean-bag from one authoritarian socialist to another. When in 1965 the L.C.C. sent spokesmen down to 'tell' the parents the school would be closed, they made it clear they had expected the children of Risinghill to pull themselves together and behave like Hampstead children.)

When one did not intend to see evil in the children, they could be delightful – particularly towards the end of the five years, the time when the L.C.C. closed the school down. That fifth year, in fact, was the first time one would be able to see what the school was accomplishing . . . the first time the school could have senior

---

*Hampstead is a mainly rich, green, spacious, and arty district, north-west of Islington.

pupils who had been educated at Risinghill and absorbed its atmosphere, and could pass it on, unconsciously as well as consciously, towards the younger ones. When a visitor came into school at that time, a boy or girl would instantly detach himself from friends and ask, not with a cold dutifulness but with a warm friendliness, if they could help in any way. They would take you wherever you wanted to go, voluntarily; they were host and hostess and you were a privileged guest whom they were glad to welcome.

I have never met this treatment in a traditionalist secondary school, for very obvious reasons. A child there is too tied by fear, by obligations laid on him from without not from within, ever to throw everything aside and look after someone; he is always afraid he will get into trouble, he will be late for something, he won't have a 'good excuse' (a typical and revealing authoritarian school phrase), he will be breaking some unknown regulation. A child at such a school is 'well-mannered' – which is to say that he stands up when the head comes into the room – but never sees his own humanity in someone else. He is 'polite' (according to his discretion, of course) but very cold, and lowers his eyes and sees nothing in the presence of a stranger.

A well-educated intelligent woman – she had chosen Risinghill for her children very deliberately – who was very large, and looked somewhat larger in her black cloak, told me that she came to the school to see Mr Duane, and at once a boy and a girl detached themselves and asked her if they could help. As they escorted her to the headmaster's study, a couple of small girls said cheekily 'Ever heard of Dracula!' The elder boy, scarcely pausing in his walk, simply said 'Ever heard of good manners!', and without another word, or any feeling of embarrassment in anyone, the group went on its way.

Five years later, when the L.C.C. had decided to close Risinghill School, I was in one of the art rooms – the same one, incidentally, that Mr Sebag-Montefiore and Mrs Townsend had by then painted as a den of vandalism. The art teacher had a book of mine he wanted to return. He looked round to see if there was a child unoccupied, and called him over. 'Jimmy, would you mind doing something for me? Here's my car key. My car's a light blue

Hillman. It's parked down there, on the right. I've left a book in it that I must give back to Mrs Berg. If you can't see it on the seat, then look in all the pockets – and in my bag at the back.' The boy took the key and was back almost instantly, very pleased with himself for his speed. This was in a district where the commonest children's crimes are 'theft' and 'taking and driving away'. An authoritarian would have called the art teacher's casual trust 'putting temptation in their way'; to him it was simply treating children as equal human beings, which neither the authoritarians nor the confused teachers do.

Earlier in that same period, I arrived to see Mr Duane. He had been called away for a few minutes to a laundry up the road that had been smashed up, the laundry people said, by one of his boys. Just as he came back, out of breath, and sank into a chair, a group of little boys poked their heads into the study. 'Was it Terry, sir?' they said. 'No,' he reassured them. 'It's all right. It was Terry's brother. He doesn't go to our school.' 'Oh *good*!' said two of them, and a third added fervently 'I'm glad it wasn't Terry, sir. I'm glad it wasn't our school.' 'So am I,' he said cheerfully, and waved them away. The concern in their voices, for Terry, for Mr Duane, and for the school, was very evident, and, I thought, not only touching but remarkable.

A Risinghill teacher had said to me, telling me how she read 'The Loneliness of the Long Distance Runner' to the older children, 'At first they only understood why he loved running – they understood this very well – and how he felt. Only three or four could grasp at all the idea of the prestige of an institution as against individual prestige, but I think more of them began to grope after this. It's an idea that's quite alien.' Yet from the love towards individuals that had been fostered in them, and that they had been encouraged to express, they had formed a love for an entity.

But I am rushing ahead. In that first year, particularly the first term when the boys and girls who had been uprooted for a pointless solitary term got their own back on a society that, to their amazement, had suddenly stopped provoking them, there was chaos.

The labour

Unlucky conflicts are not confined to inexperienced teachers. There are some seasoned teachers. . . who 'positively create problems' by their lack of perception and inability to make effective personal contact.

But did the chaos come simply from the children? Or did it also, and more fatally, come from the staff?

Can you run a school with a certain aim, when most of the staff have the opposite aim, and are encouraged by the authority to have an opposite aim?

Our teachers have been trained – and continue to be trained – to keep children silent and obedient and concentrating on getting through examinations and becoming the sort of people who are convenient for the state. This, they believe, is their job; but at Risinghill they saw their head standing in their way preventing them from doing this.

Take just one fact alone. Michael Duane refused to expel anyone. He said that since education had been made compulsory by the state, expulsion was illegal. 'In any case,' he said, 'suppose you decide to expel a boy, and you have him up on the platform, and right in front of the assembled school he says "Suits me, cock. Cheerio. What are you other mugs staying for?" Any Islington kid could do that.' So he took children other heads had expelled, refused to expel them from his own school, and unlike other heads did everything in his power, and tried to get his staff to do everything in their power, to keep them from being sent away from their homes to approved schools or borstals.

This is one reason why Risinghill had far more 'difficult' children than any other school – Michael Duane was the only head who did not reject them. And when he could not get the children who needed it into special schools, he kept them in his.

The L.C.C. was later to deny over and over again that Risinghill children were any more 'difficult' than any other. This puzzled me at first, for they were denying the figures, families in constant trouble with the police, children of below-average intelligence, families on the books of care committees. But there were several reasons for this – it would reflect on their prestige to own to such children, it might hurt their campaign for comprehensive schools, it might reflect on the *un*-difficult children at Risinghill (many good teachers, and many harassed children repeated this). But another reason was that Michael Duane, unapproved by authority, had all those children because other heads, approved by authority, threw them out. He made the inhumanity which resulted from their policy visible, so that in self-defence they sneered at him. But his staff had been trained to work for precisely those heads who threw the kids out.

*

Inspector Macgowan visited Risinghill School remarkably frequently – two or three times a week, on many occasions during the two years.

But despite the inspector's frequent visits, Mr Duane's requests – based on the fact that Risinghill had to provide not only for academic but for large-scale remedial needs – were largely ignored. In fact, sometimes they were worse than ignored. In the first year, staffing difficulties were very great and the inspector was frequently informed of them. Doubtless the inspector was having difficulty in finding teachers who would work, or linger, in a district like Risinghill. Doubtless, too, Risinghill was getting, within the context of the general teacher shortage, its share – possibly even slightly more than its impersonally reckoned share – of teachers. But the school had a large number of specialist rooms that were intended for one teacher working with only a small group of children, and it had 'heads of house' who had 'family' duties as well as their teaching duties; and for all of this, which meant a large staff, the school was supposed to have been originally designed.

When in fact a cut of eight teachers was followed by a cut of two more, this meant the school lost the use of one workshop, one housecraft room, two art rooms, and one science lab. Some people felt the difficulties in the school were not due simply to Mr Duane's ideas on education.

The inspector cold-shouldered the child-centred approach, which since this policy was rarely applied in state schools, needed help, and spent considerable time with the traditionalists, whom he approved of and with whom he sympathized. He had liked the way the two ex-heads ran their previous schools and had told them so. When they and their old staff told him their children were being ruined by Risinghill, that they were becoming impudent, impious, undisciplined, reverting to their home accents, he was as genuinely scandalized as they were.

By the way, why were the children from one of these schools in the old-fashioned habit of making dresses for an inspector? I remember many years ago this was mystically said to be good for the children's character; it was supposed to make them glow with achievement. Yet in a slum area, above all, one would expect the children themselves, and their families and friends, to be more in need of clothes than the inspectors. Perhaps it was thought to be charming; yet I cannot myself imagine these children saying spontaneously 'Do let's make a dress for the inspector!' In factories they have a name for this sort of thing and it is not charming; and I should fancy these present-day children – or their parents – knew it.

How could Inspector Macgowan ever co-operate with Mr Duane without going against his own convictions? Wasn't there bound to be antagonism – manifest antagonism – between a man who believed that 'six of the best would cure almost any disciplinary problem' and a man who believed corporal punishment was brutal and encouraged brutality, between a man who disapproved of informality between head and staff, and between head and children, and a man who thought life could only be lived on terms of friendliness; or between a man, such as Inspector Clark later, who was horrified by things 'impure' and a man who accepted cheerfully that nothing human was alien; or indeed between any man who uses power to maintain a hierarchy and any man who uses it equably to help others?

Is it not worth underlining that the inspector who denounced the school the first time was a man who was interested in 'grammar-school material' and a man who approved of corporal punishment, and that the inspector who denounced it the second time was a man who was opposed to comprehensive schools and to all large schools ? Neither of them hid these views. They were known to many people concerned with education and educational publishing – though not, of course, to the general public. I should be surprised to the point of incredulity if they were not known to the L.C.C. Education Department, or the Ministry. And certainly the teachers knew, knew at any rate that their L.C.C. inspector stood firmly for the traditionalist outlook. Did this help them towards a new vision ?

*

Some of the Risinghill children were regularly turned out into the streets quite early every morning, when their parents went to work. So they came very early to school. The teachers, who had not been turned into the streets, did not come so early. If it was wet or cold, the children, being conscious human beings not yet old enough to be docile, climbed into the school through the sliding windows, in the course of this sometimes scuffing walls or pulling down curtains (technically 'vandalism'). This caused anger and conflict among the staff, which reached a peak when a boy was found one morning still asleep in the flat in the housecraft block. Evidently he had been there all night. His mother kept a brothel and he had nowhere to go. There was a great deal of angry talk at this point about teachers' rights.

Mr Duane thought not so much about teachers' rights as about human rights. He asked the L.C.C. to look at the situation honestly – both the wider social position, and the position within the school. The damage done when the children climbed in occurred because the children were being prevented from getting into a warm dry building. He said once again, as he was to do for years, that it would be intelligent and practical to secure the windows properly both against burglaries that were now taking place, and for safety's sake; and that it would be humane to leave the doors unfastened for the 'early' children to come in, and to have rooms warmed and equipped for them where they could have extra tuition, or do homework, or read or talk, or follow their own interests. But the teachers said he was 'disorganized' and 'chaotic' and threw the children out again into the cold and wet.

I am sure that every teacher, traditionalist or not, must have been disturbed by a child's homelessness. I am sure every teacher must have been stirred to the realization that there was something very wrong with society, something very wrong with the immediate environment of the children who came to the school, if a child had to live, secretly, in the school. Why then were the traditionalists furious with Mr Duane and so vindictive towards the children? The reason is that their natural human response clashed with all their training and conditioning and all the inhuman practical conditions of teaching today which they had been trained to do nothing about. He brought them face to face with their own dilemma. (This pattern, already plain in the original announcement of 'no more corporal punishment', was to recur very often throughout Mr Duane's career. Not only was he a man who saw a problem, then acted instantly to clear it. He was also a man who took people at their word. The combination to some people, who found themselves swept into action as a result of their own words, was terrifying. They then said 'He uses people!' But this anger, though growing, was not yet large enough to destroy Risinghill.)

Someone said to me then, rather wistfully, 'He asked a great deal of his teachers.' He did; and yet at the same time he asked very little. He only asked them to be human beings; in our society that is beginning to be difficult, and a painful thing to be. And it is the opposite to the way teachers have been trained.

So they pushed the children out again into the cold and wet, spoke savagely of Mr Duane, and fell back on the protection of the System. A teacher who was very much against Mr Duane's policy and told me 'You cannot help one child at the expense of others', began every second sentence to me with 'The System is . . .'.

Incidentally this was a continual problem at Risinghill, but only the non-authoritarians tried to solve it. One might say – and I'm sure the authoritarians did, sincerely and *bewilderedly* – that the non-authoritarians *made* the problem; for the authoritarians expected to slap down a 'difficult' child; it was only when you accorded the difficult child the same human rights as the rest you had a problem.

But do you really ever help one child *at the expense* of another, if it is done with the participation and discussion of the other, and if the other knows without doubt that he too will be helped when he needs it ? That teacher meant 'You can't help one person at the expense of the System'. For the hierarchical system does indeed break down when everyone unites to group, temporarily, round one child.

Later on, in 1965, when I took a class of eleven- and twelve-year-olds at Risinghill, there was one small boy, a little worried-looking scrap of a child, who simply could not sit still; he was driven on from seat to seat, from one side of the room to the other, by an inner anxiety that would not let him rest. I thought to myself at the time that some of these children go through life tormented by fears that hold them from their path. What school that the L.C.C. approves of, I thought, what 'respectable school', is going to acknowledge this anxiety, let alone erase it ? And how many teachers today are mature enough to deal with it ? For if a teacher was not mature, though herself anxious and sensitive, such roaming and ravening anxiety would tie up with her own, would leap to join it like electricity leaping a gap, and she would become hysterical. This happened a great deal at Risinghill.

This child told me, in the course of the lesson – we were writing a story and trying to think how real children and real parents behave – that when he came home from school he played in the street till his mother came back from work.

'And if it's raining ?' I said.

'I climb in through the window.'

'And what do your brothers and sisters do ?'

'They do the same – climb in through the window.' (They were taught to do it, for their survival, at home – and thrown out when they did it at school.)

Later I mentioned him to Mr Gwyn, his usual teacher, a non-authoritarian. He told me Bobby's mother had no husband, and simply could not cope with all the children. She was a kind woman, a nice woman; but one of the boys had just been sent away to an approved school and she was *glad*, because now she had one less to cope with, one less to feed, to look after, and be responsible for. I thought to myself, my God, what does our society make of us !

No wonder Bobby was anxious! And how determined he must have been to climb into his house, not to accept that he was shut out.

This teacher unconsciously underlined for me again that any teacher who is what I would call good can tell you about each of the children, their background, their home. Mr Gwyn said to me 'People are always saying that in comprehensive schools you can't get to know the children. But this is the first school I have taught in, in which I really do know them.' But the traditionalists didn't; they looked at you in amazement if you asked them; it wasn't their job. (And Inspector Macgowan didn't think there was time for it either, and told Mr Duane so.)

Risinghill, so many of whose children were disturbed, in broken homes, or of below-average intelligence, simultaneously had parents who often would not, or could not, go with the child to an outside psychologist, and would not, or could not, co-operate with the psychologist even when their relationship with the child was warm, loving and vitally important; and the outside psychologist in a Child Guidance Clinic could not know, except at the most from notes on pieces of paper, how those children were living. A friend in a Citizens' Advice Bureau once said to me, 'What is the use of psycho-analysis to a man who cannot pay his rent?' If a woman is not putting her head in the gas oven only because the gas is cut off, what is the first thing to do? To alleviate her despair, or to restore the gas so that rooms can be warmed and meals cooked and clothes washed in hot water and the children can stop crying; and how can you dare to balance one against the other without being in constant friendly touch with the home?

What was needed was, as Mr Duane stated it, 'special teachers *within the school*, taking groups of children who need therapeutic treatment *within the school*, and nursing them back to the normal teaching situation.' But neither Inspector Macgowan nor Inspector Clark really understood Risinghill's child-centred teaching and remedial work.

One day, an ex-head coming from Mr Duane's room, where she had left him, met a little girl pushing a baby in a pram across the playground, a younger child hanging on to the handle at either side.

'What do you think you're doing?'

'Please Miss, I want to see Mr Duane.'

'What for?'

'Please Miss, I want him to sign a form.'

'He's much too busy to be bothered with things like that. Anyway he isn't in! Now go away!'

The child, naturally enough, was distressed. She had been given an aim by her parent that the teacher would not let her fulfil. But Mr Duane came up, asked what was wrong, and instantly signed the form, a pension form.

This teacher was trying to keep his study sacrosanct, to make him into the kind of head that she, like the L.C.C., believed heads should always be. But he was only concerned for the weight of responsibility that lies so heavily on working-class children, almost from the cradle, that they desperately defy it by becoming what we call irresponsible.

The teacher was undoubtedly extremely angry. He had 'demoted' her. He had not supported her in front of the child. He had shown her up as a liar. He had shown utter contempt for the System. And on a personal level he had rejected her friendship. And the fact that after he had done such shattering things he explained them in such a gentle surprised way made them even more incomprehensible.

There were so many incidents where the attitude of a human being was at variance with the position of a cog in the state machine. I think for instance of the episode of the dagger. At one stage, a flashy dagger kept appearing and disappearing in the school. Nothing ever happened . . . but every now and then someone would report they had seen it, and then it had vanished again, and no one knew anything about it. It seems to have been produced, and reacted to, in very much the same way as an exhibitionist impresses a solitary lady in a railway carriage; and one or two of the women teachers became a little hysterical. No one could tell who was in possession of the knife at any given moment. The traditionalist teachers felt it was necessary to know this, instantly; but they made no headway. But Mr Blaize talked apparently casually to a group of boys, mentioned this knife, remarked that such knives were of course illegal and were therefore apt to lead to unnecessary trouble, and suggested that if a respectable-looking person like a teacher were to find the knife just lying in the gutter he would simply hand it in at the police station, which would be pleasanter for everyone. The boys matter-of-factly informed him that the police would then melt it down and make themselves a packet. Since they believed this, it was to him natural that they should think of another plan. In the end, he and two boys – an informal delegation – went to the canal and ceremoniously threw the knife in.

But this is illegal. Weapons must be handed in to the police. That the knife was disposed of and could no longer be a danger to anyone, and that the children had disposed of it voluntarily, was relatively unimportant to the authoritarians; they were indignant that the 'culprits' had escaped the verdict of the law.

Another time, Mr Duane asked a mother to come round to the school because her son's language even by the most relaxed standard was so astonishingly lurid, and he thought she might throw light on it; and she came and said 'Christ, mate, I don't know where he gets his fucking language from, honest I don't, the bloody little bugger, but if you get any more of it you tan his bloody arse, the fucking little sod.' Mr Duane roared with laughter afterwards; he had learned something. But most of the other teachers were outraged, and very virtuous, and felt 'There you are, you see! this is what happens', as if someone had spat on the altar. All they could learn from such an incident was the need to redouble authoritarian efforts, and to separate the child from his environment.

In any case the traditionalist teachers resented the parents coming to school to discuss the children's progress. For one thing they did not feel these parents had any right to discuss education. ('That little market-stall holder thinks he has an opinion!') It was completely against the idea of the educational hierarchy and against their idea of education. How can an educated person learn anything from an uneducated one? How can a teacher learn anything from a parent?

More specifically, when a parent came to school the discussion would often, sooner or later, turn to the teacher's attitude towards the child, and the teachers felt this as intolerable criticism. One teacher, when a patient and reasonable father suggested he might get a different response from the child if he treated the child differently, simply left the room. Since such meetings, ending in such a way, must have been very disturbing to the authoritarian teachers as well as to other people, they just did not want them to take place. They did not say so, because in 1965 we have other slogans. They said, for example, believing it, that parents had no right to come without an appointment; but simultaneously they knew quite well – or they would have known if they had allowed their knowledge of people to affect their beliefs – that these parents could not make any genuine contact on a formal level, that formality petrified them. But Mr Duane was delighted to meet the parents. You would find mothers and grandmothers sitting by the fire in his study, and babies bubbling and crowing in the armchairs, as if it were a clubhouse. The authoritarians thought it very undignified, thought it dragged them down, and darkly said it was 'unwise'. They did not want the environment seeping into the school, uncontrolled, because their training had been framed at a time when the schools had to wrest children away from parents; and although times had changed and slogans had changed, they had never moved from their antagonism, which had once been part of their idealism.

But to my mind to see their parents and the family babies 'included' in the head's study was wonderfully good for the children, especially these children. They gained security, confidence, dignity and responsiveness from it. It was calming for them to know that the school was a warm, relaxed, welcoming place, and it was a wonderful social education to experience their school as the place where other people came for help, advice and information, and to play their own part in this. But the disciplinarians felt the children were being distracted from their work, dragged back to domestic preoccupations (which in many cases were not very orthodox anyway), and when the visitors were not even parents they felt the situation was fantastic.

For many teachers sex is a disturbing thing. Many of the elderly ones have had no experience of it; many of the younger ones who have can only cope with it on a jocular semi-destructive level. Many of them went straight from a single-sex school to a single-sex training college (which is, often, only a large school), and straight back into a school again, generally a single-sex one. Three of the four schools from which staff came to Risinghill had been single-sex schools.

The district of Risinghill included brothels and dubious clubs. Some of the children's mothers were prostitutes. I have been told on good authority that one of the teachers frequented these brothels, and also that the children saw him going in and out and commented on it.

Sexual words were frequent in the children's home vocabulary, but rarely with any tender connotation. They desperately needed to be helped by mature people to align sex with love. But when sex education was once mentioned to the senior members of staff 'all except one tittered and giggled like repressed children', someone told me.

One day two small girls, heaving with outrage, complained to Mr Duane that a teacher had said disgusting things to them. Mr Duane tried to calm them down, and asked them just what it was the teacher had said, but it was so disgusting they couldn't repeat it, no they couldn't they said. Quite befogged, Mr Duane asked the teacher if he could explain; but the teacher was quite befogged too. Finally Mr Duane asked him to try to go over, in detail, everything that had happened and been said. The teacher said the two girls were being rather a nuisance so he said to them 'Oh you silly prigs!' Light dawned on Mr Duane . . . though not on the teacher. Mr Duane then explained to the children that what the teacher said was *prigs*. He showed them in a dictionary what this meant. Eventually they were mollified, and he sent them away.

But he now had to explain to the teacher; and then to the traditionalist ex-head who had been disturbed by the girls' sense of outrage – for they had passionately come to her – and was now anxious for an explanation. This was much the most difficult part.

'It was a misunderstanding,' he said. But because of her genuine concern, she wanted more details.

'They misheard what he said.'

'What *did* he say?'

'He called them silly prigs.'

'Well?'

'They didn't hear it correctly.'

'Yes?'

'They thought he said "pricks".'

'I don't understand.'

' "Prick" is a colloquialism for the male sexual organ. The phrase is a phrase of contempt.'

She left the room precipitately.

Even on the intellectual level, both child and teacher had learned a little. Certainly they had each enlarged their vocabulary. This is surely good.

To me it is amazing and sad, and not commendable, that anyone can work for a lifetime among any people – let alone people in that particular district – and not be used to such colloquialisms. When a person is a teacher, I am shocked. Since when was ignorance a prerequisite for an educator?

Yet I suspect that the whole episode, as far as the ex-head was concerned, only confirmed to her that she did not want to work very much with Mr Duane. If she felt, as she possibly and understandably did, that such an episode could never have happened with the old-style head, she was correct. If she felt that Mr Duane was corrupting her girls, then she was very wrong.

And then this teacher, and many other teachers of her age and experience, was distressed by the idea of Mr Duane's humanist assemblies. (The assemblies themselves, I think, did not bother them much. I think they had anticipated something like the Black Mass. But the *idea* of humanist assemblies alarmed them intensely.) At the beginning of the school it was impossible to get the children into one room for assembly – this remained a physical impossibility till 1963 – so assembly was split into junior and senior; and this stayed so until the school was closed. The junior assembly was taken by this teacher, the senior by Mr Duane. When the children were old enough to move from her Church of England assembly to Mr Duane's humanist one, she was surely hurt, outraged, despairing. But from Michael Duane's viewpoint, the children, in his own school, had been handed religious clichés till they were bored, resentful and cynical, and he knew that it would be a long time before they would listen long enough at assembly to hear what he was saying, and to hear that it was not irrelevant cliché.

This was a school above all others where the humanist philosophy must have seemed most applicable. There were children here of every nationality and creed, and many of no creed at all. But it was precisely for this reason that the traditionalists – of whatever religion – believed they must have religious assemblies; and if those assemblies could be Church of England only, then that they must be. (In 1965, when the school was closed down, a mother was to tell me she believed it was closed because of the humanist assemblies; she had heard this said by people outside the school. I remembered this later when I discovered that Inspector Clark, whose 1964 report condemned the school, Dr Briault, and the Chief Inspector held strong religious views. Indeed, Dr Payling, the Chief Inspector, said in an L.C.C. pamphlet on London comprehensive schools 'All the heads regard taking prayers at the full school assembly as one of the most important things they do.')

Mrs Thatcher saw nothing shocking in a boy coming to her class wearing a brilliant red and black corduroy cap; he had bought it himself and was proud of it, and she couldn't believe it was anti-educational for a deprived boy to express joy. But another teacher threw him out of his class for it.

Some of the traditionalists even objected to individual music lessons. They called them 'another interference with the work of the school', which did not please the teachers who took music or other similar subjects. Yet in a different school with a different social background the children would have taken music to O Level, which would have been academic, therefore respectable, and not at all time-wasting; and the teachers who wanted the children to do music were very aware of this.

Many of the old-style teachers had a great deal to offer the children. When one gave cookery lessons to the toughest tearaways and had them cosily baking Cornish pasties for tea, when another helped the children to make rich and colourful costumes for the nativity play, the non-authoritarians were entranced and enthusiastic. But in their private life and in their professional training they were so trained to delight not themselves but an outside authority, and had been so hard hit by Mr Duane's refusal to be that outside authority, that when he praised what they were doing they were even more at sea, even more hostile. He was invoking in them the kind of pleasure in a superior's approval that he simultaneously told them he did not want them to have. Mr Gwyn said to me 'There was one group of teachers who really hated him. I think if he'd passed them in the corridor and said "Good morning", they'd have thought it was something sinister.' So more than ever they cried 'What does he *want* of us ?', which is rarely a request for information but the despairing cry of people who have lost their compass.

Intriguingly, some of the most rigid authoritarians, the most bitter opponents of Mr Duane, were Communists. Roughly speaking, within the district, English Communists tended to oppose Mr Duane, while foreign Communists (by which I do not mean Russian or Chinese; I never saw a Russian or Chinese in Islington) warmly supported him. But those Communists who opposed him did so in a much more organized way than any other of his opponents bar the L.C.C.; they held meetings and took decisions as to their next step, and they passed resolutions when they were the only people left at the staff meeting, and they had a strong tendency to 'bend' decisions taken by other (including union) meetings so that they suited their purpose better.

This was to me one of the most fascinating things about the Risinghill staff neurosis – that some of the very teachers who put themselves forward as, and I think maybe really considered themselves as, champions of the workers and the downtrodden were Mr Duane's bitterest enemies. Such 'championship' is often merely an attempt to possess. (Katerina, a Greek pupil, and therefore used to authoritarians, said to me equably of an authoritarian teacher 'He helps me a lot. He will help you if you do exactly as he says. He is possessive.' This accurately describes very many authoritarians of all or no political creed.) For these particular Communists, as for the most backward-looking Tory, people were tools, a means to an end, never individuals with a private worth. When Mr Duane gave everyone a worth as an individual, he became for these 'revolutionaries' a far greater menace than their Tory protagonists had ever been. With 'reactionaries' they could happily play a game for the allegiance of the people, like kids gambling for a bag of conkers: and to neither side did the individual people in their own personal right matter a damn. The teacher who was most enraged at the children climbing into the school and the boy sleeping there, who threw them out again with the greatest efficiency, was the foremost 'champion of the oppressed'.

It was Mr Duane and the other child-centred teachers who became aware, because they were so close to the children, that some of the kids were dogged and harried by some of the police *until*, almost in desperation, they did something they could be pulled in for; and it was the foremost 'champion of the workers' who regularly wrote the most hostile reports about these children for the benefit of those about to judge them. This is interesting and revealing. The children are still very bitter about the reports this teacher wrote, just as they are very bitter about another 'champion of the oppressed' who one child told me 'was the one who had me put away'.

I said earlier in this chapter that Mr Duane would not expel anyone. He made, simply in the natural course of things, an informal agreement with another local boys' school head that they would cooperate with each other by swapping kids. Once Mr Duane sent him a boy who simply couldn't stand women teachers; and later this head sent him a boy who was unmanageable at his school but who settled happily at Risinghill. This was simple and reasonable, and meant that everyone, including traditionalists, would have an easier happier time. But traditionalists do not approve of flexibility, which to them means 'giving the child his own way'. And besides, all the mystique of disapproval, all the threats and the power and the right to 'mould' children were being taken away from them.

Risinghill had a School Council, made up of four teachers (including Mr Duane), twelve boys and girls, and three other adults working in the school. It had been decided that complaints should be brought before the School Council and dealt with there, not dealt with privately in anger; anyone who had a grievance could ask for a meeting of the School Council. This was how the gang warfare had been stopped.

Later, cases of bullying were brought up there. Indeed one older boy in the school – David Jones – brought up grievances for the younger boys at the Council, and fought on their behalf so determinedly that he was co-opted on to the School Council, where he made speeches for the small boys, referring to them as 'My learned friend'. (It was David's nuclear disarmament campaign which caused Inspector Macgowan to say of a chalked C.N.D. symbol 'I'd sooner see four-letter words [chalked on the wall] than that!') It was obvious that the Council, even though inexperienced, had valuable potentials. It was also obvious that many of the staff furiously resented meeting the children on equal terms.

One day, at a Council meeting, the head boy said that some members of the staff were not turning up for their playground duty, as arranged, and the prefects were having to do it for them, in addition to their own. Mr Duane stopped him from mentioning the actual names of the teachers, by promising to deal with it. Immediately after the meeting closed, a deputation from the staff arrived to say they strongly objected to being discussed and criticized. Mr Duane pointed out that no names had been mentioned, but this did not mollify them; 'the staff', in the abstract, had been criticized. They went to Inspector Macgowan, and he made it one of the items in his report (which County Hall was later to describe as 'the blackest report they had ever seen'). Later on in 1965, the same destruction of democracy was to happen on a larger scale. The School Council affair was the pupils' first introduction to a democracy that offers rights as long as the rights aren't used.

In a hierarchy, some people have power and some haven't. What a child said about a teacher was often hostile, but did no harm; there was no power behind it. What a hostile teacher said about a child might go down – and often did go down – in a statement to court that could separate the child from people who loved him and send him to an institution.

Two teachers were later to libel two of the Risinghill children, perhaps mark them for life, deliberately and with complete impunity. And later still, I was to meet the boy in the market and hear him describe a teacher as 'the one who had me put away'. Even if he was mistaken – and I think he probably was not, for I learned at Risinghill that what a middle-class person living in different circumstances might dismiss as chronic paranoia was often for these children an objective fact – but even if it were incorrect, can such a relationship between teacher and child be a good one for education ? What does one learn from enemies but enmity ? What does one learn from *powerful* enemies but subjection which is almost death, or the determination to use power, when one gets it oneself, to hit back ?

There were other battle cries too. 'Cover up the women teachers!' was my favourite. It seems that one of the ex-heads, anxious about a policy that made the children more friendly (disrespectful) towards their teachers, spoke to Inspector Macgowan on the subject of bare skin. Bare skin, she honestly felt, had a tendency, when belonging to a young and attractive female teacher, to inflame adolescent boys – the adolescent boys of Risinghill, that is. (Presumably, short sleeves in other districts were not considered dangerous. Or are they dangerous everywhere ?) The inspector directed the women teachers to cover themselves up. This naturally caused further conflicts as well as laughter.

And crashing all the time into the chaos was the contemptuous mind-spattering brutality of the public-address system – authority's new method of conditioning children for the factory and the army, and, beyond that, of wiping out all individual human growth. How much alienation is generated in children, who stop trying to think or to concentrate or feel or be a person – how much sheer hate, anti-society and anti-adult, is built up in other more vital children – by that public-address system, so beloved by the L.C.C. because it is cheap ? What a weapon it is for the authoritarians! What a powerful vehicle for hate, with its cracked distortion of the tensed human voice! When a teacher is angry, even if he is unconscious of it, the whole school knows it, and is disturbed. Some of the teachers called it Big Brother.

Everyone knows it is possible to get into touch with teachers in their classrooms, quietly and privately, by a shielded flashing light system, which allows the teacher to take any message when it is convenient for him and when he will pass it on personally to his class. (This method is used in America; an American teacher at Risinghill was appalled by our system.) But oh, our system is cheap – and it needs no initiative, not one movement on the teacher's part.

'Thirty acres, quiet, peaceful' run the property advertisements in the papers for top people. But the majority of our people cannot speak, will not be listened to, and now cannot even be allowed to think undisturbed in their own secret acre of tranquillity, lest, heaven forbid, they discover themselves as individuals and act so. Blast on, loudspeakers! Contemptuously annihilate any warm bond between teacher and child and blow private identity to smithereens! If anything is needed to crystallize, to add to, to carry along, to express, hysteria, anxiety and brute force – if anything is needed to symbolize what authority, 1960, thinks of education – it is our loudspeaker system. It tore at the exposed nerves of Risinghill.

Growth 1961

Anxieties

They seem to us to need a specially favourable staffing ratio.

In 1961, the most difficult older children left. This should have given the staff a respite, a chance to take stock. But teacher shortage turned this into a bitter joke. The staff – told they would be increased – were in fact decreased by eight – then a few weeks later warned by the L.C.C. of an imminent cut of three more.

Small wonder that in such circumstances the authoritarians who wanted straight lines, no running, no talking, or you-know-what-you'll-get, were screaming at the non-authoritarians, who must have seemed to them to be deliberately denying them the only means of control. In such conditions, even people who are drawn towards non-authoritarian ideas may become authoritarian, because they cannot cope – and stay that way, turning a painful temporary inadequacy into a respectable lifelong philosophy.

Overwork and overstrain, due to all the difficulties of the school, meant staff off sick; and this meant supply teachers. And the stream of ever-changing supply teachers who did not know the names of the children and had no idea of the district upset the children, upset the permanent staff, and made things worse for the teachers who were away and would be coming back. These were the last children on earth to be subjected to supply teaching. Yet in fact, the supply teachers were never enough, and teachers were constantly taking two classes at once, or dividing up among themselves the uncooperative and depressed children of an absent teacher.

The teachers who refused to use corporal punishment because they believed it degraded the children and themselves and was part of a vanishing world were exhausted because, instead, they had to reason with the children (and many of these were children for whom a blow had begun to represent notice, the only notice they got, so that they now became even more emotionally demanding), and because simultaneously they had to face the hostility of the teachers who wanted corporal punishment. (This hostility is expressed in practically all London schools by 'Oh, Miss Brown, I beg your pardon, I had no idea there was a *teacher* with the children' – which may sound funny and trivial to non-teachers, but it has broken down many a young beginner, and perpetuates corporal punishment.) The teachers who wanted corporal punishment were exhausted because what they had been trained for was no longer getting approval from their head; and when they used the children as convenient scapegoats, as they had been unconsciously accustomed to, his lack of approval grew bleaker.

The plan of the building was a constant enemy. The duller children simply could not cope with moving frequently from a classroom in one block to a classroom in another. The more intelligent and anxious ones cannot either, really, but they do not show this so openly. The duller ones tended to get wild and destructive, and forget where they were going. Many of them actually got lost in the complexities of the building; some of them, finding that other children got lost, pretended that they had got lost too; many of the staff assumed that they were all doing as they liked and that none of them got lost. Whole periods could be burnt up in this way, with children and teachers dispiritedly or furiously sorting themselves out. It had been realized this might happen with backward children, but no one had known these would be so many. The only way to solve this problem was to cut down on the specialist classes for these children, and keep them in one main room. This would not have mattered if in their one room they could have relied on getting always first-class basic teaching. But of course they couldn't.

Open-plan buildings need a high degree of self-discipline. It was going to take these belted children years to get used to their freedom. They had come from small secondary schools that had high prison walls round them, with straightforward no-nonsense playgrounds, and, within the school, classrooms grouped round a central hall for easy supervision. Whatever they had done they had either been forced to do or had done as a rebellious escape.

Even had they had the most integrated staff no one could have expected Risinghill to run really smoothly until all the children there had come straight from primary school – and that would take five years. Before that date, which would be March 1965, the L.C.C. was to announce it was closing the school.

*

So much for their emotional development, but what of their intellectual education, if one can ever presume to separate the two ? Inexperienced, unknown teachers can't be put in charge of a laboratory or a workshop, or any specialist class; you have to put them in charge of the most vital subject of all, the 'mere' English lesson, the class where the children learn humanity's most basic, most urgent skill.

Furthermore the 'general' classes were the large ones. Classes in labs and workshops are always 'half-classes'. So these inexperienced new-to-the-area supply teachers were taking not only the most important classes but the largest classes, with wretched results for the children, the teachers – and, incidentally (this seemed to trouble the L.C.C. most), the furniture.

It is fantastic that a 'general' subject like English should be treated as something inferior; as long as one is English, as long as one is in England, English is communication. It is living. It is being a human being. It is expressing what you feel, saying what you want to say, having the words to think with. It is finding your place in human history by knowing that others have felt, suffered, puzzled and rejoiced like you.

When you watch a scarcely-educated child or adult wrestling to find the words to express what they so passionately feel or have so painfully and truthfully wrought from their own experience, feelings and ideas so much more urgent and important than the unfelt posturings of some 'educated' people, you are seeing the waste of treating English as 'a subject', an inferior subject . . . as something that must be repressed and stamped down in the baby and child too young to go to school, and something that, when the children are old enough to go, may be taught at best as a motiveless technique and at worst as a vehicle for proving to the child how stupid, contemptible, ridiculous and worthless are the things he so desperately tries to say.

These Risinghill children needed to be shown far more than the children of richer districts how to use their own language; but there were not enough good teachers constantly available. Those who were worked hard and absorbedly. Risinghill had more 'discussions' than any school I know. At grammar schools I have been told 'We have no time for discussions. The curriculum does not allow it'; yet grammar schools used to be places where people were encouraged to have independent opinions. Discussions are important in any school, if education is to mean something other than cramming with the right answers in time for an examination, but in a school like Risinghill, where the children arrived already starved of words – and therefore of ideas – discussions were as vital as food. But no mention of this, of the importance of learning one's own language, was ever made by Inspector Macgowan to Mr Duane, although he came two or three times a week. And this is no wonder, since his main professional interest lay in academically introducing second languages in primary schools. What interest to him were children who by the time they were in secondary schools could not even manipulate their own ? He lived in a different world.

He did indeed say French teachers were being wasted on the 'less able' children, and should not continue to be, but this was not because he said they should do more English.

It was difficult to arrange after-school events, though Mr Duane and several people like Mr Benson, Mr Gwyn and Mrs Thatcher went on trying. The children were not free after school; their life was not their own. And most of the staff were really content that this should be so; they did not want to stay any longer in school – or in that district – than they were forced to; so they did not want to creatively allow for the children having to mind littler ones after school, for having a small paid job to get done, and somehow incorporate these situations into after-school activities. They simply felt 'It is impossible to arrange anything for these children', and many of them added in their hearts 'Good'. Those of the staff who did arrange things, who realized the immense importance of providing socially for these children, and furthermore did it with enjoyment and not out of a sense of righteousness were few; and they had to fight not only against the inertia and in-difference of their colleagues, but against their resentment, sometimes expressed in conscience-stirring terms ('This is destroying all the rights that we have fought for . . . bringing down the working conditions of teachers all over the country'). And since the staff had been so cut down that it was at times scarcely possible to get school activity carried out it was not really surprising that few people felt energetic enough by the end of the day to do any more . . . especially as, precisely because of such things as lack of social concern, the children were so demanding during the day.

It was the same with homework. I always wondered how these Risinghill kids could ever do homework. There are no spare rooms in those Islington homes. Maybe the more fortunate children who lived in a council flat could work in a temporarily-unused room; but what about the children who lived in the houses that were tumbling down around them, a whole family in one room ? Did they do as I had once watched a boy in Sheffield do ? – in a room, unpapered and unpainted and almost unfurnished, in which five other children played, shrieked and shouted and the baby sat up in his pram and father and mother talked and a tiny television set yelled away, this boy in his first term at secondary modern school, doing algebra – a subject he had never heard of before – put the far corner of his exercise book on the one table that was crowded with the remains of high tea for eight, and wrote his homework in a book that was largely balanced in mid-air. Is this how the Risinghill kids would do it ? – adding to this the semi-darkness that so many of them lived in, and their parents' incomprehension and inability to help, and the social tradition of the district that regarded such after-school work as peculiar and worked against it ?

Mr Duane and some of the teachers provided for the children to stay and work in the library. But first the children wanted to go home and get some tea. How many middle-class children settle down to homework before tea, or immediate prospect of tea ? Tea could have been provided for the children at the school, but most of the teachers preferred to get away. In this they probably felt they had the support of Mr Macgowan since on

another occasion, in another context, he had said the social
problems of the children were not the teachers' concern.

*

Immigrants must surely be on the lowest rung of our hierarchical
education ladder – lower even than our own children. The authoritarians' attitude to immigrant children was an intensification of
their attitude to English slum children, and the conflicts that
rose at Risinghill were therefore very deep.

Furthermore since the whole basis for such teachers is measurable results within their own framework, they could not
possibly see such children, who had different cultures, backgrounds and languages, as anything other than down-dragging,
and they were bound to be anxious about them. Education mirrors
society, which was geared to see these children as a danger, and
ambitious parents see them as a menace to their own children's
progress. Yet it is a fact that at Risinghill, which had a very large
proportion of immigrants and particularly of entirely non-
English-speaking ones, measurable academic education went up
(for instance G.C.E. results went right up), measurable social
education went up (for instance, the number of pupils on probation dropped), and unmeasurable progress as shown by the behaviour of the children towards each other and towards strangers
was evident to anyone who entered the school. And the first two
Risinghill pupils to win university scholarships were an English
boy and a Turkish-Cypriot boy. What would have happened next
we do not know since at this point the L.C.C. decided to close the
school.

*

'Why do they call Greek children "Bubbles"?' said Mr Colinides
to me when I came to the school for the first time. We were both
puzzled; and I think he was wondering if it was an insult. But
later it dawned on me it was short for 'bubble-and-squeak',
rhyming slang. Consciously, I think it was not generally used
emotionally at Risinghill (though doubtless it sometimes was
by individuals, particularly in that first year). But it was like the
rhyming slang 'four-by-twos' for 'Jews', used commonly,

thoughtlessly, undeliberately, but perhaps with an undertone of lurking contempt, since four-by-twos are generally wooden planks, and bubble-and-squeak is a fried-up hotchpotch, and neither of them are people. It is revealing that by the time the school was closed the word was scarcely being used at all.

The Greeks in Islington live mainly together. They have their own butcher, their own greengrocer, even their own shoemaker. They do not feel any need to learn English.

Since the authoritarian teachers were horrified at the idea of going into the English children's homes, they were scarcely likely to visit the immigrants. Since they did not want to know the language that was the language not only of English slum children but of the vast majority of English people, but thought only in terms of imposing their own language, they were scarcely likely to want to know the language of Cypriots.

But if a Greek child is taught to speak only English, how can the family continue to communicate together? And if their children's friends, and their children's teachers, cannot speak Greek, how can the parents ever understand what the child is doing, or whether it is something they approve of, or at least can bring themselves to bear? And since, unlike many of the English parents, they respect teachers and would wish to honour them, and since in Islington they live in rooms that are not what they would wish them to be, for they are a proud people, how can they receive with ease teachers whom they do not know also, warmly, as friends?

The L.C.C., faced simultaneously with schools filled with immigrant children and a great shortage of teachers of any kind and an infinitely greater shortage of *good* teachers (though this is a reason for their decisions that they never mention), maintains that these children should be 'integrated' – meaning, in the particular context of immigrants in England, that their own identities must be wiped out. In 1963 they were to write to Mr Duane 'While sympathizing with the desire to foster knowledge of the language and culture of the place of birth of immigrant minorities, I do not feel this can in any sense be regarded as the responsibility of London schools. The task of the schools is really the reverse.' (The humane Ministry of Education booklet published earlier in the same year held a different view; and much of what is said in this Ministry booklet could have been said by Mr Duane. Unfortunately it was the L.C.C. who was Mr Duane's employer and in the Government's vote crisis the Ministry was scarcely likely to oppose, later on, their most powerful supporter.)

We delude ourselves about the brutality of this by saying that these immigrants *want* their own identity to be erased, otherwise why did they come to England ? This of course is nonsense, and no one knows this better than the English who have always gone, and continue to go, to other countries without the slightest intention of losing their identity.

But Risinghill worked out its own response. There was nothing ingenious about this. The school had children of nineteen nationalities, more than most of the children, or even some of the teachers, had realized existed. Since the school had many Greek, Turkish and African children, Mr Duane took on Greek, Turkish and African teachers.

Having teachers of their own nationality, speaking their own language, meant that the non-English children knew they were granted as much respect as the English children. Their teachers were their prestige symbols. Messages were sent to their parents in their own language, and they too could be drawn into the life of the school; now they no longer need face the conflict of feeling the school as an enemy who drew their children away from them and yet an enemy to whom they had to submit both for their children's sake and their own. It meant that the particular extra problems of these children could be explained and understood. It meant that these children if they got into trouble could be helped to give a statement in court and would therefore have some possibility of justice. It meant that ideas and conventions could be examined, re-examined, compared, and pondered over. It meant many more things; but these few are enough to show that the authoritarian idea of conforming never builds on the possibilities within a situation, does not even solve the problems of a situation, but merely gets by, by pretending no problems are there. This was why the authoritarians said – which puzzled me when I first heard it – 'Mr Duane disorganizes everything.'

*

Mr Colinides was one of the Greek teachers at Risinghill, the man who played the largest part in this continuous two-way interpretation.

When Mr Georgiou threatened to cut his daughter's throat because she had a boy-friend – for to Greek and Turkish parents, this is horrifyingly immoral, as are many other English customs – and the mother began to escort the girl to school daily, so that she should not meet the boy – how many teachers, how many employers, know that Greek parents take time off work to do precisely this ? – it was Mr Colinides who explained the situation. And though Mr Duane was at first astounded, he talked to the parents and to the girl, talked and talked, never dominating but always explaining, Mr Colinides told me, until the mother allowed Maroulla to go unaccompanied, knowing she would still meet the boy, and the father began to take Maroulla to the cinema and the theatre so that she should no longer feel shut off from the life around her and unloved by her father, and Maroulla began to understand that it was fear that made her father violent towards her. These ideas were alien and frightening to the parents, but they trusted Mr Duane, for they could see – since he took the trouble to communicate with them – that he only wished them to have for their daughter, and she for them, a concern that was true, not a concern that sprang from unnecessary fear. Now that Risinghill is closed, who will make it unnecessary for a Greek father to beat or want to kill his daughter ?

The Turkish families too had similar problems. The Turkish women never went out of their rooms. Yet here were their daughters going to school. How many headmasters would care, or even be aware, how fearful and evil this new life was to them ? And here their children were mixing with Greeks, their enemies, not theoretical enemies but experienced as such in blood and death. Many of the Greek families had been in Islington for a long time; but the Turkish families were newly arrived from the troubles or pending troubles in Cyprus; they had fled, escaped, leaving the newly dead behind them, and this was what the Greeks meant to them. It was amazing and wonderful that in Risinghill they worked side by side with Greek children. It would never have happened if Mr Duane had not insisted on being able to communicate with them and their families; and if the children had not daily seen a Turkish teacher working companionably with a Greek teacher.

In Islington all the children smoked. It was part of the background. Children of seven smoke, girls equally with boys. Fathers will get very small children to light their cigarettes for them at the stove; the child pulls away to get it lit, proud and delighted at being 'included', at being increasingly competent and adult. Of course it does not happen in every family, but it is common. To the Greek and Turkish families this was not merely disturbing – it was undilutedly horrifying.

The Turkish children, to whom these ways were newer and therefore even more shocking than to the Greeks, used to come running wide-eyed to the Turkish teacher. 'The children are smoking in the toilets!' In such a situation she would have to exercise very great delicacy and tact and wisdom.

Many English teachers did not like having non-English teachers at Risinghill, whether they were black African or white American or Australian; many of them cold-shouldered all non-English teachers in the staff room. Foreign children were bad enough; did they have to have adults too? They liked it even less when they found that, if they had trouble with a Greek boy, for instance, and could not understand him, they were expected not to hit him, which would have settled the matter quickly and simply, but to ask a Greek teacher to interpret and help. Some began to be glad that they had the foreign teachers; but many others must have felt the situation time-wasting and humiliating – particularly when they found the older immigrant children sometimes achieved more than the English teachers. (One girl said to me 'Sometimes they will not listen to a teacher. But when a Greek pupil says it they believe it.' This cut against the hierarchy with a vengeance.)

Yet this policy, although understood and fostered by only a minority of the teachers, like all the humane policies at Risinghill began to flower. The school began to be known as a place where people of all nationalities could come for advice. The Educational Attaché and the Welfare Officer came from the Greek Embassy to see the school. (In 1963, *To Vema*, the Greek newspaper, was to carry a long and warm article about Risinghill School. Later on the Cyprus High Commission's Cultural Attaché was to say 'How can you close a school which has achieved what even the United Nations has not managed to do?')

Mr Duane read Homer aloud, in English, at his morning assembly. The children learned Greek, Turkish, and West Indian songs and dances, and games. Modern Greek books were bought for the library, and Greek textbooks used. Children who could not speak English at all had special classes in the school to bring them to the standard of oral and written English where they could join the others – all in the context not of stamping out their original identity but of enlarging it, and of enriching others. English children began to learn other languages, to talk with their friends and their friends' parents, there in Islington.

If 'comprehensive education' means anything, it must mean that everyone has riches to contribute to the common treasure. How can any school that assumes the all-importance of English-ness ever do this? This was an assumption that Michael Duane never made. He hoped that at Risinghill all children – and their nationality did not matter – would find self-respect. This cherishing of differences, for a common enrichment, later blazed out in the remarkable nativity play, and those of the public who saw it were startled and moved. (But I have not found any member of the L.C.C. Education Committee who did.)

Faced with an immigrant child, the authoritarians say 'He must pretend to be something different from what he is – English, let him have a stab at being that!' They will not accept the child unless he does this, and yet all the time they know he can never be as good at being English as the most despised English child; and this joke rather pleases them.

When this joke was taken away from some of the teachers at Risinghill, they resented it. To this group children were always enemies, and weapon by weapon, Mr Duane, who should have led them into battle, was disarming them.

Delights

The schools in crowded urban areas – the potential, as well as the actual slums – should be conceived on a different design and scale, as part themselves of a community centre serving all the social needs of the neighbourhood.

Yet so it was that even within this muddle of criss-crossed aims, the school began to build up, and to acquire its own proud identity. The standard of art at Risinghill was unusually high (even though the authoritarians, as they always do, looked down their noses at the young people's natural expression of art through clothes – in a district like Risinghill it is often their only means of self-expression). Partly it was because the classes were small groups right from the start; partly because it was not one of the schools where the attitude was 'They can go to art if they're not doing something more important, like A levels'; partly because the head's attitude was that art should pervade the whole school; partly because art teachers tend to be non-authoritarian, and therefore they fitted in best with the school, were among the happiest, and got good results.

The pupils painted fascinating murals, exotic kings and strange beasts, and things familiar. These were often painted out again to make room for new ones, but three I remember in particular – the market, a fair, and an imaginary Islington park, the last so gay, exuberant and witty, proclaiming the flying hopes of the Risinghill children. They hung exquisite wire and tissue mobiles in the hall, they made enchanting felt animals, gay felt curtains, and painted decorative wood panels in the library. Their art did not stay in the classroom; it pervaded the whole school by deliberate policy; and seeped through to the home in the form of ashtrays, printed cushion covers, skirts. They learned, for later days, how to cook, how to choose furniture, how to make attractive curtains cheaply. 'I know one teacher, at another school,' said Miss O'Dea, 'who used to have a public gnome-smashing; but I can't see that the kids could learn anything from that, except not to trust you.' They made masks, and mosaics, made puppets and held puppet plays, working out the script for themselves and improvising colloquially; now and then they charged the audience threepence each and gave the money to Oxfam. At Christmas time, they hung fantastic decorations in the hall – 'By far the best decorations I've seen anywhere, in any school,' said Miss O'Dea. They had a remarkable exhibition that parents came to, and exclaimed and puzzled over. They helped Zvia make the coloured slabs that the sun now shines through at Ken Wood . . . but that came later.

The two members of the L.C.C. Education Committee who in 1965 were to describe a Risinghill art room as though it were used by gibbering morons managed to miss all this. And the other members did not know enough about the school to deride them, for few of them had ever been there.

The library too was extending these children. Until the school opened, books meant for most of them only magazines, or children's pulped-up annuals. Most of them had no background of other-than-supermarket books at home – no books on shelves, books casually on armchairs, books borrowed from children's libraries, or bought and read in the evenings. At the beginning of the school, books had been handy things to throw at people, or to bang someone over the head with. When the children at last began to be interested in books for reading, the books simply disappeared from the shelves and never came back. Once, Miss Sloan, a gentle person, who with Mrs Bright concentrated with tremendous persistence on introducing the children to books, felt so despairing at the damage, the pilfering and the incessant noise that she furiously wrenched the radio switch out of its panel, appalling herself. But in 1961, she was writing:

The school seems for long periods uncannily quiet. . . . We have science and art clubs, a canoe club, a school orchestra, choirs and sports teams. The Greek, Turkish and West Indian children along with the other six nationalities which make up the school are rehearsing a nativity play for a cast of over a hundred – costumed by the needlework people. The difficult boys who are due to leave this year have taken their programme of work so seriously that they have cleared a local bomb site and laid out the foundations for a house – while at the same time learning how to make Cornish pasties. The girls change on Fridays from noisy gigglers to young social workers who visit and help old people. Our sixth-year mathematicians are applying their knowledge to the designing of a machine which plays noughts and crosses. . . .

In the library the children do as children do in any school library – they read books of their own choice, have stories read to them, pursue their own studies and learn slowly how to use books and libraries. At dinnertimes and after school they come up to read, to do their homework, to help me run the library, either because it is warmer than the playground and more peaceful than the houserooms or, simply, because it has become a habit.

The children were reading with Mrs Bright – Maupassant, Sillitoe, Shelagh Delaney. They were discussing books about genuine human problems. Even the 'lowest ability' children had learned to use books as tools as well.

The house system helped to build up warmth and vitality and that true self-importance that leads to creativity. Mr Duane felt no desire to imitate public schools; nor were the houses simply to facilitate football matches. They were organized wholly for the many Risinghill children who needed a warm homeliness, an assurance of belonging, of being included and being considered. (Not that this need is felt only in districts like Risinghill. There are plenty of children in clean suburban districts who long for this too.) Very often women teachers proved the best heads of house; but this was not always so. It was a matter of temperament and character. What was needed was a mixture of capacity for affection and understanding and the kind of patience that goes with that, plus a capacity for organization and constructive practical action. This was a blend one tends to find in women, but not by any means all women – especially now that patriarchal authoritarianism and a struggle against it had driven a rift between the two qualities. Although the governors originally tried to keep the sexes balanced when choosing heads of house, they eventually realized this was irrelevant. It was one of the women heads of house who made the 'early children' welcome, when no one else did; but it was another woman head of house who threw them out with the greatest competence.

The damage within the school was noticeably less. What did take place was mainly accidental, often due to children having to lug furniture about, because no adults were being paid to do it, and to the furniture and the structure not being solid enough or well enough designed. (The schoolkeeper said to me 'The old schools were built for strength and endurance; the new ones are built for looks.' And an architect told me that council architects always try to economize on the smaller things, in an effort to placate authority, which is why, for instance, door handles so often come off. So people say 'There you are, you see. You give them something that looks nice, and they just wreck it.')

Outside the crowds in the playground were mixing tranquillity and happiness into their astonishing liveliness and vitality; little groups talked with the unfolding expectancy of adolescents everywhere.

The crowd outside the playground, the curious spectators who had been drawn by wild reports to this vulnerably visible school as to a fairground, now found less to inflame, amuse, worry, or titillate them, and in turn no longer provoked the pupils by words, gestures or mere sardonic presence; they drifted away.

Parents were encouraged to come to school at any time at all, unheralded. And at a further distance from the school, the people of the district who had no connexion with it began to speak affectionately of it. Resentful already at the life they had been condemned to they had been even more resentful when the new school was built. The open plan of the school had given a focus to their resentment, because they could observe and comment on everything that went on in the playgrounds . . . and also they could wander in and out of the school, and some of them did. Many of them, including people who were not parents of the children at the school, had now been won over by Mr Duane's spontaneous helpfulness.

Risinghill began to be the place where the whole district sorted out their difficulties and brought their latest joys. It was already developing into a community centre and an arts centre. The children of the school may not have realized it at the time, but they were specially privileged because they were part of something bigger than only themselves yet something of which they formed the warm, living, important nucleus. Many of the teachers did not like this. They had come to get children through examinations; that was their talent and their interest; they had been trained for this and they had always been respected for this. They resented anything that distracted from their work. If the arrival of someone in distress could have been pinpointed on the timetable as social education, so many minutes, and dismissed conclusively when the bell rang, if it was something you could take A levels in, they could have looked at such episodes with a professional eye, kindly. This is what our education system had made of them.

Inspector Munday, who has been given less attention than those two inspectors who blasted the school sky-high, but was in fact the regular Ministry inspector, came for his yearly visit in July 1961. He agreed with the policy of abolishing corporal punishment, said he thought no clear improvement could possibly be seen until the toughest children – the ones from Gifford – had all left, and congratulated the head on doing the job certainly as well as anyone could and probably better than most. He sympathized with the problems, and he took it on himself to ask whether any anti-faction had developed, as he said was common in big schools, and whether any of the staff were unsympathetic to the idea of 'comprehensives'. He made it clear he enjoyed visiting Risinghill very much, and found it stimulating.

But the fear and hostility of certain teachers had been passed on to the governors and on to Inspector Macgowan and so to County Hall. The politicians held their position very precariously; they needed 'the right image' for allaying fears and attracting votes. And they were in a particularly awkward position, since comprehensive schools could not be true comprehensive schools, covering all ranges of ability, temperament and background, could not in fact be good successful schools, if the most intelligent children with the most favourable backgrounds were being creamed off to the grammar schools; but they could not say this, or reveal what it was doing to comprehensives, since many of the people whose vote they needed wanted grammar schools. Comprehensive schools were one of the main items in the

Labour programme, and the Labour politicians were now trying to maintain that they were as glamorous as the public schools many of them sent their children to; indeed, 'Eton was only a comprehensive school.'

Some people say that even as the school began to blossom it was already marked for cutting down. The children say this too, less delicately, less abstractly, more despairingly. Miss Sloan said it to me, later in 1965, more specifically. 'It naturally took us a long time to find out what we could do. And we had only been doing it for a year or two when the school was closed down.'

First warning

They need to develop a sense of responsibility for their work and towards other people, and begin to arrive at some code of moral and social be-haviour which is self-imposed.

In 1961, a year after the school had opened, the chairman of the governors, a conscientious, responsible and able Labour Party member, who knew the district extremely well and warmly supported Mr Duane, was removed from the L.C.C. Education Committee, by what was described by them as 'an unfortunate misunderstanding'; i.e. her name somehow did not appear on the ballot paper. She was now out of contact, and had no pull with officials.

Later that same year, she was summoned by the chairman of the L.C.C. Education Committee (who was then known to be campaigning for 'the right image' for comprehensive schools) and told that she was to be removed from chairmanship of the Risinghill governors, irrespective of the governors' wishes. About the same time, two governors, both enthusiastic supporters of Mr Duane – one of whom turned up at every governors' meeting, which is worthy of remark – were also superseded.

The new chairman was an ex-H.M.I. He was undoubtedly intended to provide another 'brake'. So the L.C.C. must have been infuriated very shortly afterwards, when the Great Sex Row broke out, and the new chairman warmly and unexpectedly sided with Mr Duane.

I give the original episode of this row in Mr Duane's own words, from an article in *Family Planning*.

For several weeks after the beginning of the Autumn Term, 1961, I had been taking groups of adolescent boys and girls for discussions. My aim was to try to get to know them in the slightly more informal atmosphere of such discussions better than could be possible in a series of lessons more tightly bound to a set syllabus. It was clear from the first that discussions were a bore. They were not interested in 'Jobs' or 'The H-bomb' or 'Current Affairs' for more than a few moments at a time. The horses died and remained very dead no matter how hard I flogged them.

One day I overheard a girl telling a friend what her mum had said about the daughter of a neighbour alleged to be about to have a baby by a schoolboy. I broke in and asked what the father had said. They looked startled that I had heard and that I had asked the question, but replied that the father had 'nearly killed her'. They followed this up by asking me what I would do if my own daughter (aged fourteen) told me that she was going to have a baby: 'Well, only such a thing would really test what I would do, but I hope I would have the sense to realise that she must have passed through a very unhappy time of worry, doubt and fear of discovery. I would try, therefore, to make her realise that her mother and I would be there to help and that she should not waste time and energy in regrets. What would happen to the baby would only be decided when she was in a calm frame of mind, and would depend on all kinds of things such as her feelings for the young man, on his age, on her feelings for the baby and so on.'

By this time the girls were all ears and plainly astonished that there should be anyone who could regard such an event with anything but horrified shock. The end of that lesson followed soon after and I was not able to pursue it. That same afternoon I had a double lesson with the boys. It should have been Maths but I wanted to follow up the idea that had occurred to me while talking to the girls. I told the boys what had been said during the morning, and then said:

'It's very clear that you find our discussions dull. Now ask me any question you like and I will promise to answer it truthfully if I know the answer.'

At this there were some incredulous sniggers and muffled whispers.

'*Any* question?'

'Yes.'

Not a move apart from giggles and further whispers. I realised that they were afraid of the isolation demanded by asking a question.

'If you prefer you may write the question on paper and you needn't write your name. I will go out of the room for a few minutes. Put the papers on the desk before I return.'

When I returned there was a pile of papers on the desk. I read out each question and answered it directly.

Except that I have corrected grammar and spelling to make them intelligible, the questions that follow are exactly as framed by the boys, and the answers as nearly verbatim as memory will allow.

'What is a — ?'

'The common or vulgar word for the outer parts of the female sex organs.'

'Is — a swear word?'

'This is what your father and mother did to produce you, my father and mother did to produce me, and all fathers and mothers do to produce any baby. Because nowadays we have got to the unhappy state that we speak of — as if it were something dirty or evil instead of what it is, a normal and natural act, we use the word to shock people or to make them embarrassed, and so it is used as a swear word.'

This statement was punctuated by titters, guffaws and plain roars of laughter, but the boys were staring at me with a new interest. I went on: 'Naturally you will find it embarrassing to speak so plainly about things that are commonly regarded as improper or rude or bad, but if you feel like laughing, do so; I shall understand.'

'Is it bad to take yourself in your hand?'

'I take it that you mean "masturbate", that is to cause sexual excitement by rubbing the penis with the hand. You have probably heard a lot of old wives' tales about masturbation making you unwell or weak, or even driving you mad. That is not only rubbish, it is harmful rubbish because it makes boys nervous and anxious about the possible results, or it makes them feel guilty and ashamed about what is a harmless act. If I found that a boy was practising it a great deal I should be inclined to think that his life at home was lacking in the ordinary affection that a boy should find there, or that he had not enough friends among boys and girls of his own age, or interesting things to do in his spare time.'

'Why do girls have periods?'

I gave a simple explanation, with diagrams on the board, of the menstrual cycle and its function. This was interrupted by various questions about the details of my explanation. By now all the boys were absolutely serious and could scarcely wait to ask their supplementary questions.

'How does a woman have a baby?'

Again, a simple and illustrated explanation. At one point I was explaining the function of the testicles and saw a look of puzzlement pass over their faces at the word 'testicles'.

'You probably know them as "balls".'

At this they became speechless with laughter. One boy had tears rolling down his cheeks and some were literally doubled up. I was a little taken aback. I had certainly expected them to smile or laugh but

I was not ready for the extreme form of their amusement. When I could get a word in I asked them why they had found my remark *so* funny.

'We've never heard anyone like you say a word like that.'

'What is a bastard?'

'Strictly speaking a person who has no legal father, though he must, of course, have had an actual father. Because a bastard could not inherit the property of his father and could not take his place as a normal child of his father it became a term of abuse and so a swear word.'

'What is sexual intercourse?'

'The act of inserting the penis into the vagina and releasing the sperm into the vagina.'

This was followed by many questions about the words used and the details of the act of sexual intercourse.

'Why does a boy get the "horn"?'

'The "horn" or the erection of the penis is necessary to make sure that the sperm is placed well inside the body of the woman. Since the sperm and the egg are so delicate and will only join and make a human being if the conditions of temperature, moisture, supply of blood with food, oxygen and so on are exactly right, and since those conditions are possible only in the sheltered place we know as the womb, then it is obvious that the erection of the penis is a method that has evolved to ensure that the sperm is brought close to the womb.'

'What is a "homo"?'

'A person who has strong feelings of sexual attraction towards people of the same sex instead of towards people of the opposite sex. May be caused by the normal balance of chemicals in the body being disturbed, or by the child having been brought up by only one parent and by people of the same sex as that parent so that the child cannot experience affection for people of both sexes. People do not choose to be "homo", so it is wrong and foolish to punish them for what they cannot help. Some people like this have been great artists or very kind and brave in helping others.'

'What is — ?'

'It is sometimes used to mean copulate and sometimes to mean "masturbate".'

'What is a ponce?'

'A man who employs women to go to bed with men for money. He takes the money in return for paying them some wages and "protecting" them or making sure that no rival women interfere with them.'

'What is "love-juice"?'

'The liquid produced in the vagina of a woman when she is sexually excited. It has the function of making it easy for the penis to enter the vagina.'

'What is V.D.?'

'V.D. stands for venereal disease, and strictly speaking refers to any disease affecting the sex organs, but it normally is taken to refer to one particular disease which if not recognized and treated in the early stages may lead to complete breakdown of the nervous system and death.'

'Can V.D. be caught from a toilet?'

'That is very unlikely unless you have a sore place or a cut through which the germs could enter your blood stream directly. However, this is one more reason for being fussy about the cleanliness of cups and glasses used in cafés and restaurants, and about the cleanliness of toilets.'

'What is a "Lesie" [Lesbian]?'

'Roughly a female "homo".'

The number of questions relating to the less normal or more perverted manifestations of sex is a sad reflection of the unhealthy surroundings in which so many of these young people are compelled to spend their youth, and where they are too often brought into contact with attitudes that are unhealthy, depraved or merely financially determined.

'What is the difference between a "pro" and a "whore"?'

'Not much. A "pro" usually does it for a living whether she enjoys it or not. A whore does it for enjoyment. The words are, however, often interchanged since neither base their activities on anything we would normally call "love" or affection.'

'How long do you keep your prick in the girl?'

'Since the actual ejaculation lasts only for a matter of seconds it is strictly necessary to have the penis in the vagina only for the time during which this occurs, but if the man and the woman care for each other at all they will normally enjoy being together before and after the ejaculation and will wish to give each other the greatest possible degree of pleasure.'

Immediate Results

By the time the double lesson had come to an end the attitude of the boys had undergone a dramatic change. Whereas at the beginning they were restless, ready for a 'lark' or a 'muck-about' or a 'giggle', horsing about, overfull of undisciplined energy, loud in volume and

manner, by the end they were quiet in a way I had not hitherto experienced, leaning forward intent on every word, listening carefully
(this a remarkable change!) to questions asked by other boys, and in
general displaying a self-control such as I had not observed in them
during other lessons. On other occasions I had had to bully them into
making the desks tidy, into picking up the odd scraps of paper from
the floor, and into leaving the room in a reasonable state for the
incoming class. On this occasion to my surprise they did these things
without being asked. Further, they went out of the room in a relaxed
and quiet manner, said, 'Cheerio, Sir' and walked down the corridor
instead of galumphing. One boy found an excuse to loiter after the
others had left and asked me whether long hair prevented intercourse.
I checked that he referred to pubic hair and told him that I had not
heard of such a thing.

Some days later George, a notorious dodger with a long record of
appearances in court for truancy and violence, backward and idle,
with two older brothers in prison for assault, with an aggressive bully
for a father, went to the Second Master and asked to see me. He was
told that I was busy at that moment, but he insisted on trying to see
me. Eventually the Second Master persuaded him to tell him what
was the matter:

'Can sperms cause a baby?'

'Of course, nitwit, what do you think they are for?'

'Yes, but in a boy of my age?'

'Certainly.'

'Oh, Gord!'

For the few days immediately after the first lesson the boys wanted
to have questions in every lesson and I agreed. The questions were
largely repetitive of the earlier ones but I thought I detected a wish
to reassure themselves that I was serious in my attempts to satisfy
their needs for reliable information, and particularly to be certain that
I would not suddenly turn on them and denounce their questions
as 'dirty' or 'wicked'. Gradually the questions died down and normal
lessons were resumed. Now only very occasionally does a boy ask a
question and when I reply that I will deal with it at the end of the
lesson he seems content to wait.

The change of attitude that began on the first day has continued. I
had to revert to my daily bullying to get the room tidy, but I found that
attendance at my lessons improved and has continued to remain good,
that the boys will listen more attentively to the routine material of
teaching, that they seem to feel less resentment when spoken to
sharply for poor work or carelessness. In general there seems to be an

air of greater relaxation and less tension in the normal lessons. The boys smile more easily; they seem less anxious to impress me or their fellows with how big and tough they are. They are clearly more amenable. As a result I am able to cover more ground in the syllabus more easily.

A few days ago I heard one of the boys shout abuse at another which included the word —. I told him that I did not like to hear a good word misused and made him write it out six hundred times after school. He appears to bear little resentment. I hope that I have not damaged his sex life irretrievably.

Sex Education — One Definition

Clearly, the 'lifebelt' operation described here and carried out in what I considered to be a state of emergency in view of the little school time left for these boys, could in no real sense be held to be 'sex education'. It was designed merely to begin to break down the barrier that I have too often found to exist between the adolescents and our middle-aged generation.

Sex education is not something learnt from books or lectures. It should, in my view, embrace a wide range of experiences and activities including all of the following:

a. the answering of all questions posed by children from their earliest years in the fullest and frankest manner possible consonant with the ability of the child to understand intellectually and imaginatively and to absorb emotionally.

b. the bringing up of children in a family atmosphere of affection and happiness where curiosity and plain speech are not restricted and where natural modesty is respected.

c. the instruction of school children in the rudiments of anatomy and biology including the processes of reproduction in animals and humans.

d. the discussion at home and at school of the personal, social and ethical problems raised by sex in modern life, and of the structure of family relationships, material, social and psychological, and their bearing on the development of a healthy and autonomous individual.

e. the study, from the beginning of adolescence, of literature dealing with the relationships of men and women, and of works of art in all media inspired by such experiences. Study to include acting and singing in mixed groups.

f. the expression by adolescents of their own feelings in writing, painting, sculpture, dance, music or any other medium felt to be relevant by the young artist.

g. the sharing, from their earliest years, of experiences in work and play by boys and girls under both men and women teachers.

h. the freedom for boys and girls of all ages to form friendships without interference.

At the actual time Mr Duane duplicated an uncensored account for his staff, and also gave copies to Inspector Macgowan and the governors. The new chairman said it was an excellent piece of work, and added, 'Have you got anyone who can do the same for the girls ?' Inspector Macgowan, however, was distressed and horrified, and went off to County Hall to show the Chief Inspector his copy of the document that proved that when the boys of Risinghill said 'What is a cunt ?' Mr Duane told them.

The result of this was that when, about eight months later, *Family Planning*, a conscientious and thoughtful magazine published by the Family Planning Association and containing articles by doctors, printed the censored account by a headmaster, *unnamed*, at a school *unnamed*, of 'Sex Education – a Small Experiment', which incidentally received favourable comments afterwards from their readers, the L.C.C. at once summoned Mr Duane to County Hall to account.

He was given a furious dressing-down by the Chief Inspector of the time, who was not affected by the fact that the school was not identified in the article, nor the fact that the questions, though not the answers, had been censored (so that you had the enchanting position of a boy asking 'What is a — ?' and miraculously always getting the right answer).

Was the position that the L.C.C. did not know what — was, or that they did know but didn't want anyone else to know ? Or was the reason the one given by the Education Officer to Mr Duane at a stormy County Hall meeting – that comprehensive schools are a hot political issue, and that the L.C.C. must have 'the right image', and didn't want to give 'their enemies' any handle ?

Sniping from inside

Our schools will not be what they should until we give them the teachers they need.

It seems to have been about this time that one or two teachers began to spread scurrilous sex rumours about Mr Duane.

It is true, of course, as a school governor has said to me, that sex fantasies are always invented about co-educational schools, by people who do not go to them. But the Risinghill stories had an extra twist – they were invented in the first place by one or two teachers who *did* go to the school at least as teachers, but who had not chosen to go to a co-educational school, or perhaps didn't like its stand against corporal punishment. And only later were they invented or spread by others. I asked one teacher how these sex stories arose, and she shrugged and said 'Some people hate to see other people happy. Some people see others having freedom and don't like it. Some want it themselves and think they shouldn't want it.'

The stories were spread by one teacher to newcomers on the staff, and were planted by another among the staff at evening institutes. Mr Duane, who was worrying not about his own reputation but about other people's, finally threatened this second teacher with an injunction unless he told people that the stories he had told were false; this he promised to do, and Mr Duane took the matter no further.

But the stories sent out could scarcely be collected in again, and in fact have continued on their way with embellishments. If Mr Duane had been thinking of self-protection, he would have taken out an injunction, right at the start.

These stories were still circulating at the time of the closing of Risinghill. They were circulating among teachers and among head teachers and among members of the L.C.C. Education Committee; they were being spread *by* teachers, *by* head teachers, and *by* members of the Education Committee. I first heard some of them from a teacher who had heard them from primary school heads. They were very ludicrous and sad. One goes something like this. 'Did you hear that a boy at Risinghill said to one of the teachers "When's the sex lesson going to start, Miss?" And she said "Well the classroom door's open. Take your girl in there. Both of you strip down and get started. Then you can write about it".' What is the emotional situation of educationalists who either believe these stories, or who spread them maliciously not believing them? I have heard quite explicitly that people involved in the Risinghill move who queried the L.C.C.'s publicly stated reasons for closing Risinghill, and who therefore were being awkward about getting things moving, were told of 'sexual irregularities' which were too scandalous to be spoken of publicly but which, undescribed, were good enough to bring any faint rebels to heel; 'a nod is as good as a wink, old man.'

Attack 1962—5

First blow from outside

Problems of poverty, health and delinquency are involved.

New Year 1962, making an exception for Risinghill, rang in the old, rang out the new. Twenty L.C.C. Inspectors descended on Risinghill in January for a most gigantic 'visitation'.

This rather high-powered word is used by the L.C.C. for an informal visit by inspectors that is not followed by a printed report presented formally to the Education Committee. Rising-hill had – apart from frequent visits by single inspectors – three 'visitations'. It never had a formal full-scale inspection; and none of its three reports were ever presented, formally or informally, to the Education Committee. It seems it was possible to close it without that.

By the time the twenty inspectors arrived, the teachers who most rigidly opposed Mr Duane had spent a lot of time with Inspector Macgowan (who spent a lot of time at County Hall); at least one of them believed, perhaps mistakenly, that he had promised a reorganization of the school from Head to toe.

The anxious teachers were more humble. They merely hoped that the authority would say that when they tried to carry out Mr Duane's policy they were doing right; they hoped to get a good mark for really trying.

A report, even a duplicated not a printed report, of a state school is highly confidential. No parent has any right to know what is happening at a school his child goes to, or what an inspector believes to be happening (a belief which may be wrong, and which the parent may know is wrong, but on which the inspector will take action affecting his child). No citizen has any right to know what the education for which he pays rates and taxes consists of, or what it is thought by authority which spends his money that it *should* consist of. No parent, or prospective parent, has any right to see the documents that might best help him to choose a school for his child. No voter has any right to know what educational policies are put into operation, and *how* they are put into operation, by the people he votes for.

As a parent and someone interested in the welfare of children, and as one who has always paid rates and taxes without demur, I find this unacceptable. Fortunately I am in a position to quote from the report.

. . . The Headmaster has pursued a policy eschewing corporal punishment. . . .

. . . Graffiti [*sic*] of the most obscene sort proliferate . . . the ubiquity of indecent writing . . . appalling signs written on the walls as in some public lavatory. . . .

. . . An acute epidemic of partial truancy. . . . The scattered site made this easy and neither the system of internal registers nor an increase in staff supervision has wholly cured the vice. The tougher elements did not feel that the sanctions they might incur were severe enough to make attempted flight unprofitable. . . .

. . . [The headmaster] esteems cordiality among the major virtues. . . . His approach to Staff and pupils is informal. . . . It is difficult to say that he carries the aura of the Headmaster around with him and though he inspires some liking, he fails largely to inculcate respect. Indeed, he may well regard this respect as basically unnecessary in human relations. . . .

. . . [She is of] outstanding integrity and character. . . . Much of Risinghill's success is due to her, and she has not always been sufficiently consulted or considered. It must be said that she is unfortunately not the professionally happy woman that she was once. . . .

. . . is equally commendable. She holds the trust of the Staff and is an outspoken presenter of their views. She handles people with tact and skill, and has had to carry a heavy weight of cares. Her role in the school cannot be over-estimated. . . .

. . . Among the senior Staff are people of remarkable dedication. Several of the Housemasters and mistresses are exemplary. They too carry a disproportionate weight of responsibility and do not always feel themselves integrated parts of a community. They all have from time to time expressed fears that they may be compelled to look for posts elsewhere where conditions are less exacting. . . .

. . . a high standard of competent teaching. In some subjects it is outstanding. . . .

. . . the children do not hold authority in any awe. . . . It seems useless to initiate a campaign against smoking when members of staff are to be seen smoking in public. Similarly, girls are unlikely to abandon stiletto heels, if three members of staff wear them in class. . . .

. . . In spite of the heroic efforts of some senior staff, the school's personality remains amorphous, fugitive and ambiguous. A greater measure of central control and direction is essential. . . .

. . . The Headmaster holds the conception of the School Council in high esteem. . . . There can be no doubt of the goodwill of all concerned; but a careful study of the Council's minutes suggests that the conclusions reached by the Council are not carried out. During the Visitation, the door marked 'For Visitors, Staff and Prefects only' was a way of common tread; yet this question had been fully discussed in Council and the decision to reserve this entrance communicated to the Houses. It was perhaps also tactically unwise to record in the Minutes that the Headmaster disapproved of corporal punishment; his attitude may have been interpreted as weakness among the chronically ill-disposed. There is moreover some suggestion that some members of the Staff feel that the Council discusses matters which properly are the affair of the Staff. It is clear that the fledgling democracy of the school is in need of firm and discreet guidance by responsible adults. . . .

. . . Instructions to the Staff lack precision. . . .

. . . It is odd to find that such titles as . . . *Sex Instruction in Swedish Schools* were being purchased [for the staff] from the allocation for the school library. . . .

. . . The other two full-time [art] teachers are leaving at the end of the term because both find the school too undisciplined to give of their best. . . .

. . . There is an atmosphere of indiscipline which is difficult to describe. . . . its effect in the Art Department is almost catastrophic. As far as can be seen it appears that only some of the children work at all and then for only some of the time. The loss of productive hours of work because the children are so uninterested and to put it simply, quite unruly, is enormous. Added to this is of course the frustration of the teaching staff who have so much to give, and also the tiredness of the Staff which is very evident. . . .

. . . Few Headmasters have so many undaunted colleagues in a team. . . .

. . . There is no doubt that day by day superficial behaviour has improved. It could hardly have grown worse without disaster. . . .

. . . The efforts of most of the Staff are beyond praise. . . .

. . . There have been too many signs of strain among staff, among good staff, too great a feeling that there is neither unity of purpose nor strength of leadership. Even in the matter of discipline, on which the Headmaster holds lofty and inflexible views, there is no uniformity from house to house. The only thing of which children can be sure is that punishment will normally be benign and the Staff hesitate to take upon themselves responsibilities which properly lie elsewhere. It may well be that friendliness too frequently degenerates into un-dignified informality; the regular clutter of children outside the Head-master's door is perhaps not the symbol of comradeship but the reve-lation of confusion. . . . Sometimes in avoiding terror the school has abandoned awe. . . .

I read this report with mounting incredulity. It drew *officially* a firm line between the head and his staff, denounced and sneered at the one, praised and sympathized with the other while carefully isolating, disapproving of, or warning, the younger teachers. It praised work that was being done in the school while at the same time saying the head was working against it. It spoke of instruc-tions to the staff lacking precision, which is very strange since Inspector Macgowan when he first saw Mr Duane's initial routine instructions to staff – a most unusual and conscientious document at that time – was heard to remark that Mr Duane had done everything for his staff bar tell them how to wipe their noses.

After this report even more of the staff felt free, even *obliged*, to work against Mr Duane's policy; they had the expressed views of the inspectors to guide them. At last, they had been 'told'.

The inspectors did not mention that the School Council had broken up the gang warfare; perhaps they were not aware of it. But they were aware that it was not supporting the hierarchy – letting people come through the wrong doors. After the visitation, most of the staff, with great satisfaction, chose to boycott the School Council, with the result that it, helplessly, died. This was another omen.

In the autumn of 1960, 184 children had been accepted by Risinghill and, of these, 156 were below average in 'ability' rating. Inspector Macgowan, though he did say this was 'a difficult area' and spoke of 'chronically ill-disposed elements' among the children, did not mention this, nor did he mention brothels and rats and broken sewers. He knew that corporal punishment keeps them out of sight.

He mentioned 'graffiti' (another self-conscious word) but not the ones scrawled all round these children's homes. Nor, apparently, was he aware that in the telephone kiosks in the Institute of Education they are etched, it seems, by graduate teachers. Mr Duane mentioned this.

So Mr Duane was told he would have to take 'certain urgent steps', and was summoned to County Hall, confronted by seven or eight officials, told this was 'the blackest report we have ever seen', warned by one of them he had better get legal representation, and ordered by Dr Briault to bring back corporal punishment and public expulsion. He refused.

Two and a half years later, the Swedish book that so worried Mr Macgowan that he named it in his report was among those recommended to teachers in the L.C.C.'s booklet 'Some Notes on Sex Education'. So were seventeen other books available at Risinghill.

The booklet however was in unmistakable L.C.C. style, and warned that sex instruction should not be given by anyone who had 'an undue interest' in it. (Imagine applying this criterion to other subjects, say maths or religion.)

Re-grouping

The less his school, or any school, is an island to itself the better. If it is to serve this generation it needs to be joined to the mainland of life by a causeway well-trodden in both directions.

The Macgowan report was a bugle-call. It made the traditionalists feel part of an institution again, made the anxious jump, and made the creative teachers grit their teeth.

The all-out traditionalists of course believed quite sincerely that they had been proved 'right' – as if the inspectors were pieces of litmus paper that had dispassionately turned blue; one of them rejoiced openly at the report. They expected an instant change of personnel and organization. Teachers who disagreed with Mr Duane and who but for the report would have left for other easily available jobs in schools more congenial to them now stayed to fight him.

The anxious 'middle section' of teachers who had been trying hard to do what they felt was wanted of them, now changed from supporting Mr Duane to being hostile. Furthermore, being generally more sensitive than the traditionalists they had become aware that they were involved in a 'political matter', and that the approval of County Hall now rested on matters in which educational efforts were irrelevant. Naturally this played on their nerves, and distracted them from carrying out policies they were just beginning to find creative.

'The staff is always keyed up when inspectors come,' said someone to me. 'It was depressing to feel out of favour at County Hall. I began to feel myself that things said defensively to inspectors, excusing what was inevitable in the social circumstances (that the children weren't reading, for instance), were being interpreted and used as criticism of the head. It was most damaging to morale.'

The teachers who had throughout been using a creative policy

with the children had been misinterpreted, their growing supporters had been routed, and their opposition consolidated, enlarged and perpetuated.

'It was wicked', one of the staff was to say to me later, 'that
Mr Duane should have been undermined in this way.' And
undermined not only within his own school. For she also said
'When it became known that inspectors and the L.C.C. were
gunning for the school, the primary heads knew they weren't
supposed to send children.' In view of the things that were said
later, I found this interesting . . . almost as if the school began to
be closed in 1962, two years after it had opened.

Six months later, three of the inspectors returned, to make a
follow-up report. It was as remarkable as the original report —
as glowing in praise as the first had been damning.

They said they felt very flattered that their advice had been
accepted . . . the headmaster had inspired his colleagues to
remarkable achievements that suggested there had been most
encouraging team-work . . . they congratulated the headmaster
and his colleagues . . . glad to see the head was co-operating with
them . . . they felt very differently about the school now . . . and
so on. They seemed to reverse everything they had said in
January.

Surely a school as bad as they had felt Risinghill to be could
not have taken on 'the approved pattern' in only six months, with
the same head and staff? How had the 'lack of leadership', 'lack
of unity of purpose', 'the confusion' turned so swiftly into 'most
encouraging team-work'?

After this second report, Inspector Macgowan oddly enough
disappeared from Risinghill. But perhaps even more odd was
that, all the time he was speaking so alertly and so gravely of the
position at Risinghill, the L.C.C. Education Committee members
didn't all visit the school to see for themselves.

Intriguingly, his disappearance threw the authoritarian
teachers into a tumult of anxiety. They had pinned a great deal
on what they believed he had promised them, and were now very
disturbed. I think they then determined to use any weapon that
came to hand to make sure of victory, believing perhaps that he
sanctioned it.

I have been told he is now concentrating on the subject he enjoys – modern languages viewed from an academic standpoint, and particularly the idea of teaching a second language in primary schools. He had high qualifications, but they were inappropriate to Risinghill; indeed his interests were such that he very likely felt Risinghill as a frustrating place. Why, one wonders, was a specialist in French ever sent there?

First blow from inside

Discussion should be used to develop judgement and discrimination. This may apply to enjoyment in music or art or literature; to taste and craftsmanship in the workshop; to a sense of what is appropriate behaviour in a particular situation, which will generally involve some consideration of other people's feelings and points of view.

A conversation at Risinghill between four girls and a teacher:

JOY: I think the blacks should go back, cos there's old people who want homes and there's all darkies in 'em – and Greeks.

MARLENE: My mum says if they all went back to their own country there wouldn't be no trouble about it all.

LINDIE: Some of 'em got money off the National Health, and they have a lot of kids –

JOY: And they get all the best rooms and everything.

MARLENE: They don't. You know how much they pay for one room?

LINDIE: Yes, but fifteen of 'em live in two rooms.

MARLENE: There's some I like and there's some I can't stand.

LINDIE: And these Indians earn a lot here, and if they were in their own country they wouldn't earn nothing.

JOY: Yes, when whites are in black countries there's a war, isn't there?

LINDIE: They should chuck 'em all out of this country, and just have our country here. When we go out to their country they start complaining. They start wars and that.

TEACHER: It's not quite true, is it?

JOY: They've got wars over there, haven't they?

TEACHER: Over where?

JOY: Look at the soldiers they're killing in their civil war. They're our soldiers.

TEACHER: What about the American Negroes fighting against Hitler in the last war?

MARLENE: They fought because they like fighting.

LINDIE: There are some make me sick.

JOY: Look, in this school it's about fifty-fifty, blacks and whites.

TEACHER: No, it isn't.

JOY: You look at the crowd of girls downstairs. It's about three black and one white.

LINDIE: And they don't half reckon themselves.

MARLENE: And altogether, Greeks and all, it's fifty-fifty.

RENE: They get a better chance than whites.

MARLENE: You know that Annette Brown's Dad? Well, when his wife died he went down the Labour Exchange and he got two pounds. And there was a wog going down there and he got five pounds, and all he'd got were his wife and two children.

LINDIE: They do. They get more money. They have all the big cars an' all. They have all those kids so they get the money on 'em. That's all they come here for – the National Assistance.

MARLENE: My mum reckons when she's walking down the Cally* on a sunny day, it feels like she's in Jamaica.

LINDIE: My mum reckons she was waiting at the bus stop and there was this girl expecting a baby and a coloured lady, and she said 'You ain't getting on this bus' and pushed her off, and she lost her baby. Ever since then she hates 'em and won't talk to none of 'em.

TEACHER: That can happen with a white conductor too.

LINDIE: No, it wasn't a conductor. It was another lady. She said 'You're not getting on before me' and pushed her off the step.

RENE: They eat Kit-e-Kat, monkeys, bananas, green bananas. They eat garlic and even pigeons.

MARLENE: And they get snails and they crack 'em. Oooh, it's terrible.

TEACHER: I've eaten pigeon pie. They eat it in Gloucestershire. They shoot wood pigeons.

MARLENE: I hate Ching Chongs too, but there aren't many over here.

LINDIE: And Jews –

MARLENE: Oh yeah –

TEACHER: How do you know I'm not a Jew?

LINDIE: Are you? We don't. You haven't got a big conk like them.

MARLENE: Some are all right.

TEACHER: If I was a Jew would your attitude change towards me?
[Three noes; Marlene, 'yes' – then]

MARLENE: Not if you was nice.

LINDIE: I've never known a Jew who was nice. Have you ever met a Jew who you like?

JOY: There's a Jew next to us and I went in there once –

LINDIE: They own all the clothing factories and have people working there.

*The Caledonian Market.

TEACHER: If you were going to send all the foreigners home, those who were not English –

LINDIE: Oh yes, the Irish and Scottish could stay, or my dad would have to go.

JOY: Anyone who lives in the British Isles is all right.

TEACHER: – you would have to send me too, because my father had a Jewish grandmother.

MARLENE: Yes, but you're an English Jew though. Was your Dad a nice man, or was he a horrible old miser?

TEACHER: I think you should see people just as they are – for what they do, not their colour or nationality.

MARLENE: No, I'm not against colour.

LINDIE: But I mean, some coloured people you could wring their necks.

TEACHER: But you could wring some white people's necks too.

LINDIE: Yes!

In January 1962, about the same time as the Macgowan report, the Institute of Education asked Mr Duane if he would allow one of Professor James's research students – a Lebanese teacher – to investigate relations between white and coloured children at Risinghill. (It was as a result of an investigation by Professor James and Dr Tenen at Mr Duane's Howe Dell school that the book *The Teacher was Black* was published.) Mr Duane agreed and as a result Mr Jedda came to Risinghill.

For six weeks or so, Mr Jedda got to know the pupils, the staff and the school. Then he began discussions with the children: what did they feel about children of other nationalities, different coloured skin? . . . had they seen such-and-such a newspaper report, and did they think it was accurate, or fair? . . . Finally, in consultation with Professor James and Mr Duane, Mr Jedda drew up a questionnaire, which he now asked children who wanted to do so to fill in; Mr Duane was always present.

'Parents and society at large set the tone,' Mr Jedda said. 'The children say "They take our jobs" – obviously taken from adults – and then go on to say "and they're dirty in the toilets." At one class Mr Duane had an argument with a boy who said "They steal our jobs and our houses." The other children were against Mr Duane and argued back. The Cypriot boy in the class took it as a joke. . . .'

Mr Duane questioned ten of his most experienced and perceptive teachers, during and after these sessions. Eight saw no effect of any kind on the children. Two had found the questionnaires provided useful starting-points for discussions. (It was noticed at this time that several children said they liked 'blacks' but didn't like 'Greeks' – which for them means Cypriots. Mr Jedda thought this was maybe because the Cypriots preserved their own culture.) Mr Duane himself believed that open discussion '*in circumstances where calm inquiry can prevail*' leads to a reduction of tense feelings; and this was borne out.

The authoritarian teachers did not like it; they had a horror of 'things coming out'. One of them deliberately read, almost on the spot, the written answers that Mr Jedda had promised the child would be confidential . . . as a demonstration of contempt. Another said 'You come here, and destroy what it has taken us ages to build up.' Another said 'You have no right to ask the children anything. That is our job.' Although racial questions were openly discussed by the children in the playground and commented upon openly on local street walls and lavatory walls (and equally offensively in the staff room by some authoritarian teachers), the authoritarians became increasingly hostile.

What happened next was bizarre. First of all, a man with an educated voice telephoned Mr Duane, and said he was a lawyer, and that a parent had instructed him to order Mr Duane to stop the survey. When Mr Duane asked 'Who are you ? Who is the parent ?' the man rang off. No more was heard from him . . . at least, in this guise.

Next, half the Communist teachers at Risinghill, a small but formidable group, accused Mr Duane of spreading racial hatred. This was obviously lunatic, and indeed other Communists, the ones who supported a non-authoritarian policy, seem to have been very embarrassed and even angered. But, undeterred, they took the matter to County Hall. The L.C.C. told Mr Duane the survey must stop immediately. (Interesting that the Socialist L.C.C. paid more attention to the Conservatives and some of the Communists than to the Socialist chairman of the governors, and the Socialist leader of the parents.)

The group, having used the L.C.C., then went on to make use

of the London Teachers' Association (a branch of the N.U.T.). They roused them to heights of fury against Mr Duane for his 'racial hostility' (taking care to 'pack' the meeting with Communists; Communists like other authoritarians have a tendency to support each other for the sake of the System). The meeting passed a resolution deploring what was going on at Risinghill. At this point Mr Duane resigned membership, but was persuaded by union leaders to remain.

I was struck over and over again by the hostility of this small group towards Mr Duane, a hostility that was well-organized and implemented. I hesitate to reckon how far it was, with one powerful teacher at least, entirely personal. But I think too they were jealous of the respect and affection he drew from working-class families, and angry because he did it without their leave.

And some of them were ambitious, and had done well for their careers at their earlier authoritarian schools. Besides Mr Jedda had once defended Mr Duane in the staffroom, when some teachers were attacking him, 'not to make trouble, simply expressing my opinion. I was made instantly aware I had put myself into one ideological camp. It was a bad mistake.' And then Mr Jedda was an Arab, when they in this little group were Jews, and the Arab-Jew conflict could be as intense as the Turkish-Greek one. There were so many different conflicts at Risinghill and if they were not openly admitted, which would have made them harmless and constructive, they bumped and buzzed like angry bees who would one day swarm out to sting like fury.

The next year, the Greek newspaper carried the glowing account of Risinghill's work which I mentioned earlier; and later, at a Greek-Turkish party where Michael Duane was a guest, the editor, a Greek poet, talked enthusiastically to him about Risinghill – and introduced him to a friend who particularly wanted to meet him, to express appreciation and friendship and ask him questions, who turned out to be the Secretary of the Greek Communist Party! But the resolution of the L.T.A., English-Communist-packed that night, still, I presume, stands.

Mr Jedda, by the way, being thrown out of Risinghill, went on to other London schools, where the staff did not mind him at all. His relations with them and the children became very informal, which was the atmosphere he needed for his work; the children would come to him with family problems. (Once a boy came to him, almost in tears, and said 'Mum left Dad last night. What am I going to do?' They talked about it for a long time. Then the mother came back, and he and the boy celebrated riotously with fish and chips.) At the last school, the staff asked him to come back; many of them kept visiting him until he was too busy with his thesis to see friends any longer. A few days after the government had agreed to close down Risinghill, the newspapers carried the story 'A thousand schoolchildren to be questioned on racial attitude'. A survey was to be carried out by Dudley Training College. It had become respectable.

Looking back at the conversation that began this chapter, it is laughable to remember that some Risinghill teachers claimed Mr Jedda and Mr Duane were putting ideas into the children's heads. The kindest thing one can say is that they must have been incredibly ignorant of the children they were teaching, and the wider slogan-scrawled district they were living in.

It is worth remarking too that a conversation exactly like that would no more take place at A. S. Neill's Summerhill than it would at Eton. These children came to Risinghill, not with the Nanny-nursery-prep-school background of Eton, nor the Susan Isaacs, Freud and Homer Lane background of present-day Summerhill. They came with years of brutal environment behind them, years of hostility in which only power had counted, years of hate which look forward to adulthood only because 'that is when *we* will be on top and that is when it will be *our* turn to make children pay for being small and vulnerable.' You cannot change the environment overnight.

But their environment goes on existing. However much you put uniforms on the children, make them stand up when a teacher comes in, cane them when they swear, and threaten them with expulsion, they are still going back to a home that is next to a brothel, or a home where they have to climb through the window to get into an empty kitchen. Is all we can do to teach them to say 'Bother this frightful life' instead of 'Sod this fucking life!'?

*

The nativity play put a glorious end to an appalling year . . . a year which had started with an inspector talking of certain children as 'chronically ill-disposed elements'.

It is one of my greatest regrets that I never saw it, this play in which every child's nationality was something to contribute, to delight in. I heard so much about it, questioned so many people, heard about the West Indian children's calypsos and the Turkish children's graceful belly-dancing. I studied the photographs of the children and imagined the jewelled gold of Herod, the embroidered purple of his queen, their tiny Cypriot attendants bare to the waist, with Turkish trousers, peacock fans and turbans like silk melons, with their one-string Turkish mandoline, and the Chinese emperor in pale blue silk, entering to his fascinating music, the African king dignified and graceful, carrying assegais and furry spears, and the loutish British king, his men stumbling uncouthly in leather and brass tunics, helmets with horns and tartan trousers, with their jester riding his hobby-horse . . . and the songs, like 'Bethlehem on a Saturday Night', idiomatic, starting from the children's own life, but soaring away.

The *Islington Gazette* loved it.

Not for Risinghill the worn-out gimmicks – the paper wings for Angel Gabriel and cute kiddies wrapped in yards of mummy's discarded curtains and a cardboard star while parents smile affectionately. For Risinghill – the impact of luxurious costumes just like King Herod and the three kings from the East must have worn. For Risinghill – the impact of a thunderingly majestic orchestra which accompanied a grandiose choir. For Risinghill – the impact of a multi-racial cast adding oriental splendour and striking authenticity to this most exciting of tales. As I left Risinghill Street and walked in the chilly December night air down Chapel Market, I wept slowly with emotion at the greatest nativity play I have ever had the honour and privilege to see.

(For Risinghill too, of course, a real baby.)

Lady Armstrong came from the Royal Academy of Music to see it, and enjoyed the music and the dancing and the use of the different nationalities, though she found the colloquial atmosphere a little irreverent.

The woman chairman of the governors said to me:

This was the first of the two extraordinary performances that were given at the height of the school's powers. It just isn't possible to organize things like that unless there is some beneficent influence at the back. They were tremendous occasions. Everyone thought so. When you talk to people about it, they say 'Oh that's all very well but that isn't the purpose of a school.' I myself think that it is a very large part of education. The difficulty is you can't measure it. The whole school was involved. You felt you'd really been through an experience. I am associated with other schools, and have some means of comparison, and what struck me was the way the whole school – children and staff – were welded into a unity.

But there was no one there from the L.C.C. Education Committee. I was told, by someone who had considerable contact with them, 'There were a few important people on the L.C.C. who were against the school – maybe three. Other members, therefore, did not go to the school, because to go would imply not only unhealthy interest but even, perhaps, approval.'

For a short time, then, the whole of the Risinghill staff were united in a brief vision, delighting themselves and the children. Yet at the beginning of the year, one of the teachers who contributed a great deal to this performance had openly rejoiced at the Macgowan report that attacked Mr Duane, and another who contributed much was to say, in 1965, to a bewildered parents' meeting, that a child had shot at him, and help get the school closed down.

That Prize Day, Mr Duane said:

Examinations are necessary in a highly technical society like ours, but to measure a school by exam results is like estimating the quality of a man's life by the number of calories he burns, or the number of footpounds of energy he expends. They bear no relation to the real purposes of living. Real life is bound up with other people, with personal relations, with love and man's need to serve.

I do not by any means claim that the school is yet running in the way we would hope to see, but at least a beginning has been made, and in such a way that the children seem to be retaining their vigour, their spontaneity, and their zest for life. These are important.

*

1963 was a good year for Risinghill School. That year the children were able to hand over the job of moving dining-room furniture to the school-keeping staff. But it was still the children, who obviously were not strong enough or controlled enough in their movements to shift heavy furniture skilfully, who had to move the furniture for assemblies, as there weren't enough school-keeping staff to cope with this too. When eventually a sympathetic senior official in charge of equipment was taken round the school by Mr Duane and actually saw what was happening, he was horrified, and ordered hundreds of extra chairs. But mainly the L.C.C. did not see what was happening, and later was to talk about the children having damaged the furniture. They did not say then that they were using the children as an unpaid labour force.

It was the year too of the magnificent *Easter Cantata*, based on the Bach *St Matthew Passion*, written by the same teacher who had written the music for the nativity play. Again the different national characteristics of the children were used creatively, again the whole school, children and staff, were united, everyone contributing what they could. The orchestra, mainly an enormous body of string-playing children, were mostly beginners, but playing in unison on bare open strings they produced an astonishing spine-chilling effect. This was the second 'extraordinary performance'.

And for the whole country it was, of course, the year of the Newsom Report.

Mr John Newsom, who had followed Mr Duane's work in Hertfordshire and Suffolk with sympathy, though perhaps some trepidation, was now chairman of the Central Advisory Council for Education. The government had given the Council the job of reporting on the education of children 'of average or less than average ability' aged between thirteen to sixteen. These children, said Mr Newsom,

constitute half the pupils of our secondary schools; they will eventually become half the citizens of this country, half the workers, half the mothers and fathers and half the consumers. . . . We are concerned that there should be a change of attitude towards these young people not only among many of those who control their education but among the public at large and this cannot be achieved solely, if at all, by administrative action. It involves a change of thinking and even more a change of heart.

The Newsom Report was called *Half our Future*. (I wonder how many people think of our rejected children as *half* our children.*) It was a most valuable document, and on the question of staff, it had this to say:

Here we must urgently draw attention again to the special difficulty of securing and retaining good teachers, for schools of all kinds, in slum, heavy industrial and other ill-favoured areas. The children of these areas, because of their surroundings, are severely handicapped at the outset of their education, and *they stand in need of especially gifted teachers*. In these times of teacher shortages, however, to which we see no early end, highly gifted and experienced teachers can choose where they will work; and, although some with a strong sense of vocation fortunately do choose to work in the least attractive areas, many, understandably, do not. These areas in consequence tend to have more than their share of teachers who cannot secure other appointments, coupled with a formidable turnover of teachers who are only there until they can move elsewhere. [The italics are mine.]

Everyone acclaimed the Report, though some got the cheering over quickly.

It came out a few days before the Robbins Report on university education, which interests any British government of the present day (in 1963 it was Conservative) far more than 'average and under-average' children for it affects more immediately our competition with other countries. *Labour*, the T.U.C. magazine, said '... the Newsom Report was received politely but non-committally by the Government as though it were the cart sanding the road for the Lord Mayor's Show'. Mr Charles Carter, chairman of the Schools Broadcasting Council, remarked much later 'The

*They are really far more than half. Professor D. V. Glass, writing in his symposium *Social Mobility in Britain* (Routledge), says 'British sociologists have sometimes been accused of being obsessed with the underprivileged. But I regard the 80% of children in secondary modern schools as underprivileged, and in the circumstances I am prepared to be viewed as obsessed.' Dr J. W. B. Douglas, in *The Home and the School* (MacGibbon & Kee), says 19.1 per cent of all children in England and Wales go to grammar schools, or 20.9 per cent of all children who compete for a place. This makes four fifths of our children rejects!

Newsom Report on "Half our Future" appears to have received rather less than half our attention.' The *Guardian* realized that the Newsom Report was a matter of making 'not just better scholars or better workers but better people' (this of course was exactly why it was landing in the waste-paper basket). And later, in an extremely thoughtful talk, Mr D. H. Morrell, secretary of the Schools Council formed in 1964 to examine new teaching methods, said at Jesus College, Oxford, 'From the point of view of Government, this is in many ways a very awkward report. . . . It concerns the casualties in a situation of severe tension within our society, a situation in which we are becoming more loving – more moral, if you like – but, at the same time, more competitive . . . In a sense what John Newsom and his Committee have asked us to do is to think about abolishing sin.' The new Conservative Prime Minister, Sir Alec Douglas-Home, invited Mr Newsom to Downing Street, assured him that the government was giving the Report close attention, and knighted him.

At Risinghill Mr Duane bought six copies of the Newsom Report for the staff, but only Mr Gwyn, Mr Benson and a few others were eager to discuss it.

Later the L.C.C. was to ask forty schools to answer a questionnaire in order to show what London schools were doing that was of relevance to the Newsom Report, and these answers were collected into a printed document. No schools or heads are mentioned in this document by name; but in fact Risinghill has two specific unique mentions, apart from numerous activities mentioned which Risinghill as well as some other schools were carrying out; in addition, the whole section on the house system is a direct quote from Mr Duane. It was safe to make use of the school to show how the L.C.C. was implementing the Newsom Report, since no names were mentioned; when the L.C.C. closed the school down, the document would be untouched, and their 'image', which they treasured above all, would still be shining with the help of Risinghill which they had destroyed.

That Prize Day, Walter Allen, the novelist, who later became one of the governors, gave out the prizes. Mr Duane spoke of the need for a child in school to have 'the freedom to concentrate his full energies on the problem in hand; but only a child from a secure and loving home has the necessary emotional calm and stability to do this.' He could have spoken of David Jones. David Jones had been caned at his previous school with the result that he had become a truant, and eventually got into trouble with the police; his probation officer had asked Mr Duane to take him in; at Risinghill he had gone straight into an A form, and had played a proud part in the School Council. Just as he was due to take his O levels, he had gone home as usual, and his father – a chronic invalid and a very difficult, bitter man – had come in and started a furious row with him. David simply disappeared – wrote a letter to Mr Duane saying thank you, and please don't ask any questions, and disappeared. Eventually, in dubious company, he was picked up by the police. Because of the intervention of the Risinghill staff who wrote to the Magistrate, and of Mr Duane who personally went down and talked to the Magistrate, David now has a job. But Mr Duane said this boy could have gone to a university.

In that same speech Mr Duane said:

> How do you sincerely teach 'Love thy neighbour' when we look around and see just how little love has been extended to our people in this part of London. . . . You cannot educate against the climate of opinion or attitude in the family, the neighbourhood or society. If our society were to give up the hypocritical pretence that this is a Christian country actuated by Christian principles when the difference between the wealthy and the poor is so blatant, and were to bend its efforts to making Christian love or basic democracy a reality, then there would be no limit to the progress we could achieve with our children.

Mr Duane was evidently going to have to be cut down to size. A few months later, a group of H.M.I.s would arrive and for the second time Risinghill was going to be beaten down to its knees, and this time counted out.

*

By now the school was for the first time getting A level results. The staff was beginning to consolidate, and to hold on; only the supply staff was still changing. Of course the children were still a very unacademic crowd – the new arrivals in the autumn of 1963 were made up of only 0.7 per cent in Group 1, the top ability group (no intake at Risinghill had ever had more than 0.8 per cent, that is to say eight children out of a thousand, in the top ability group), with 38.8 per cent in Group 4 and 42.7 per cent in Group 5, the two lowest ability groups, so that the A forms still had to include Group 3 and even Group 4 children, but Mr Duane had by now insisted on advertising differently for staff, and gearing the education to the children, with the result that the school was becoming more tranquil, imaginative and satisfying. The prefects had stopped seeing their role as 'power to bash', and were behaving as older members of one family would ideally behave, protecting the younger ones (though not sentimentally) while firmly extending their social education; this quality of concern for each other was beginning to be the most noticeable characteristic of the school.

By now people were coming to study what was going on at Risinghill – students from English training colleges ('I think a great deal about your school,' wrote one lecturer, after visiting with her students; 'one cannot but be aware that something fine is stirring') and teachers from other countries, America, Israel, South Africa. 'I strongly recommend you to include this school on your list of interesting educational experiments for the benefit of visitors to your country,' wrote a teacher from abroad to the British Council after a visit to Risinghill:

This school's problems are very close to the problems in many of our schools. The problems facing the headmaster are immense, and I was very impressed by the effort and devotion by the headmaster and his staff, and by the fantastic enthusiasm of that difficult type of child for their school. It was clear from our talks with many of the children that they had been physically punished in their previous schools. The staff had to face an enormous problem of freeing these children from fear and from a deep hatred of society. The amount of delinquency that is evident in the neighbourhood shows clearly the emotional disturbance from which these children suffer.

Already Mr Duane was accepting invitations to speak, to a Committee of M.P.s at the House of Commons, to the National Association of Mental Health, to the Royal College of Nursing, to the Royal Society of Medicine, and many other bodies – invitations that, as official opposition to the school became public, booked him up for years ahead; the Central Office of Information sent a representative to the school to prepare a booklet for use in Cyprus.

One teacher said 'The spirit of the school was at its most optimistic in those months. All kinds of plans were being made.' Then, in one swoop, eight of the most outstanding teachers left. One had retired, and seven had been promoted. And the L.C.C. told Zvia to go.

For some time, Zvia, an Israeli artist, had had the more difficult boys who were on probation working with her on some plastic sculpture which she had been commissioned to do. The material was experimental and besides this the conception was a thrilling risk, in the sense that any work of art is a risk, having its own growth; and the boys shared in the excitement of this risk, and gradually felt their own positive and beautiful capabilities. If the L.C.C. had the slightest vision they would have seen this is what schools should be – places where sculptors, painters, engineers, and all artists, craftsmen and artisans worked, and discussed work, with the children who would work beside them. Schools should be places for apprentices – not apprentices as we know them now, asking questions of a man who hates their guts because as likely as not he's on piece-work, so that he sets them making pots of tea all day long to keep out of his way, but apprentices in the old sense, who help and share and work and experiment, who learn the intrinsic needs and the intrinsic possibilities of different materials (which is how any work of art, from a book to a metal instrument to a human relationship, is made) and absorb the answers and the solutions to the questions they ask at the time they want to know, going further into whatever seems important and absorbing at the time.* Anyone with vision would have moved heaven and earth to keep Zvia at Risinghill. But anyone with vision would have kept Risinghill. The Divisional Officer wrote to say that it appeared she had what amounted to a private studio at the school, free of charge, and that she would have to leave.

Zvia's experimental plastic columns stand today in Ken Wood, shining and bubbling in the slanting sun. Risinghill pupils, boys

---

*Later on, John Holt in his book *How Children Fail* (Pitman) was to outline something very similar.

on probation, worked on that first one. But there is no plaque to say so. True, the columns are at Ken Wood only 'temporarily'. But if the closing of Risinghill had really been a matter of 're-gretful' reorganization (as I was told), would not the L.C.C. have seized the chance to perpetuate in public memory the creative work of the school just for another year, or two or three?

Second blow from outside

Very high on the list must come the corporate life of the school. In its most intimate form this means the way its members behave to one another. The assumptions on which the staff and pupils meet – friendliness or hostility, for instance, grudging legislation or generous helpfulness – show themselves in speech and gesture and conduct.

In February 1964, *Punch* gave three pages to an article called 'Bubble and Squeak', surmounting it with a drawing of a group of white and coloured children near a street wall scrawled with a Fascist slogan. Nearly one half of the article was about Risinghill school.

It was written by Elspeth Huxley, who had come to Risinghill about four months previously when Zvia was still there, and there the Divisional Education Officer had, at Mr Duane's invitation, met them both. The article was one of a series about immigrants in England, and this one dealt mainly with Islington, and concentrated mainly on Risinghill because Risinghill was known to have established a remarkably good relationship with the immigrant communities – though, in fact, neither the school nor the head was mentioned by name.

Within a week, Alderman Sebag-Montefiore, Tory Whip on the L.C.C., was reading part of the article aloud to an L.C.C. meeting. It made sensational reading, since he stopped at the sentence which would have altered the effect. As a result pressmen and cameramen roared down to the school.

This is what the Alderman read out:

Even Narkover, Beachcomber's famous academy for young criminals, can't have beaten this school's record for delinquency – 243 appearances by its pupils in the juvenile courts in three years. Yet the Headmaster, himself an immigrant – his father was killed in Ireland by the British and the survivors of his family fled from Black-and-Tans – observes one inflexible rule: no corporal punishment.

'You go through a period of sheer chaos with each incoming batch,'

Second blow from outside 153

he said. 'The children don't believe there's no cane. They have to test your statement. They shout and yell and fight and make life impossible. You have to stand there and let them call you all the four-letter words and every obscenity in the language. You've got to go on talking and whatever happens keep your temper. It's a nightmare for the teachers and some of them can't take it. I don't blame them. But it's the only way.'

The next sentences read:

'When the children grasp the fact that there really *isn't* any cane they calm down. In any case they get tired of chaos eventually and then you can start to talk to them like reasonable human beings. It works in the end.' It seemed to. At any rate the school was orderly – the children appeared to be usefully employed and not carving up each other or the Staff.

But the Alderman did not read this out. In fact what he did read out was the *past* of Risinghill, but it may be that no one except Mrs McIntosh, the chairman, who of course had to be notified of questions in advance so that she could have answers ready, knew this. (The members of the L.C.C. Education Committee could enlighten no one, for, out of about forty Committee members who later were to condemn the school and close it down, I could find only two who had visited it at all when it was functioning and in school hours.) Before the formal answer came, the extract must have created some alarm. Yet other people outside the L.C.C. had read the *Punch* article before it was brought up at the Council, and many people had talked to Mr Duane about it, without any of them realizing there was anything shocking about it, since they had read the article in full.

The *Daily Mail*, which, like all other newspapers, gave large headlines to the L.C.C. row, and again like the other newspapers (I can only recall the *Evening News* columnist as an exception) became a sympathetic and generous supporter of Risinghill, continued its report: 'The no-caning policy won support from Mrs Marjorie McIntosh, chairman of the Council's Education Committee. . . .' The press could not know, but I am afraid that Mrs McIntosh's smile, like that of Dr Rieu's Lesser Lynx, may have been on this occasion rather insincere.

> She smiled of course – but oh, the rude
> Remarks that crossed her mind!

to paraphrase the verse. In fact, Mrs McIntosh was in a very awkward position on two counts, firstly because by then the L.C.C. must have already decided ('*unofficially* decided', someone said to me) to close Risinghill and it must have frustrated them to have to defend it, and secondly because Mrs McIntosh was no enthusiastic supporter of a no-cane policy. (I happen to know this, because a friend of mine once wrote to her when we had had three mass canings within one month at a local comprehensive school because the older boys were coming to school without their caps, and enclosed for Marjorie McIntosh's interest a copy of the West Riding report.* She replied in the usual L.C.C. style. I have read her first paragraph twelve times and still do not know what it means. In her second paragraph she says the West Riding report makes it clear that 'the subject is so much a matter of personal conviction' – whereas the whole point of the report is that it is taking the matter completely out of the sphere of personal convictions, and basing it on facts. In her third and final paragraph she says she encloses 'the Council's own pamphlet' (*Punishment in Schools*) and 'would not favour supplementing it with any other publication.' But when she wrote that, she was perfectly aware, as chairman of the L.C.C. Education Committee, that the L.C.C. *had* supplemented it with another publication – *Corporal Punishment in Primary and Secondary Schools*.† But this latter is, of course, marked 'Confidential within the London Teaching Service'. Did she mean, then, she did not favour making this second publication so public as the first? Certainly nowhere in her letter is there any hint of shock at three mass canings, the first of which alone was reported by the local paper to last fifty minutes.)

The L.C.C. was certainly in strange company when they decided to close Risinghill, but I doubt that this bothered them much. Much later on, when I asked them if their actions towards Risinghill had been political, they misunderstood me and assumed I meant had they been influenced by Mr Sebag-Montefiore's speech; they laughed sardonically and with a certain amount of enthusiasm as if they were glad to find something they could

*See footnote on p.20. †See p. 20.

shrug off. What they meant was that no Tory had told them to close Risinghill; they had decided to do that long before, entirely for their own interests, and they felt superior at having beaten the Tories to it.

Mrs McIntosh did however inform the L.C.C. members that the figure of 243 juvenile court appearances in Risinghill's three years' existence included care and protection cases. I doubt that this made much impact, but I am glad she drew attention to it. Possibly it may have made them realize if only for a fleeting second that these children were not in quite the same position as their own children.

The result of the Sebag-Montefiore row was that the press and television descended on the school and reported on it with a tremendous sympathetic warmth. The *Herald* spread it over five columns, and included a three-column photograph, the *Mail* gave it a four-column special feature 'Does Sparing the Rod Breed Crime?' the *Mirror* splashed it as 'Wild School is Tamed by Love', with another photograph, and the next day gave it a leader 'That Four-Letter Word'; the *Express*, the *Evening Standard*, the *Telegraph* gave it two columns each. All were sympathetic.

It was extraordinarily revealing of the hold authoritarianism has in this country that so many people believe that the press treated Risinghill badly. In fact, it was Risinghill's good press not its bad press that made the authoritarians so angry – the L.C.C. were very angry indeed – and authoritarian anger made people more irrationally anxious, so that they fell on Mr Duane as a scapegoat and said that because of him the press had attacked Risinghill; but the press had done nothing of the kind.

(Later on, in 1965, the same thing was to happen again; the authoritarians attacked the school, the press rallied to support the school, and even the parents and the children of Risinghill, in their anxiety, because they were fearful of what the authoritarians could do to them, believed the press was hostile to them, even after reading the actual reports. This kind of anxiety is infectious, and I myself assumed the press had been hostile; so that when for the first time I read all the reports I was surprised at their generous partisanship.)

Many of the teachers, because in them fear of authority ran very high indeed, were disturbed when reporters and television people arrived, though some of them rationalized this by saying it made the work of the school impossible. A teacher said to me 'The right-wing press descended on us' – again this was un-consciously distorted by her own anxiety; it was *all* the Press – 'and this deluge upset the staff terribly. They thought it would upset their careers, and make them look ridiculous, and, instead of attaching the blame where it belonged, fastened it to the nearest scapegoat, Mr Duane. . . . And once this became evident, that there could be *political* results, everyone became anxious, stopped trusting their own judgement, and began to look for a lead from Authority.'

The most ironic thing is that since Mrs McIntosh had rebuffed Mr Sebag-Montefiore's attack the press may have thought that when they supported Risinghill they were supporting the L.C.C. or at any rate Mrs McIntosh. How maddened the L.C.C. must have been.

At this very time, as I later heard, someone employed at County Hall was saying to a friend 'The L.C.C. are going to close Rising-hill. Some people who are kinky about caning have been running a campaign. I suppose they'll do the obvious – get H.M.I.s who are stern disciplinarian types to do an inspection.' This was in February 1964.

But there was still a little time before 'the obvious' could be done, and the L.C.C. continued to be alert. Dr Payling, the new Chief Inspector, arrived at the school, angrily warning Mr Duane that there must be no further press publicity, and that the facts about the children's circumstances and behaviour must be kept out of the newspapers because it was so important for the L.C.C. to get over a 'good image'. (Later on that year, a certain music teacher at another school was to feel the full impact of this, and to take her place in the headlines.) This statement might have been considered enough for any one conversation; but there was some-thing even more startling to come. At this conversation the Chief Inspector revealed he was under the impression that Risinghill had been going for four years longer than it actually had. Whether Dr Payling ever got this out of his head, I do not know.

Dr Payling was misinformed – or uninformed – on other points too. He looked startled to hear of the school's growing G.C.E. results – including A levels (which makes one wonder, as I was to do myself on more than one occasion later, how often action is taken on the basis of complete ignorance); but he still continued to say what he had come to say. His speech ended with the warning that since the Ministry inspected schools every seven years – he had still not grasped that Risinghill had been in existence only four – such an inspection was overdue, and would take place very shortly.

His attitude to Risinghill may perhaps be explained by the fact that his own headmasterships had been in Grammar Schools; plans were laid years ago for one of these to be turned into a comprehensive, and the headmaster who followed Dr Payling resigned in protest; the school is still a Grammar School.

There were still some weeks to go before the big guns arrived, and I think it must have been during this period that an incident occurred which no one, not even the participants, thought important at the time, but that later became a vicious weapon. A teacher, Mr Simon, told Mr Duane that, thinking he heard someone playing with an air-gun in the playground, he put his head out of the classroom window to see who it was just as a slug from the gun cracked a window nearby. 'Might it perhaps be dangerous for a child to have an air-gun?' he asked Mr Duane.

Mr Munday, the H.M.I. attached to Risinghill, had visited the school several times, sometimes coming with other colleagues.

In his first visit he had been interested in Mr Duane's policy but had said he had reservations; he would wait and see. Quite steadily he had expressed belief that the policy was working. By 1963 (this was a year after the Macgowan report in which he had no hand as that was an L.C.C. matter; Mr Duane had shown it to him in the presence of two other H.M.I.s and he had laughed and said, 'Oh, you don't need to bother about *us*. We won't be bothering you with an inspection for many years') he had said that all his reservations had gone, that he was happy about the progress of the school, and that he would come back in June 1964 with one or two colleagues. The school was now trying to pick up the pieces after the smash-up of 1962, and it was very pleasant for many of the staff to feel that despite everything someone approved of them; they looked forward to his next visit with a certain amount of humble hope.

But Mr Munday, looking markedly uneasy, suddenly informed Mr Duane that he would be arriving with more inspectors than he had anticipated. In fact, seven arrived, which was very startling for a 'visitation' (it could not have been an 'inspection' for that is notified and organized within the school many weeks beforehand – Risinghill never had an inspection), and among them were well-known authoritarians (one of them a man who, shortly after the school opened, at Mr Duane's morning assembly which consisted of the older, wilder pupils, announced he had discerned some noise, and 'I would have it so that you can hear a pin drop'; and another who was rapidly to take charge of the proceedings – Inspector Clark). Inspector Munday did not appear his normal genial self – he must have known he was to be involved in a showdown he did not support – and this in itself was enough to put on edge teachers who yearned for approval.

The inspectors spent four days in the school and during this time at least one episode occurred that made the outcome uncomfortably clear.

Mr Gwyn was taking an English class, using the ballad of 'Frankie and Johnny' in a school anthology of 'tough' verse. Mr Clark marched in and sat down in the teacher's chair, leaving Mr Gwyn standing. After Mr Gwyn (left standing throughout) had read the ballad aloud, discussed it with the children, and then set them to dramatizing it, Mr Clark (seated in the teacher's chair) demanded of Mr Gwyn why the children were being given this sort of thing to work on. They got plenty of this in their daily lives. The children – quite a few of them, since Mr Clark's remarks were not softly spoken – listened. (Mr Gwyn commented later that the children behaved surprisingly well. As children often do, they had sensed from the beginning that something hostile was going on and had behaved rather better than they usually did. They were not usually children who could be left to get on with anything by themselves.) This was their only chance of getting something great, declared Mr Clark. 'Frankie and Johnny' was immoral in subject and coarse in vocabulary. Why

weren't they doing Shakespeare? Until they were ready for
Shakespeare, his own new anthology would bridge the gap.

When I first heard this I confess I was astounded. After all,
Mr Clark must have a good knowledge of English literature.
I suppose he was thinking only of school editions of Shakespeare,
though even then unrespectable things tend to slip through.

As for Inspector Clark's anthology, this raises another matter.
Mr Clark is of course bound to have his own preferences where
poetry is concerned; Mr Gwyn himself has preferences within
the anthology; all of us have preferences. But I wonder how
many schools are brave enough to follow their own preferences,
and not to use anthologies of poems by an inspector, particularly
when he is one who is likely to walk in at any moment?

When this heated discussion was over and the class and Mr
Gwyn released, Mr Gwyn was noticeably angry. He said later he
felt the inspector's conduct had been contemptuous towards
both teachers and pupils. I have talked to teachers in different
parts of London about this inspector, and have found this kind
of behaviour is not uncommon with him. I heard of two schools
where complaints were actually made to the education authority
about his behaviour.

It should perhaps be said that Mr Clark had made it clear
that he disapproved of comprehensive schools, and that he
disapproved of large schools. Also he was a well-known cam-
paigner for 'purity' among schoolchildren (though some literary
critics might say his school poems are a little irrelevant to
such children as are white-faced the whole school day when a
man is being hanged in the prison down the road, and whose
own creative writing is about an old man sitting on the stairs of
the flats swigging methylated spirits.*)

On the last day of the 'visitation', the senior inspector, who
has had no other mention in this narrative, had to leave early,
but he spoke to Mr Duane before he went, and he was cordial,
constructive and friendly. Was he unaware what was going to
happen, or was he glad to be out of it?

Mr Munday was in charge, as 'the conducting inspector'. He

*See piece by Josephine Winter in *Starcross* magazine for 1966, that school's first
year in the Risinghill building.

prefaced the verbal report which was to be given by the remaining inspectors with what could only be called an apology. He said that this was not a complete inspection; that they had, in fact, concentrated only on the academic side of the school; and that had they inspected all the school a very different picture would have emerged. Did Mr Duane think at this stage that Mr Munday meant that the report was not going to be given much weight? After all, if the inspectors really wished to have a full-scale inspection, there was nothing whatever to stop them staying in the school as long as they liked and looking at everything. Or did the extraordinarily large number of inspectors together with this rather odd apology disturb him?

Mr Munday then called upon individual inspectors to give their reports, and they did – reports of rude drawings in the margins of books, unmarked exercises, a bottle in the lavatory pan, and other very hostile comments.

Then Mr Clark took complete charge. First of all he asked Mr Duane what he thought of one of his teachers, an elderly man on the point of retirement. Mr Duane was startled, but spoke kindly of him (as a matter of fact, I happen to know he was at that time doing a great deal of the teacher's work for him), but I imagine not very enthusiastically, perhaps even gently critically. Mr Clark then launched into tremendous praise of the man.

Mr Clark then attacked Mr Gwyn (whom Mr Duane had planned to make Head of Department) – and said of the editor of the anthology Mr Gwyn was using that he was not fit to be in the teaching profession, and that he, Mr Clark, would see to it that he was hounded out for good. (The man concerned, like Mr Clark both an editor and a writer of poetry for schools, is also an educational lecturer.)

Mr Clark also said that he had been to an Islington primary school when the head had been interviewing parents about secondary schools, and that the parents had refused to send their children to Risinghill; that the head as a result had written to the Divisional Office, complaining about the school and about Mr Duane. But this head told me later, 'there is no truth in it whatever'; he had never written such a letter, never criticized Risinghill to parents, and Mr Clark had never been present at his interviews with parents.

I found there was indeed a letter to the Divisional Office – but it was from the school management committee, commenting on the attitude of Mr Clark. One of the managers (equivalent to the governors of secondary schools), a scrupulous and fair-minded person, told me, 'I put his behaviour down to a lack of knowledge of how things are done in London, and to ignorance of the district and how people here live.'

Mr Clark concluded with: 'Mr Duane, do you consider yourself fit to be a headmaster?'

What does a man reply – after his school has been misjudged by being considered only academically, and his own ability denied by a blasting attack on his appraisal of his teachers – does he say 'Mr Clark, do you consider yourself fit to be an inspector?'

This report was given by Inspector Clark verbally and privately (for a visitation report is never printed and issued for discussion) to County Hall.

After the visitation Mr Duane got out a document headed 'Risinghill: The Problem before us' for staff discussion. The staff mostly did not want to discuss it. They were too agitated. Most of them threw it away. It was of such value that I have re-printed a small extract in the Appendix.

Some questions remain. Why did seven inspectors turn up for an informal visitation? Why was the most important of them – at the very least, on his own reckoning – a man who was known to be against comprehensive schools, and even against any large schools? Why were so many of them known authoritarians when the school was known to be non-authoritarian? Why did they examine only the academic side of the school, when it was known that the school could not be academic? Why did Mr Clark, who was not attached to the school, take charge of the visitation, and why did he give the report to County Hall, when the regular visiting H.M.I. was present and supposed to be conducting the visitation? What had happened in those few months between Mr Munday's saying he was happy about the development of the school and this visitation that condemned it? The answer to the last question, and perhaps to all the others, is the article in *Family Planning*, the article in *Punch*, and the publicity that flew into the national press from Mr Sebag-Montefiore. Mr Duane had shown that he would not allow the social position of so many of our children to be a state secret.

The H.M.I.s' report on Risinghill would go to the government. The government would now back the closing of the school.

The next month, July 1964, Mr John Newsom wrote to Mr Duane: 'You have obviously done a heroic job at Risinghill and should have a glow of satisfaction at having achieved such a success out of an unpromising situation.' While he was writing this, a mother who wanted her child to go to Risinghill was being told confidentially by a friend close to the L.C.C. that the school was being closed down.

This mother was the cousin of a university classics professor. She had been trying for weeks to get her son entered at Risinghill.

I had taken Miles away from his choir school because there were children being beaten there every day. One day Miles said he couldn't stand it any more. He was wretched. I said 'There's no reason why you should. We'll find a better school.'

'I spent three weeks traipsing backwards and forwards. I couldn't find a school in the district where they didn't beat the children. I went to the District Education Office, but they wouldn't help. They said it wasn't their job to find me a school that didn't have corporal punishment. The woman there said sardonically 'I suppose you want vegetarianism too!' Then I read in the paper about Risinghill. I went to the Education Office and said 'Why didn't you tell me about this school?' They said 'It's full.' I went down to the school, and the deputy head, who was responsible for taking on new children, said there were no vacancies. Even if there were, said the deputy head, I wouldn't want to send my children there; if I thought it was a nice easy school I was very much mistaken; there was hooliganism, sex crimes, and so on. That person did everything possible to prevent me putting Miles down for the school – finally telling me I would have to wait at least two years. In the end I went back to the Education Office and told them that if I couldn't send Miles to Risinghill, I wouldn't send him to school at all. The deputy head wrote to me after that, saying that 'with great difficulty' she had found a place for Miles, but 'he would have to go in a B class', obviously thinking I was an educational snob, and that that would settle it for me. But Miles said 'I want to go to that school, and I don't mind going in the B stream. If I turn out to be brighter, they'll have to move me to the A stream some time.' So we accepted. He went in September.

Later on, I told Mr Duane about this. He was astounded. He said Miles could have started that day. And now they're saying the intake went down because parents didn't want to send their children to the school!

Six months later, at the angry parents' meeting in January 1965, five or six parents were to say they had been recommended by primary school heads *not* to send their children to Risinghill. (These were parents who had disregarded the recommendation. How many had followed it ?) Had the intake of the school, which the L.C.C. said was a reason for closing it, been going down partly because the L.C.C. had decided to close it ?

Later, at County Hall in 1965, I mentioned both these incidents to Mr Turner, Assistant Education Officer, and he said in both cases the parents were lying.

The mother of Miles was lying, he said, since the Area Education Officer couldn't possibly have said that because it would have been untrue – an interesting argument; but perhaps at this very moment, so far undestroyed, there lies in the files of this boy, in the education office in the area of his choir school, a paper that shows a whole term's gap between his leaving choir school and starting at his new school, Risinghill; this was because he was not given a place at the school he insisted on going to; his parents were never prosecuted, no action whatever was taken as would normally be done in cases of non-attendance; authority knew the situation was far too tricky, because unfortunately for them Miles's mother was educated and articulate, and could not be browbeaten.

And the parents at the January meeting were lying, Mr Turner said, since at the February meeting with the L.C.C., the L.C.C. had asked them to give the names of the heads, and no parent had done so. Now this Feburary meeting, as readers will see later, was scarcely a meeting where the parents looked on the L.C.C. as a friend in need. And furthermore, even in a more hopeful situation, no parents with other children at local primary schools (which covers very many of the Risinghill parents) were going to

make open trouble for the primary head, most particularly in a
district where the children have been shunted backwards and
forwards since they first started school. And yet even so, I know
that at least one parent did do exactly what the L.C.C. claimed
no parent did. The parents of one child asked Mr Duane to
write for them, and he did so.

Furthermore by the time I mentioned these matters to Mr
Turner and had his somewhat unconstructive reply, he must also
have known that certain statements of Inspector Clark had been
denied; though he did not know I knew.

I do not think the teacher who tried to turn Miles away was
deliberately doing harm, in the belief that it was harm. At first I
simply thought that such a teacher would tend to assume that a
well-educated woman would not want to send her child to Risinghill (showing the contempt that lies, sometimes unconsciously,
behind authoritarianism), and would not realize that it was precisely a school like this that many a well-educated parent was
longing for in the arid desert of meritocracy. (After all, it is well-
educated parents who keep the independent progressive schools
going; and some educated parents cannot pay private fees. Close
on Miles's footsteps was to follow the daughter of an Australian
painter, next the daughter of another painter, and then Miles's
sister, and children began to be withdrawn from grammar schools
to be sent to Risinghill; the well-educated parents of these children
were among the strongest supporters of the school. It was only a
trickle, but I have no doubt it would have become a steady
stream.)

But I know that some people who heard of this incident soon
after it happened began to wonder if there was some agreement –
a tacit one perhaps – between such teachers and the Divisional
Office to turn people away; whether in fact a 'run-down' was
arranged. I began to wonder about this too, for it would tie in
with teachers who have said to me they think a run-down in staff
was deliberately arranged, to make it impossible for the school to
function properly. All of course was done with the best of intentions, and possibly almost imperceptibly; as Bob Dylan sings,
'You don't count the dead, when God's on your side.'

But this sequence is not yet finished. For I then discovered that while Miles's mother was still battling to get her son into Risinghill, she recounted her experiences to a friend, an educational worker, who listened and said 'I agree it *is* the right school for Miles, but to save you both some heartbreak later, I think I ought to tell you, in confidence, that the L.C.C. is going to close it.' The mother simply could not believe the authority would do such a thing. She said to me later 'I admit, I had my head in the sand. I had found my school, and I didn't want to believe they could do this. I didn't dare to ask Mr Duane, when, later, I met him; I didn't say a word to a soul. Months later, Miles came home from school and said "Something terrible has happened", and I thought "This is it".'

Of course if the L.C.C. had decided secretly, against the spirit and letter of the Education Act, to close the school, it is understandable that they would not want to take any more children, or teachers, or spend any money, if they could possibly help it. They would even feel they were acting like this for everyone's good.

But just about the time that Miles's mother was receiving the news and not believing it, Mr Duane was being summoned to County Hall. Here he was received by Dr Payling, the Chief Inspector, and Dr Briault, the Deputy Education Officer. Dr Briault told him, not that he had not created a good school, but that he had not created a 'good image'. Because of this, he said Risinghill would have to be drastically reorganized, and Mr Duane's future with the L.C.C. would come to an end.*

Later the L.C.C. was to translate this affair to Starcross governors and all others who were not helping the dispatch of Risinghill as enthusiastically as they should have been, as 'It was impossible to complete the 1964 visitation. It was so bad . . . the position it revealed was so appalling . . . that it had to be called off to save the headmaster's face. That is why no report was printed. That is why we must close the school, as quickly and quietly as possible.' Similarly Starcross governors have told me that there were 'sexual irregularities' too shocking to detail – this I have already mentioned – and also (as a final sledge-hammer

*In February 1966, the Inner London Educational Authority inserted an advertisement in the *Times Educational Supplement* for a headmaster/mistress for Hampstead Comprehensive School: 'A head is required with . . . the ability to project an attractive image of the school to the general public.'

blow if innuendoes failed) that if they didn't move into the Rising-hill premises another local girls' school (which had a decrepit building) certainly would, and they, Starcross, would be 'absorbed' (i.e. liquidated).

Dr James Hemming, the educational writer and broadcaster, gave the prizes that year. Sir John Newsom had promised to do so, but the interest aroused by the Newsom Report had brought him so much work and so many engagements that he had to postpone his visit. He said he would give the prizes next year. That would have been the autumn of 1965. Unfortunately by then the L.C.C. and the government had closed down the school he was interested in, which now had a West Indian head boy and a Greek Cypriot head girl.

It is very instructive, in the light of Risinghill, to read through the H.M.I.'s report on Summerhill, A. S. Neill's private non-authoritarian school. It was said by several people during the 1965 storm that Michael Duane was a pupil of A. S. Neill. This is not so; Michael Duane went to a Jesuit School; but he had become a friend of Mr Neill's, and admires what he has done. The report on Summerhill was warm and friendly. For Summerhill, not being a state school, does not endanger anyone in power.

Rallying

Most schools are making strenuous efforts to establish contacts with parents.

Imperceptibly – long before the matter was openly discussed, long before the parents reached for their democratic rights under the Education Act – the school was grinding to a halt. By now, many people in the educational world, but not the Risinghill children and parents who (except for one) were completely in the dark, knew that the L.C.C. was going to close the school.

Staff had begun to leave, and new staff became almost impossible to get. At the beginning the school had not got the teachers it needed because the L.C.C. insisted on using the staff of the original four authoritarian schools (of whom only a few were able to support a new 'permissive' policy). Now it could not get them because of the rumours that the L.C.C. was closing it down. 'In the last twelve months,' a governor told me, 'we have had very little choice. We have just had to make do with what the Divisional Office sends.'

For the children therefore that last year was completely disrupted. (After that year, they would go to a new school – those who did not give up – and a further term, or maybe even a year, would be disrupted. What had these kids, many of whom had already been moved several times before they came to Risinghill, ever learned from the educational authority except that society judged them worthless ?)

Within the school, the staff were on edge, the authoritarians becoming more determined and therefore more authoritarian than ever, in an effort to dissociate themselves in the eyes of authority from what authority considered the failure of the school. Scenes between teachers, in the staff room or in front of the children, were becoming frequent.

In the early autumn of 1964 – still a year to go before the school was officially closed, and only a little over four years after the school had begun – the deputy head was retiring and it would now have been possible to find for this position someone who was more in sympathy with Mr Duane's ideas and methods; but although the advertisement was drafted by Mr Duane and sent to the Divisional Office, it was never published; it got as far as County Hall and stayed there. County Hall knew it was not necessary, though they did not say so to Mr Duane.

About this time a letter from Mr Duane appeared in the *Daily Telegraph*. It challenged points raised in an article by Angus Maude about comprehensive schools which had congratulated Conservatives on their educational record, and it was signed 'Michael Duane, Headmaster, Risinghill School'. The L.C.C., saying it was an infringement of the Council's Standing Orders for a head to write such a letter, which had 'direct political implications', without submitting it to the Council's Press Officer, demanded an explanation. As it happens Mr Duane had, in fact, tried four times without success to speak to the Press Officer on the telephone; and having had previous experiences of the Press Officer's keeping submitted articles or letters for a fortnight without making any comment, by which time they were useless (an experience which can be duplicated by other people), he decided to send it off, having, he felt, something important to say.

It is interesting that the Labour-controlled L.C.C. should have been so angry about a letter that supported – and drew to public attention – their original declared policy.

About three weeks later, they summoned him to County Hall to tell him Risinghill was to be closed, and that he had better think about taking up teacher training. (For the next twelve months, the L.C.C. was to deny they had made this latter statement – until the autumn of 1965 when, after turning him down for all other available headships, they finally offered him – teacher training.) Dr Briault, the Deputy Education Officer, said Mr Duane had made slanderous statements about various people concerned with Risinghill including members of the L.C.C. and that they were considering taking action against him, and that he had made irresponsible statements about corporal punishment in L.C.C. schools in the *London Schoolmaster*. (He had written saying that several girls in their first week at a London secondary school had been caned for forgetting their P.E. kit. They had. I can name the school.) His letter also said that Risinghill children had been beaten at their primary schools; and this aroused the anger of certain local colleagues.

By now the anti-Duane half of the Communist group of teachers had a movement well organized. They would meet new teachers when they came uncertainly out of their first lesson, trying as every such teacher does to find the reason for failure, and would say with huge sympathy 'Of course you couldn't manage! No one can teach with him running the school!' In this way the inexperienced and possibly inadequate teachers, comforted, befriended, and raised in their own estimation, one by one were drawn into the battle. A Risinghill teacher described this to me in detail, and added 'This nucleus operated at Common Room meetings. They were extremely clever and cunning. . . . But surely, if you don't like the captain, you change your ship. You don't sink the ship and everyone else on it?'

Mr Duane, in order to save the school, and very much aware that certain teachers were gunning for him personally, asked the chairman of the governors (now again the original woman chairman, since the second chairman had too many other duties) to offer his resignation to County Hall. She was very distressed, and at first refused. But he said he felt enough of importance had been done in the school for the authorities to allow it to remain as long as they had got rid of him; he begged her to go to County Hall. Finally she did so. She offered his resignation to Mr James Young, Chairman of the L.C.C. Education Committee. But Mr Young refused to accept it. This enabled the L.C.C. to tell the press later that Risinghill was simply 'one of several schools involved in a complicated reorganization plan' and that 'There is no question of personalities being involved.' They had their plan worked out; they felt secure in their power to carry it through, and they were going to stick to it.

But across the river, the reason for closing Risinghill was showing very clear indeed, although we did not know then that Risinghill was going to be closed. A music teacher in Kidbrooke, a South London girls' comprehensive school, speaking not at a public meeting but to a professional group of other music teachers, said she had difficulty in applying her academic methods to the girls in the school who had poor backgrounds, girls whom she described as 'the sisters and girl friends of some of the unpleasantest gangs in London'. This meeting would normally have been reported in the quiet, professional pages of the *Times Educational Supplement*; but someone saw the sensational political possibilities, and grabbed it for the next day's *Times*, splashing it at the top of its main news page: 'Comprehensive Schools a Failure'. The following day *The Times* published a letter from her, in a very much more obscure position, saying she had been misrepresented; but by then the other papers had picked up the story and splashed it big. The L.C.C., far from being concerned about the points she raised, hinted very strongly that she would be dismissed. ('Perhaps she will want to reconsider her position in view of her strong feelings about the school.') Fortunately her head stood by her.

Now this could not have affected the Risinghill issue, which must have been decided long before the parents tried to exercise their democratic rights; but it clearly revealed the motivation of the L.C.C. It showed their extraordinary bullying hamfistedness which was to astonish me later on when I met it personally; and it showed that they had determined to clamp down instantly on anyone who revealed the truth, as he saw it, about the social conditions of comprehensive school children and the irrelevance to many of them of academic education. When the Risinghill row followed, taking a far more serious turn, it also became clear that in a district that was solidly Labour, as these two were, the Socialist leaders would jettison the poorest people who voted Labour automatically, and woo the people higher up the social scale instead.

The same month, the L.C.C. told the governors of Risinghill that the need of Kingsway College of Further Education for more accommodation was 'urgent', that secondary school accommodation must be released for this purpose, and that since Starcross School was at present occupying a building that had originally been intended for Kingsway, the L.C.C. proposed that Kingsway should take over the Starcross building, Starcross should move into Risinghill, and Risinghill should vanish; they made this suggestion, they said, because it was evident that Islington parents did not want Risinghill School.

A few days later, Dr Briault came to the school, after school hours, to talk to the staff. A Deputy Education Officer might be expected to visit a new school once, while it is functioning. When it is a school known to be in a difficult area, he might perhaps be expected to visit it twice while it is functioning. When it is a school that is reported to be in difficulties, and when it is taking the headlines in the national press, he might even be expected to visit it, say, three times while it is functioning. But Dr Briault never once, to Mr Duane's knowledge, came to that living school during school hours.

He outlined the L.C.C.'s 'proposals', as they were called throughout, and said the principal of Kingsway College kept warning him that Kingsway would no longer function unless it was given the Starcross building at once. He asked for comments from the Risinghill staff. All the staff who spoke, spoke against the proposals; most of them said they were very concerned for the children, particularly the backward and disturbed ones. Not one member of the staff spoke in favour of the proposals.

The next week, forty-seven teachers out of the sixty at Risinghill signed a petition saying:

We, the undersigned staff of Risinghill School, deeply concerned at the grave social, emotional, educational and environmental handicaps with which so many of our children are burdened, and undeterred by the impact of those handicaps on our work as teachers, affirm our desire to continue that work at Risinghill, and most urgently request the Education Committee not to close the school.

That same day Dr Briault paid a second visit to Risinghill, again after hours. He had never seen so much of at least the building as when he was closing it. This time he addressed the governors, who had already received a copy of the staff petition. Finally the governors, some of whom were on the L.C.C. Education Committee and some of whom had close personal friends on it, accepted the proposals. The press were told they 'accepted' unanimously; this was technically correct but gave a somewhat distorted impression; in fact, the discussion was very long, and their official resolution stated that 'We accept the necessity to close Risinghill School with deep regret.'

Still on the same day, the head and eight members of the staff of Starcross visited Risinghill to see it for themselves; on their return, the Starcross staff voted against accepting the 'proposals', and also passed a resolution deploring the closing of Risinghill School which they said had accomplished so much educationally and socially.

On the same day, the governors of Starcross unanimously rejected the 'proposals'.

I have no knowledge of actual voting at Kingsway, but I was told by someone at the college 'We *do* need to move. We desperately need space. But what we need is a new block near Southampton Row. In fact we had planned, and the L.C.C. had planned for us, to move in another two or three years' time. Why have they suddenly put this date forward? We do not want to move to Starcross. Starcross will be nowhere near big enough for us, in any case. We are actually going to have to lay on buses to shunt people regularly from Gower Street and back.' I asked the principal of the college what his feelings were, but he refused to comment.

After that weekend, on the Monday, an incident occurred that was as innocuous as the incident about the air-gun, but similarly, was to be used viciously against the school. A thirteen-year-old boy who for some time had been on the files of the Borough Medical Officer as a child who should perhaps be sent to a boarding school for maladjusted children, whose father was in prison and whose mother had just abandoned him, a child with a speech defect who could not easily communicate in words, got out of his seat in the classroom, saying he was leaving the class because he had a stomach-ache. His teacher, a large powerfully-built woman, got hold of him, took him forcibly back to his seat, and told him to sit down. The boy wouldn't. The teacher tried to push him on to the seat, skidded and slipped, laddering her stocking. The boy was obviously worried that she might be hurt. She took him to the deputy head, who sent him out of school. (I have formed this description from official accounts, including the teacher's own, made at the time.)

The sub-committees of the L.C.C. Education Committee and then the full Education Committee were scheduled to meet on 15 and 16 December to consider their proposals and make a decision 'in the light of the reactions of staffs and governors'. However, possibly 'in the light of the reaction of staffs and governors', these decisive meetings were not in fact held until the end of January, and before then the whole country was to be reacting too.

Early in January, Michael Hamlyn of the *Sunday Times* heard through personal contacts that the L.C.C. wanted to close the school, and went down to talk to Mr Duane. Mr Duane received him at first with a certain amount of reserve, but finding he already knew the position discussed it with him. Michael Hamlyn later asked if they could take photographs of the school. Mr Duane said that as far as he was concerned they could, but they would first have to get the permission of County Hall. Michael Hamlyn got in touch with County Hall. County Hall said 'Certainly not!' and instantly got in touch with Mr Duane to ask how he dared to give the *Sunday Times* permission. Mr Duane said he had not. While this interchange was going on, the *Sunday Times* was taking its photograph from the street.

On 10 January the *Sunday Times* splashed the story of Risinghill on their front page and on page three – a big news feature by Michael Hamlyn, 'L.C.C. Is Closing Toughest School', and a large photograph explained underneath by the sentence 'The picture was taken from the street because the L.C.C. would not allow photographs on school premises' (which County Hall could take as courtesy, explanation, or cocking a snook).

One might not have expected the *Sunday Times* to have a very high readership in the Risinghill district, but Bob Redrupp, parents' leader and potato-seller, reads it and he alerted other parents.

By the next day, Monday, the more widely-read papers were running the story. The *Mail* carried a detailed feature by Roy Nash, with pictures, 'Ban-the-Cane Head in Clash. Parents fight to Save School'. The *Sun*'s story was headed 'Headmaster Who

Banned the Cane May Lose the Tough School He "Tamed"',
and had a small box at the bottom saying 'SHOCKING if such a
successful experiment as Risinghill is brought to an end – whatever the reason.'

It was the *Sun* and *Guardian* that quoted 'a local Labour
Councillor' as saying 'Some people feel that Mr Duane's lack of a
deterrent is a prime cause of masters being beaten up by pupils
and the number of schoolgirls who become pregnant.' Perhaps I
should mention here that no masters were beaten up by pupils,
though certain teachers were to fight hard later to provide evidence; and as for pregnancies, one girl was four months pregnant
before Risinghill opened, and another girl was made pregnant
by the lodger at her home and left the school. This was in five
years. Compared with a local girls' school which had five pregnancies in two years, and a local mixed school which had two
pregnancies in one term, Risinghill was evidently unusually
responsible.

The *Express* headed theirs 'Parents Will Fight Move To Close
School'. The *Telegraph*'s was '"Tough" School's Future under
Review'. *The Times*, typically unimpassioned, headed their
meagre four inches with 'Change Likely at Risinghill'. (Claud
Cockburn once described a 'Dullest-headline-you-can-actually-
get-published' competition with which he and some other members of the *Times* editorial staff used to alleviate boredom; he
once won with 'Small Earthquake in Chile. Not Many Dead.')
They were only equalled in impassivity and an apparent complete
absence of curiosity by the *Daily Worker*, who had evidently taken
a decision to keep clear of a tricky situation; throughout the whole
affair, they did not even once, to Mr Duane's knowledge, send
their able – and, I would guess, friendly – educational reporter to
the school to find out what was happening. The *Express* and the
Sun both said Risinghill's motto was 'Love Conquers All' (although the *Express* was not sure it agreed to this).

On the Monday evening, the *Evening News* ('Head is Asked
to Give Up Teaching') and the *Evening Standard* ('At "Tough"
School the L.C.C. Threaten to Shut Down - Head is Asked to
Give up Teaching') carried the story further, saying also that
'an L.C.C. official' had told Mr Duane to bring back the cane

and expulsion, and he had refused to do either. (A day or two later, the L.C.C. was to deny that anyone had made any of these three demands or suggestions; and papers were to print the denials. But at a staff meeting on 15 January, Dr Briault was to make it clear to the teachers that he resented that statements and suggestions made *in confidence* had been reported in the press.*)

The next morning the *Guardian* carried two stories, perhaps to make up for its lateness – a big news feature with photographs (one of which was to rouse the anger of parents) headed 'Headmaster Defends the Controversial Comprehensive', and a news story headed 'Probation Officers Want School Kept Open', which featured a letter signed by eight probation officers from local courts, who said, 'We have known children who hated school and were persistent truanters who have become deeply attached to Risinghill and hated leaving.' The *Sun* had an enormous photograph and a news story – 'The Defenders. Four Prefects Plead for the Headmaster who Banned the Cane', and also a leader – 'Rebel with a Cause'. The *Mail* on their VISION page carried the same huge photograph, with an even bigger news feature – 'Revolt at Risinghill. In the Head's study . . . four prefects discuss plans to save their comprehensive school', and on the back of that a further feature by Roy Nash, with a headline taking seven inches in depth – 'The High Price of Being Ahead of Your Time'. The *Express* had a slightly smaller version of the photograph headed 'Fighting Four' and a news story 'Marching Prefects Back Headmaster'. The *Mirror*, a little behind at this point, had a story – 'No-Cane Head asked: "Give up Teaching"'. The *Telegraph* ran, ' "Insults to our Head" Protest by Prefects. "A Personal Vendetta"'. The *Times* story was headed 'Headmaster Denies Assault Stories'.

The previous day, four senior prefects had asked Mr Duane's permission to march to County Hall. He told them, 'Do what

*I discovered later that the L.C.C. and Mr Duane had always disagreed about this question of 'confidentialness'. The L.C.C., when it makes appointments, expects to be given 'confidential reports' on its teachers as well as open testimonials. Michael Duane refused to give confidential reports – unless it was understood that he sent a copy to the person concerned. The L.C.C. was scandalized. This is an excellent example, with all its implications, of Michael Duane's 'tactlessness'.

you think is right. That's what I've always taught you.' Nine prefects marched taking the letter, which asked the council to keep Risinghill open; it was signed by thirty-seven senior pupils, and ended 'many of us have exams at O and A level G.C.E. in the near future, and we plead with you to reconsider your decision, if there ever was one, to reorganize the school.' The Parent–Teacher Association arranged for an emergency meeting. Mr Duane and Mr James Young, chairman of the L.C.C. Education Committee, both appeared on television. Mr Duane also spoke on radio.

The press reports were the first the parents and children had heard of their expendability. Some of them had missed the *Sunday Times* revelation and did not know till the Monday. As for me, reading the *Guardian*, I did not know till the Tuesday. In fact, this was the first time I had ever heard of Risinghill.

Fighting back

As long as they teach at all . . . they teach by the way they behave, by what they are. That is why one of the absolutely essential qualities of a teacher is integrity.

I am interested in children, and because of this I sometimes go to visit a school that for some reason has attracted my attention. I phoned Risinghill and asked if I could come down, and was simply told 'Certainly'.

The situation within the school was apparent to me the moment I got there – the friendliness and concern of the children . . . the head's study, which was more like a clubroom for all ages . . . the head himself who let me do whatever I liked, and stayed out of his study for as long as I wished while I used it to discuss him and the school with his pupils. No, this was not the L.C.C.'s idea of a head.

That evening the parents were meeting. I decided to go along. I took very full notes of everything that happened, knowing no background then beyond what I had heard and observed for myself that afternoon. It was impossible to write down everything because questions were fired non-stop for hours. Sometimes I scribbled questions for myself, to follow up later; sometimes when a comment or question was my own and not the speaker's, I put my initials after it. Here, then, are those notes:

Actually called to discuss Education Today, and to see some sex education films which M.D. suggests showing to the children. (Can see this is typical of the easy way he educates parents along with the children.) But obviously it is going to discuss, instead, the horrifying news that has burst on them in the press – that the L.C.C. are considering closing the school.

A very noisy, intense, passionate meeting.

My immediate impression – I have been to many parent–teacher meetings, but never to one where the parents are so passionately involved in education as this; tremendous and inspiring.

Between 150 and 200 people; hall packed. Due to start at 7, but by time parents are home from work, washed and changed, had bite to eat, it is always well past the hour, people next to me explain; in fact, meetings never start till 7.30. Many parents work odd hours – many mothers are office cleaners, and work in the evening; also, many parents have no belief in education, or even in their children. Yet this meeting is certainly as large as I have seen at grammar schools, and infinitely more involved; their involvement is not based on the fear that tends to be called conformity, but on self-respect; a wonderfully stirring and inspiring thing to see, this belief in themselves, this passionate acclamation of their right to education.

Sat next to parents who had taken their boy from a grammar school to send him to R. At his grammar school, his parents say, he was learning nothing. He was supposed to do swimming and didn't want to. He had had an operation for hernia and was afraid of using the horse in the gym. Finally, because other boys in the flats told him so much about R., his parents sent him there instead. Now he is interested in everything, has learnt far more than he ever did at grammar school and loves swimming. He wants to learn, because of the way he is treated. Even though he could only be placed, at first, in a C form, his parents sent him; he is now in an A form, and he and they are delighted. (All this his parents told me.)

Parents spontaneously said 'Skip the film-show tonight.' There was a lot of anger against press (see cuttings for that day. L.B.), parents said press were hostile, and distorting, but parents said 'Press can stay if they speak the truth.' (They keep saying this – 'speak the truth'.)

At this meeting M.D. explained to the parents that no decision had yet been taken; the L.C.C. Ed. Co. will consider the matter at the end of January and will then take a decision. He is very calm and seems quite unworried – as always, I fancy. Parents leaped up to speak, sometimes several at once. There was no break in questions – no pause.

PARENT: What is the future of the school now?

M.D.: There are administrative difficulties in fitting children into existing schools. The L.C.C. will decide about this at the end of January.

PARENT: Is their decision final?

M.D.: Parents can appeal.

PARENT: How can they go about it?

M.D.: Do you mean after the decision has been made? It hasn't been made yet –

PARENT: To what do you attribute the notoriety that has been attracted to the school?

M.D.: The difficulties and disturbances of the early days; and the fact that comprehensive schools are now a matter of very great importance – it is the fact that R. is a comprehensive school that has brought us to public notice.

PARENT: What are the proposals of the L.C.C. Committee?

M.D.: As far as we know them, that a certain reorganization of a group of schools is made necessary by the fact that a day college has to be rehoused.

PARENT: Can you tell us what would happen to the pupils of the school?

M.D.: I don't know.

PARENT: Won't the move upset children, when they have been settled so long?

M.D.: Obviously, yes. But I am certain the Education Committee will consider this difficulty.

PARENT: Could we have one of the L.C.C. officials to come and tell us why they have these proposals in mind?

M.D.: Parents and teachers are normally informed of any decision. A public notice is inserted in the press at least six months before any change is made. Until the Committee has discussed the various proposals, I am not sure whether officials will be in a position to discuss them.

PARENT: Why have you been singled out for so much publicity on your teaching methods?

M.D.: Our colleagues of the press have to interest their readers. Some of the things *we* are doing here (*we*, not *I*; nothing can be achieved in a large school without the staff sweating their guts out, in conjunction with the parents) seem to be slightly unusual.

PARENT: I read in one paper, if the Ministry had its way it was intended to reopen the school as a comprehensive school for girls only. What connexion has this with all the talk about day college?

M.D.: Most members of the Committee seem to prefer single-sex schools. If this is also the wish of the parents, the Committee can say they are carrying out the wishes of the parents.

PARENT: When are they going to ask the parents what they want?

M.D.: In a sense they have that already, by your selection when your child is 10. But clearly, when 500 parents select a school that only has 300 places, some have to have a second choice. The L.C.C. looks back over these forms.

PARENT: But this is going back over a period of years. We are dealing with R. *now*.

M.D.: This is a point which you as parents are at liberty to say to the L.C.C.

PARENT: My daughter started at this school at the age of 13, and is going to take G.C.E. What opportunities will she have?

M.D.: If this school is made into a girls' school, she should have as good, perhaps a better, chance as now. You, as parents, have a right to demand equal opportunities. If the decision to close is taken at the end of January, we would instantly start to build up records to hand over to the child's new school – including saying 'This is what the child – and the parents – want to do.' We would therefore point out to the L.C.C. that the child must go to the school that fits her wishes. That is our duty as staff to the children.

PARENT: What is all this in the press about the No-Cane Headmaster?

M.D.: When we first started this school, it was possible for heads of the houses to use the cane, according to Ministry Regulations. During the first week, a boy was caned for stealing. Of their own accord, the staff had a meeting . . . [see other notes – L.B.*].

PARENT: Have you ever regretted this decision?

M.D.: No, never. At my previous schools, I had used the cane. But the more I looked at the Punishment Book (which contains a public record of canings), and at entries which went back generations, I saw the same children's names coming up over and over again. One name came up 59 times in one year. So I decided to try other methods.

PARENT: What are your methods of punishment?

M.D.: I personally have no time for punishment at all. But we are a state school; I and my colleagues are equally able to be sacked by the L.C.C. If I and my staff are to get along, I must modify my views when necessary; the same applies to my staff. The punishments used are detention – the giving of report cards or attendance cards (the first for bad behaviour, the second for lateness or skipping lessons). The person who knows the child best, the head of his house, is the best person to discuss with the child how he's getting on.

PARENT: Do you find you get more satisfaction when you give love and affection, especially when somebody's in trouble?

M.D.: When a child's constantly in trouble – in and out of court –

*I had made notes about the staff meeting that decided against corporal punishment, earlier on in his study.

there is something seriously wrong; and you don't solve it by beating. My experience of twenty years is that there is almost always something in the background that has brought this about, and this entails discussions with parents, doctors, social workers and so on. Our job is to help the child.

PARENT: What do you do if you don't get the co-operation of the parent?

M.D.: This is one time when we fail – though even then, we don't always.

PARENT: Isn't it true to say that those few are the ones who are bringing this trouble to the school?

M.D.: This is true. But this is where press publicity is valuable – they can show how few can damage many. . . .

PARENT: Why don't you get these parents – and these councillors – to see Open Day . . . the lovely things the children here have done?

M.D.: These parents are the ones who won't come. But more and more councillors are doing so.

PARENT: Why does the L.C.C. want to close the school?

M.D.: The L.C.C. has officially said nothing yet. The position is that some officials think these proposals might solve a problem of theirs.

PARENT: Surely they'll take into account the results you've achieved?

M.D.: I'm sure they will.

PARENT: One paper said the decision on Risinghill will not be taken for some time yet. How long does this give us?

M.D.: It depends on the date of the meetings. The L.C.C. Education Committee meets twice a month; but other smaller committees would also be involved. All the committees would meet, and then put their recommendations to the big committee.

PARENT: Have you noticed, since all the publicity, that there has been a disturbed atmosphere in the school?

M.D.: Yes. I had a special assembly this morning, to try to explain to the children what this position was meaning to the staff. The present situation causes worry among children and parents, and teachers find it difficult to control. That is why the L.C.C. should decide as quickly as possible.

PARENT: What was the trouble that got Risinghill into the press this week?

M.D.: No trouble. A reporter discovered these proposals, which had been confidential.

PARENT: Why do the press always report the bad, instead of highlight the good?

M.D.: Because vice is always more exciting than virtue.

PARENT: Have you ever had any complete failures?

M.D.: You can't ever say a child is a complete failure. This is putting yourself in the place of God sending someone to hell.

PARENT: The interviewer on TV said something about 243 cases.

M.D.: This referred to the number of children who had appeared in court over the full four years. As I explained, many of these were in court because their parents had neglected them, not because the children had committed any crime. In fact, our comparative figures were fairly close to the national average. In other words, this school is no different from other schools in comparative areas. But the children here all came to us from other schools. And if they were in trouble, it is partly the fault of the other schools.

PARENT: If the policy of the L.C.C. is to have comprehensive schools for girls and comprehensive schools for boys, how many other schools are being changed?

M.D.: I think the L.C.C. wants all three types – boys, girls, mixed –

PARENT: Do you think the press has been irresponsible in this matter? And that you have been indiscreet in talking to them? They showed photographs of slums that have been empty for goodness knows how long, with windows broken years ago –

[Yells here against mass-circulation press. Parents very angry. Took a while before meeting quiet enough for M.D. to answer. L.B.]

M.D.: Quite honestly, my impression is that a fair picture of the school has been presented *on the whole*. The reporter from the paper that printed that photograph said 'What a pity the school has these surroundings.'

[More shouts, and anger expressed from people who didn't accept the newspapers' good motives. L.B.]

PARENT: Is there nothing we can do *before* the decision is taken?

M.D.: Certainly. If the meeting feels the school should go on, this meeting can say so.

PARENT: The children are going round with petitions – some of them were carrying banners saying 'We want our headmaster' . . . 'What is going to happen to our school?' This is contrary to other schools where the kids want the bloody school to close down. I think we have to *thank* the press, because people who only knew bad things about the school now know good ones. I say we should first of all send a letter to the Education Officer and the Chairman of the L.C.C. and our M.P.s for Shoreditch and Finsbury, and the Prime Minister. I don't think the L.C.C. or anyone else has the right to close our school. Thank God classes *have* got a bit smaller; why is the L.C.C. complaining about this? [Cheers from parents.] I'd like to move a motion that this parent–teachers association has complete confidence in the head and the staff, and deplore any action to reorganize the school, or to request Mr Duane or the staff to accept other positions.

[This was voted on, and carried with 17 abstentions. Cheers from parents, shouts of 'Let's get out a petition with signatures tonight.' The meeting also insisted that a copy of the parents' petition go to the Prime Minister and to the Ministry of Education; and that they send a deputation to the Education Officer of the L.C.C., before their meeting, 'to put *our* views'.

At the end of the meeting, I went back in my notes and scribbled this here: at this point the meeting was happy. They had worked things out, and their anger was turning into self-confidence. What followed was extraordinary, because it was deliberately destructive – so very startling. L.B.]

TEACHER: After school this afternoon, the common-room staff met and agreed on the following statement:

'We are firmly in favour of comprehensive education in this area, because we think it fulfils the educational and social needs in this district. We think any of these changes proposed . . . would be educationally harmful to the children and the staff. We believe that very much good has been done in this school. . . . But we are not satisfied. We are disturbed about the question of the first choices of children who come into the school. They have fallen. We feel that this is because the school has an unenviable reputation. The press has not helped us. . . .' [Can't make out if this is staff statement or if she's speaking off her own bat. L.B.] It is not true that no teachers have been attacked. They have been attacked, and I have been attacked. [Shouts.] I sometimes don't sleep for nights. I have nightmares about the school. [Shouts. Parents are very confused. L.B.] Forty teachers stated: 'We wish to dissociate ourselves from certain statements about the school that have recently appeared in press reports.' [This is the meeting on 12 Jan. that issued statements I have a copy of. L.B.] We feel that when mud is slung about, it sticks to everyone, justly or unjustly. . . . We worry will the children be able to get worthwhile jobs, will the school be able to get the staff it demands. . . . The Common-room Council decided to ask this meeting, for the sake of the children's education, the children and the staff, to call for a public inquiry into the school, conducted by the Ministry of Science and Education.

> [Parents confused. Some clap and cheer. Some stand up and ask questions all at the same time. Shouting. L.B.]

PARENT: But won't a public inquiry further increase the insecurity and prolong the period of indecision?

M.D. [meeting very turbulent by now. L.B.]: In view of so much coming into light, no more harm can be done, and sensationalism may be cut out.

PARENT: From my own experience on the buses, of public inquiries, public inquiries can go on for a very long time – perhaps two years. . . . I know everyone talks about the school's academic record, and this is fine; but I think there should also be talk of the work of the school with the also-rans – this should be stressed too.

PARENT: When were you attacked? [Various shouts – from parents, and from group of teachers at back.]

EX-BOY: I don't think any amount of time is too long to bring out the truth about this school. [He spoke very warmly about school. Everybody talking at once. L.B.]

PARENT: My child is fourteen. I assure you that if anything happens to this school, he will not go to any school at all.

ANOTHER TEACHER [apparently senior mistress]: I know that all truth is only approximate. We must fight for the truth to come out.

> [This phrase roused the parents more. They had been very badly jolted, but there was a tremendous feeling that truth must come out, plus fury against the teachers. Shouts. L.B.]

M.D.: The boy in question was found to be in need of psychiatric treatment. His father had died of cancer, his mother tried to commit suicide on three occasions. The family has been in very sad circumstances for a very long time.*

PARENT: Is it not possible that as a result of the deputation a public inquiry will be held?

M.D.: It is possible.

PARENT: Let's ask for it.

PARENT: Anything can be magnified, when the school is not compared with other schools.

PARENT: What is going to happen to our children if the teachers start stirring up things that happened years ago?

PARENT: Was it a unanimous demand from the staff?

*This was the only boy M.D. could think of, then.

TEACHER: From the staff who were there.

TEACHER: The teachers' decision was made for the sake of all the children at the school.

> [Parents clap. Extraordinary generosity of parents. Or is it because of their confusion? L.B.]

PARENT: Would a public inquiry bring more adverse publicity to the school – bring out more about things that happened years ago?

M.D.: It would bring out more of the difficulties and more of the good.

TEACHER [Man]: I was shot with a slug-gun in the playground last year.

PARENT: It seems that the teachers want to kick you out.

> ['You' being M.D. Angry shouts – 'Yes, it does' – from parents. M.D. insisted on disciplining meeting. (I think some of the staff are at loggerheads with each other. Were all the staff told of the meeting in the common room? Was Mr Duane? . . . Staff are more concerned with the 'image'.) At 9.10 meeting insisted on going on with the discussion, though it was supposed to close, worked up by their anger at the teachers. L.B.]

M.D.: It is a fair comment that the reputation that this school now enjoys is due to a very small minority of children. If you were parents in an *imaginary* school, would you criticize the head and the staff for not punishing this small minority, because some people might say this would do away with this minority? We must decide to draw the line. Some people would argue that stealing is wrong and must be punished. This is our dilemma. . . . This matter of punishing and not punishing was discussed among the staff. [Interesting that the parents present are more humane than the staff present – excluding the head. L.B.] Since heads of house have considerable autonomy, they deal with 'crimes' in different ways; and also they know the background of the individual child . . . The alternative to punishment is doing something else.

PARENT: Is it the same staff now that voted against corporal punishment four years ago?

M.D.: Some are the same. . . .

M.D.: If anything goes wrong, the head is responsible, whether the staff supports him or not. If I accepted a staff decision although I myself didn't agree, I would have to justify this to the Education Committee.

PARENT: When one talks about abolishing *capital* punishment, one group always believes that you don't want to support the police and you want to mollycoddle criminals. We have all sympathy with teachers and we are not here for a lark. We are entitled to our point of view. Pushes and shoves existed when I was at school. What about the parents who get annoyed when children are caned and want to sort teachers out? Some of us here are not gentlemen. This doesn't make us criminals. As I see it, the object of caning is a deterrent to others. Why was it then that five or six boys who I used to see caned every week, and all the others who saw it, went on getting the cane? Of course, our youngsters are not perfect. We aim to make them into good citizens. You teachers work like Trojans to do it. But some people believe the cane is outmoded. These people try to bring their children up in a normal decent way to be good and the kids come home with weals on their hand or their backside.

ANOTHER MAN TEACHER: Corporal punishment is a red herring. The teachers are concerned with the future of the school. I've only been here less than a term. I'm concerned with the future. The L.C.C. says the prestige of the school is going down; and therefore the school must be closed. I agree with them. [I blinked at this. L.B.]

PARENT: You can't change the attitude of a child overnight.

[Evident that teachers *of the right kind for comprehensive schools* are very difficult to get. Is this so? Or are we trying to get the wrong kind?

The meeting *had* to be closed at 9.45, though everyone still wanted to go on. It was at first impossible to stop it, and to clear the hall. Parents went on. L.B.]

PARENT: If there is a public inquiry, would it prolong the life of the school?

M.D.: Yes. . . . In case parents feel that there is any large measure of disagreement between the teachers and me, I should tell you I put my resignation before the L.C.C. in December. The reply came back: this relationship of the staff and the head had nothing to do with it. My resignation was refused.

TEACHER: I find it difficult to understand why parents are against a public inquiry. If the public inquiry decided to change the way of the school working, I for one would be out of a job. I'm not afraid. So let's have it.

[Risinghill inquiry may be a springboard for a discussion on the whole question of comprehensive education. L.B.]

M.D.: I asked for a full inquiry two years ago.

[At this point, the meeting decided to vote on suspending the discussion to decide whether the press would be allowed to remain. Teachers wanted L.C.C. to forbid press access to

school – 'so that real work of school can go on.' It was over-
whelmingly agreed to let the press remain – but some parents
shouted 'As long as they speak the truth.' L.B.]

PARENT: Before the war, we had the Angel Boys and other gangs.
They ruled us in school with a rod of iron. This school is doing
something different. They are consulting parents, bringing them
into education, helping children of lesser educational abilities.
Teachers perhaps don't live in this area. For a school to try to do
something different . . . ! I do a job where I meet hundreds of
children every day, piling on buses – grammar school, public
school children – they behave worse if anything!

TEACHER [he said he was teacher of Greek-speaking children]: The
Greek children are all very happy. Since they have come into this
school, they have found hospitality among English children. They
come up to me crying and sobbing and saying 'Sir, we don't want
our school to close.'

M.D.: There *are* disagreements between different groups of the staff,
and between groups of the staff and the head. But this is not necessarily an unhealthy thing. There is more time and energy spent on
discussing education and on what is best for the children than in
any other school I have known. If the school closes, the work that
is being done here will finish. If it goes on, it will be possible for
these meetings to go on, working out the best thing to do. . . .

TEACHER: We do *not* want to see this school closed down. We have a
great regard for the good that has been achieved. We want a mixed
comprehensive school here. But we want impartial people to come
and say 'This is good; keep it. This is bad; scrap it.'

[A vote was now taken on the public inquiry (67 for, 49 against,
9 abstentions). It was also agreed that a small deputation take
the demand to the Ministry. And a resolution was passed dec-
laring complete confidence in the headmaster and the staff, and
deploring 'any action to reorganize the school or the staff'.]

I wrote immediately afterwards, sitting in a café, still with no
further knowledge of the school:

A passionate and extraordinarily warm-hearted meeting. 'So that
the truth can be told.' No speech from the platform. Questions fired
non-stop from the floor. Headmaster Mr Duane acting as a quiet
obstetrician, speaking only when the need arose and then very briefly.
Gone on two and a half hours. Meeting finally cleared – very reluctantly. Still arguing, and *passionately discussing education and what*

education means, the parents suddenly got into knots, others bumping into them equally engrossed, streaming into the streets still talking.

It was very clear that parents have a tremendous active loyalty to a school – and particularly to a headmaster – who has given their children love and respect and drawn themselves, the parents, into their children's education; and that teachers, while stressing that they believe that a mixed comprehensive school is needed in the district, are not so sure that everything done at Risinghill is right. Both parents and teachers are very sensitive to the reputation of the school – parents because this reflects on the children's present and future, teachers because it reflects on the children's future and on their own. The minority of parents who voted against the inquiry did so because they were afraid that incidents that happened at the beginning of the school's life and were now done with would be raked up again, to the detriment of their children; those who voted for it seized on the fact that the school could not be closed as long as an inquiry was pending.

The inquiry may reveal that it is not sufficient to say 'Yes, comprehensive schools are a good idea. Let's have them,' and to imagine we can staff them with the same sort of teachers as staffed grammar schools. Once you believe, or say you believe, that all children are of equal value whatever their intellectual attainments, you are changing the whole concept of school, and it is becoming something much more akin to home – an ideal home into which the real parents, too, are drawn.

*

In fact, no inquiry has ever been held.

I did not, on this my first day, know the discrepancies between the stories of the two teachers who said they had been 'attacked' as they were originally told to Mr Duane* and as they were told at this meeting in front of the press. For months these stories were still reverberating – probably they will do so for ever. The *Times Educational Supplement*, by and large very sympathetic to Mr Duane, headed their restrained news report, 'Blackboard Jungle', and spoke of 'this week's bout of evidence'. On 25 April, three and a half months later, the *Daily Telegraph* was saying 'One teacher announced recently that he had been wounded by fire from a shotgun.'

Nor did I know that the teacher who said he had been at the school less than a term, and that the school should be closed, had

*See pp. 157 and 172.

been there only a fortnight. He arrived at the beginning of January, talking rather mysteriously about being 'victimized' for 'militancy' at his previous school. He was elected Secretary of the Common-room Council because it was claimed (by whom, I later wondered?) that, being new, he would be impartial. A week after his election, he considerably startled other teachers by claiming that Mr Duane was 'unethical, immoral and criminal'.

In July, when I had decided to write a history of the school, I wrote to these three teachers, pointing out very mildly and politely that I had come on some discrepancies (for instance, surely it had originally been an air-gun not a shot-gun, and hadn't the teacher been misreported?) and suggesting a meeting. From two of them there was complete silence. My letter to the third – the teacher who claimed he had been shot – was answered by a solicitor who wrote that this teacher 'feels very strongly that the recent publicity given to Risinghill has seriously disturbed both the teachers and the children of the school. In view of this, and the fact that he does not want to perpetuate the unpleasantness so caused, he has requested that you do not address any further correspondence to him in connexion with this matter.'

Nor had I seen the statement, 'signed by forty of the staff', 'demanding a public inquiry', that spread chaos among the parents, and took the morning paper headlines. What I did see was a statment that had been given at the end of that school afternoon to someone who particularly needed to be impressed. It had twenty-nine signatures and it did not ask for a public inquiry. What twenty-nine teachers had signed was a statement deploring inaccurate and sensational statements about the school given to the press.

I would not have recognized this as the statement announced by the teacher at the January meeting were it not that the first sentence in the paper I held in my hand and the sentence I had noted down as the teacher spoke at the meeting were exactly the same.

I gradually got the history of this statement, which had been cooking for some time. At one staff meeting after another, this teacher had tried to get a resolution passed demanding, in some form, a 'reorganization' of the school – that is to say, demanding that Mr Duane be thrown out; but over and over again the resolution was defeated, and had to be remodelled for the next time. Eventually, at a staff meeting in December, Mr Duane said to this teacher (I am not here quoting verbatim) 'Concentrate first on keeping the school going; *then* you can concentrate on getting me out. Get your priorities right.' She did not take this advice. He drew up a statement asking the L.C.C. to keep the school, and asked if anyone would like to sign it. She refused. Forty-seven out of the sixty teachers did sign. (This is the statement I referred to in the previous chapter as the staff petition.) She then drew up yet one more version of the 'reorganization' demand, which twenty-nine teachers out of the sixty signed, which gave eleven lines to a deploring of inaccuracies and sensational distortions in the press, followed by three lines asking for an official from the Education Department to come down and talk things over with the staff. This was the statement which, at the January meeting, in front of the pressmen whose presence had been underlined by previous discussion about them, the teacher announced was signed by forty who demanded a public inquiry.

For days after that meeting, not yet knowing this history and still being new to the battleground, I turned the incidents over in my mind; there had been a blindness and a wild irrelevance in those teachers' actions, but also a calculatedness that puzzled me because I knew I had the key to it in my mind. Days later, I remembered where I had experienced this combination before – at political meetings, where someone arrives with a decision that has already been taken and now needs to be implemented; such a person hears nothing that goes on, absorbs none of the atmosphere that seeps from his neighbours, but within his private sealed-off world waits for his moment to pounce.

Later an idea struck me. I went back over all the newspaper reports of those five fermenting days before the parents' meeting, and found in the Tuesday *Daily Telegraph* this sentence from Mr Duane: 'No one on the staff has been assaulted "even in our toughest days".' So this was the sentence the group had decided to fight on, recalling those two small incidents which now would be so useful.

When those three made their statements at the meeting,

knowing they were making them in front of the press, had they not realized that the L.C.C. would not tolerate anyone, even a strange ally, drawing public attention to difficult conditions in a school ? The schools might be state schools, but the L.C.C. made it clear they liked to keep them private. Or had they taken a decision that if they could drive out Mr Duane only by destroying the school, then destroy the school they would, the school being 900 children, plus their parents and their belief in themselves ? Was their whole battle by now an unpleasant and calculated farce, an attempt to get in on the murder scene for the glory it might bring – for had not the L.C.C. decided a long time back to close this embarrassing school ?

At that meeting I had met for the first time parents who were deeply involved in education. But after that meeting deterioration was already setting in. After that meeting they knew that everything was being settled behind their backs, cynically and secretly. They already saw that they counted for nothing; and everything that was done from this point on – deputations, protests, meetings – was done with this growing undercurrent of despair and a sense of their own expendability. Will they ever go to parents' meetings again ?

As for the children, later a teacher said to me 'The children must feel so much more insecure, when they see that adults can so easily destroy what they have come to depend on. After that meeting, several teachers said to me that the children feel they have been completely betrayed by their teachers.'

Desperation

These girls and boys must somehow be made much more active partners in their own education.

By the time the parents met, three thirteen-year-olds, two boys and a girl, had already been out in the market, collecting signatures to a plea written out on pages torn from an exercise book. It read (I have polished up the spelling):

We are self-deputized and strongly object to the attempted closure of our school. The rumours about fires being lit in the school, pregnant girls and so on, we all deny it. I would like to add that Mr Duane is great. He does not need to use the cane. If he can stop the fight between Risinghill and Tudor which you know was very fierce, he can easily handle children.

People living near a tough school (or an orphanage, or a nursery school, or an approved school) are generally the first to sign a petition against it. These stall-holders, whose openly displayed goods often tempted the kids (and indeed, Mr Duane had got at least one to agree not to phone the police if a kid nicked anything from his stall but to phone *him*, and he would come round instantly), would not have roused surprise if they cheered the closure. They didn't. In one lunch-hour those three children collected 178 signatures and handed one copy to County Hall; then, carrying home-made banners shouting 'Hands off our School' and 'Mr Duane Must Stay', with eight more young representatives they marched to Downing Street with another. In the four days between the *Sunday Times* story and the parents' meeting, four separate pupils' petitions and two separate parents' petitions (one from Greek-speaking, one from Turkish-speaking parents) were already circulating and long and deeply-felt letters were being written to the L.C.C. and the government by present and past pupils who did not even know where to address them. The press continued to support them and to photograph them –

and one group of ex-pupils, rendered circumspect by the outside world, decided to take their own petition to Downing Street without letting the press know, so that no one could say they were wild exhibitionists. The *Mirror* alone took up a point that had struck me from the beginning – the L.C.C. had long been unctuously deploring the size of classes in state schools, and now that they had a school with fewer numbers they were closing it.

A fortnight later, the L.C.C. wrote to give parents the news which they were furious the parents already knew. (It must have seemed strange to many people that Risinghill had to be closed down because Starcross was in Kingsway's premises. The L.C.C. explained this to the parents – as they explained to the press – by saying that Risinghill's intake was going down. What they did not say was that the intake of *all* London secondary schools was going down (by about 32,000 since 1960), and that since the grammar schools, of which there were several locally, were always given one-hundred-per-cent intake and therefore filled up before other secondary schools, and of those that remained the single-sex schools filled up before co-educational ones, and of those that remained the ones in a better district filled up before the ones in the worst district, and the familiar ones filled up before the new ones, the decline was bound to show up strongly in Risinghill. In fact, there was a *newer* local school that had an even smaller intake;* but the L.C.C. never mentioned this. Nor did they say that in four or five years' time, the 'bulge' that was now in the junior schools would have moved into the secondary schools, and we would need more schools; doubtless they will mention this later.)

On the same day they released the news to the press. The release contained the sentence 'Confidential discussions have taken place with the heads, staff and governors of the schools and college concerned about the proposals and the Council has taken into account their views before making its decisions.' This could only mean the L.C.C., having heard their views, deliberately flouted them.

I was in Michael Duane's study when reporters spoke to him.

*Actually an old school given a new name and in a new building.

*

One of them asked him, 'What are you really aiming at here?' He said, 'To remove fear from children in schools.'

The *Mail* carried the news right across its front page, the headline 'Risinghill WILL Be Shut' surmounting a huge photograph of a flag-draped coffin, people in the street sadly saluting it on 'the last journey to Westminster'. (The coffin was Sir Winston Churchill's.) This is how a sub-editor makes his comment.

In the meantime the group-of-three was still working hard and with tactical success. The teacher who had now been at the school three weeks and was secretary of the Staff Council framed the most fantastic letter to a headmaster from his teachers that I have ever seen, telling Mr Duane that he was to abstain from discussion of Risinghill School or of general educational problems in public, in the press, on television or on radio, and demanding 'undertakings in writing within twenty-four hours of the time and date of delivery of this letter'. As usual (see the revealing statement in the last chapter – the unanimous demand was made by 'the staff who were there'), this action was passed by a staff meeting which had, through prolongation, dwindled to a size small enough to pass it. And typically, the president of the School Council, who had also signed it, came to Mr Duane immediately afterwards, saying he was very worried about it and wished he hadn't signed it. One teacher who later saw it suggested to Mr Duane that he hand the letter over to the press as an indication of the sort of staff he had, but Mr Duane didn't.

On 2 February, the Cyprus High Commission's Cultural Attaché visited the school, talked to the children, and later said 'Risinghill has succeeded in doing something the United Nations cannot do. . . . He has children of all nationalities in his school, living together in harmony. If we all believe in international co-operation and understanding, why close the school where these principles are being applied?'

The next day the L.C.C. came down to talk to the Risinghill parents. The parents were furiously angry, and shouted down the L.C.C. spokesmen. 'Can't you feel human, instead of shoving people around like chequers?' shouted someone. Someone else shouted 'Our children are brought up here in an atmosphere of kindness. What will happen to them when they go to some schools where there are brutes who will use the cane on them?' 'Why did you come here if you have already decided?' called out someone; and Mrs Helen Bentwich answered, 'Because we wanted to be polite. We didn't come to hear from you. We simply came to tell you.' She shook an admonishing finger at a mother who kept asking questions – 'I've heard quite enough from you!' The *Times Educational Supplement*, which like many other papers described the stormy proceedings in detail, thought the roaring audience was nevertheless good-humoured. I very much doubt this. The English have a terrible jocularity that is equivalent to despair; it is the 'smack my arse, Carter' of the child in the first chapter; it starts very young.

A mother told me:

The County Hall representatives said 'In view of the fact that there had been so much press publicity, we feel we should explain to you *why we have decided* to close the school.'

They then told us, in words of one syllable, about Kingsway, about preference for single-sex schools, about low intake. Immediately a mass of parents got up. Some said they had several children and they intended to send them all to Risinghill; some said they were told by primary school heads not to send their children to Risinghill because it was a rough school and they wouldn't like it, but they had still insisted on their children going there, and now the L.C.C. talked of low intake. I said, and some other parents said, that we had chosen Risinghill because it had no corporal punishment; so could the L.C.C. guarantee we would be able to send our children to another school that had no corporal punishment? The L.C.C. said 'No, we cannot guarantee that, we cannot tell you of schools that do not have corporal punishment, but we can assure you Risinghill is not unique.' Parents said 'Then tell us which schools do not have it.' And the L.C.C. said 'No.'

Some parents said 'Our children are taking exams. They'll be very hard hit' – and the L.C.C.'s reply was 'I'm sure they won't be if you co-operate and don't make a fuss.' They made it clear it was completely settled.

I got up and told them about Miles and the 'two-year wait'. They said they didn't know anything about it, and the deputy head wasn't there to be asked.

Parents said the Education Act said they should be consulted. The L.C.C. said it was too big a matter for that.

The parents were furious. Bob Redrupp had to get up and say 'Shut up, everyone. Let one person speak at a time.' If Bob Redrupp hadn't been there, and made his influence felt from the back of the hall – trying to keep people under control and saying 'Okay, we can see what the situation is, we'll put this through the proper channels' – I think someone would have picked up a chair and hurled it at the platform. They spoke down to us, all the time; it was insufferable. When the parents said they would appeal, the L.C.C. spokesman said 'Good luck to you. You have the right to appeal. That is our glorious English tradition. But it won't get you anywhere – it's all settled. You'd do much better to make up your minds to it and settle your children at new schools.' I came away thinking a lot of thugs had got together in the power position and democracy was not working at all.

What had happened, in fact, was that the parents insisted they would appeal, the L.C.C. spokesman intimated quite clearly that they could of course do so but it would be a waste of time, the parents became extremely angry and shouted that they would go ahead just the same; and then, actually on the move, leaving the hall, with parents surging around, the L.C.C. spokesman said, 'Good luck to you'. One or two of the parents tried to find hope in this; an experienced newspaper reporter found it 'most offensive'.

On the same day the L.C.C. spoke to Starcross parents – equally angry. The L.C.C. could scarcely get a word in edgeways. The parents said they would boycott the school if it moved to Risinghill. It was a bad district, and they did not want their children to inherit 'the stigma'. To this the spokesman replied that the L.C.C. was asking Islington Borough Council to remove the name Risinghill Street.

Also on the same day, Mr Duane was writing to Mr Anthony Crosland, Secretary of State for Education: 'The human problem presented by Risinghill has been pushed aside by the L.C.C. but it has not disappeared and will not disappear by an administrative fiat. Before you make the irrevocable decision, come and see the school for yourself. Meet the children and the ordinary parents and look at the neighbourhood.'

And still on the same day, Mr Ron Brown, the local Labour M.P. and brother of George Brown, Cabinet Minister, said Mr

Duane and his staff had done 'a very good job' – and he supported the closure.

Less than a week later, Mr James Young attacked Roy Nash of the *Daily Mail* for saying that the Risinghill parents were not consulted. 'They *were* consulted', said Mr Young. Furthermore, he said, he had no evidence whatever that the majority of the parents objected. Yet by then the Risinghill parents were already holding another protest meeting to appeal to the government.

At this meeting the parents based their protest on the rights they were given, or thought they were given, by the Education Act. Section 76 of the Act states that children are to be educated in accordance with the wishes of their parents. Section 68 says that, if any person can show that a local education authority proposes to act unreasonably, the Minister may intervene. Parents thought perhaps they could prove 'unreasonableness' by stressing the evidence of probation officers, youth club leaders, and others who had spoken, during the last few days, of the happiness, the sense of true responsibility, and the widening interests that the school had brought to the local families.

Trying to draft this appeal and having no idea how to do it, the parents became despondent. Someone said 'We need a lawyer to do this for us. We don't know. . . .' Others agreed. There was a feeling of futility and disintegration in the air. Then a mother stood up, and said stoutly 'We're citizens. And we have certain rights. We're not asking to be considered as lawyers – only as citizens and as parents.' It was extraordinarily moving. She carried the meeting with her, and they felt confident again.

The appeal was finally drawn up, the parents signed it, it was sent off. A deputation from the Parent–Teacher Association was invited to discuss their points with the Minister. A deputation from the pupils was similarly invited. Both were received wth courtesy and assured that all the points they made would be considered. I talked to members of both deputations afterwards. A parent told me 'I felt we were being very politely listened to by a man whose mind wasn't on it because he knew the issue had been decided long ago. He was simply listening all the time for the division bell.' What nearly all the deputation members had in common, children and adults, was a sort of desperate hope, that was no longer concerned simply with their school, but with their own expendability; they simply could not bear to believe, openly, that they had no rights. Miles's mother once again talked of the 'two-year wait', and said 'The man seemed embarrassed.'

The group-of-three (they had two or three more adherents as well) had thrown in a final spanner. They were furiously angry at not being elected by the February meeting of parents and teachers to take the appeal to the Ministry. At a staff meeting afterwards, they demanded that a resolution be sent to the Minister saying that the majority of teachers did not want to associate themselves with the viewpoint that the Parent–Teacher Association was going to put. Mr Gwyn said this was utter nonsense since, firstly, they didn't know what the majority of teachers thought, and, secondly, they didn't know what the P.T.A. would say. But the motion was carried in the usual way. When the vote had been taken, several teachers came up to him and 'again in the usual way', he told me, they said, 'You were right, of course; it is nonsense. But the others voted, so I thought I should. You know how these things are. . . .' We all know how these things are. When the delegation got to the Ministry, the Minister had the resolution already in his hand.

Death blow

Even more fundamental are the personal relations which exist between teachers and pupils. . . . 'The great thing is to like them. If you don't, they'll know instinctively and you'll get nowhere with them.'

There would now be at least two months to wait. In fact, they extended into four.

Mr Crosland wrote to say, very politely, that he couldn't possibly visit the school during the next two months for they were legally laid down for receiving objections to the L.C.C.'s proposals; nor could he come in the time after that for that was for making his decision, he added.

In the meantime the letters were pouring in. About three hundred and fifty arrived at Risinghill. I took a pile to my house to read, feeling very depressed, and was still reading them with a new elation at half past two in the morning. They came from all over the country, from Wales and Ireland, from Athens, New York, Paris, Stuttgart. They came from the High Commission for Pakistan, the High Commission for Cyprus, the High Commission for India . . . from schoolchildren, university lecturers, mothers, teachers, child guidance workers, headmistresses, probation officers, grandmothers, educationists, teaching students. Requests came, too, for Mr Duane to speak, from training colleges, universities, working men's clubs, schools, Labour Party branches, Liberal Party branches, Humanist Societies, and he travelled all over the country talking of education; indeed, he booked himself up to halfway through 1966. It would never have happened if the L.C.C. had not been so repressive; it seemed to me typical of their hamfistedness, and I admit it delighted me. At last people, some people, were standing up to be counted.

Letters were being sent simultaneously, many writers said, to the Ministry, to the L.C.C., to M.P.s, and to newspapers. The *Sunday Times* printed an interesting letter from a teacher who had spent three years at Risinghill, and spoke of the qualities a teacher needed, which were not academic qualities; and Mr Hemmings, lecturer in Education to the University of Leicester, wrote a letter to the *Guardian* suggesting that either the L.C.C. lacked vision or wit, or else it did not like London children to be deprived of the opportunity to be caned. This annoyed the L.C.C. very much indeed, and Mr James Young wrote to the *Guardian* on their behalf to complain of Mr Hemmings's impudence and to say corporal punishment was practically non-existent; but simultaneously with Mr Young's letter, the *Guardian* printed a piece in their Diary concerning letters they had received from parents and from teachers, complaining of the amount of caning that went on in London schools.

*

I had been thinking about this subject myself for some time, and this waiting period seemed to me a good time to write an article about it.

I had already filled in some of this waiting time by studying the Ministry of Education's two excellent reports on education under social handicap,* follow-ups to the Newsom Report. They were humane, intelligent and valuable; they might have been written by Mr Duane. The third and final report† ending '. . . local authorities should be required to provide a social work agency within their schools. . . . I am convinced that to neglect this field would lead to continuing growth in the delinquency figures and life failure of many of our future citizens', came out just as the Ministry of Education closed down Risinghill.

I got down to my article. The Advisory Centre for Education told me that a London primary school near Euston had banned the cane. I was delighted to hear it, as I needed someone with an optimistic philosophy to balance all the dreary tales of hitting with cane, ruler, slipper and hand that had been coming to me from various schools. I phoned the head, and said I would very much like to talk to her.

'I am not allowed to speak to you.'

*Reports on Education, No. 17 (December 1964) and No. 20 (March 1965).
†No. 22 (June 1965).

'But – *is* it true that you don't have caning?'

'I am not allowed to speak to you.'

'But can't you even tell me that?'

'I'm afraid not.'

There was a silence. Then I said, 'Doesn't the L.C.C.* realize that people actually talk to other people outside their jurisdiction? Doesn't it occur to them, for instance, that I talk to parents, teachers, and children, in my own house, as friends?'

The head said, 'I'm sorry you're so angry. Why don't you phone the Area Education Officer? He might let us speak to each other.'

I said 'No, thank you. It is too stupid.'

'Well, I don't like the way you're so angry. . . . I'll phone him myself and ask him.'

In the afternoon, the phone rang.

'I did phone the Area Education Officer and I asked him if we could speak to each other. He said no.'

'Thank you very much.'

'Well, you still seem so angry. . . . Why don't you phone Headquarters, County Hall, and ask them? I'll give you the phone number.'

'No, thank you. It's too ridiculous, and I'm too busy.'

'*Please*. . . . I wish you would. . . .'

'No.'

I continued to gather in my evidence on corporal punishment, and later recounted this conversation to my husband, who said, 'I think you should phone County Hall, and see what they say.' So I did.

The Press and Public Relations Officer at County Hall was completely charming. I explained what the position was, and he said that naturally I couldn't talk to a head. A lot of nonsense, he

---

*On 31 March 1965, the London County Council ceased to exist. On 1 April, the Greater London Council, which covered a wider area, was officially born; and the Inner London Education Authority, covering the same area as the old L.C.C. Education Committee and therefore mainly the same personnel, took over from the committee. From 1 April, the previous year, instead of the old Ministry of Education we had had a Department of Education and Science, headed by a Secretary of State, and, serving under him, two Ministers. I have mainly kept the old names throughout the Risinghill affair, deeming it less confusing for readers.

said in a warm, friendly way, was being talked about corporal punishment. People like that man, Mr Duane, talked as if the hitting, slapping, and pushing about that goes on in schools was corporal punishment. Corporal punishment didn't really exist. But he would see if there was anything that could possibly be done to help me. He would talk to his Chief Inspector and see if the Chief Inspector could see any possibility of allowing the head and me to talk to one another. He couldn't promise, but he was going to try.

A little later, he phoned me. He had talked to the Chief Inspector (and I think several other important people, but being by then a little tired, I don't seem to have made a note of the beginning of this conversation), and after a long discussion (there was definitely a feeling of flattery here) it had been decided that the head and I *could* be allowed to talk to one another. But of course this would need special arrangements. And these County Hall was prepared to make. They would arrange a meeting for me at County Hall, where the Press and Publicity Officer and the Chief Inspector and various other important people, and several specially picked heads including the one I had wanted to talk to, would all be present, prepared to talk to me.

I said this was extremely kind of him and the Chief Inspector and that I appreciated it, but it seemed to me it was going to take rather a long time to arrange. He said naturally it would; the Chief Inspector was very busy, he himself was very busy, heads were very busy, examinations were coming up. I said, 'Well, thank you, but I've finished my article on corporal punishment in state schools, and I'm just ready to send it off. I had saved some space for the head of this primary school that I was told had banned corporal punishment, but it seems the article must go off without a word from her. What a pity!' At this point I am afraid that the charm of the Public Relations Officer broke down; but only momentarily. It was then agreed that my article would go off – how could it be stopped? – but that I would attend 'an informal, friendly discussion' at County Hall on a later date, on the lines already suggested, for a follow-up article.

On the date fixed, I arrived at County Hall. The Publicity Officer sent a last-minute message to say he couldn't come. In the Chief Inspector's ante-room, I was introduced by his secretary to several heads. We were then all shown into the Chief Inspector's room. He opened the meeting. His words were 'I think it is very kind of us to give up this beautiful summer morning to come and talk to Miss Leila Berg –'

Everyone I related this to immediately afterwards said 'Why didn't you let him go on!' I think I would have done if I hadn't been aware of the embarrassment of the heads who knew who I was. Not that they showed it. Not a trace of emotion showed throughout on their faces. I regret it now, and if I had the time again I would let him hurtle heavily into irrevocabilities. But I interrupted him.

'I'm so sorry, Dr Payling, I'm afraid that's me.'

A brief silence. Then –

'I didn't know you were here already. You look like a head-mistress.'

'I should just like to remark on what you've just said –'

'NO! NO! Wait till I've finished! I will not have you speaking whenever you feel like it! You'll listen to me!'

I was rather surprised at this, when I had been asked to come to 'an informal, friendly meeting', and I looked round expecting to see the heads were surprised too; but they weren't. And throughout that astonishing meeting, nothing surprised them.

So I waited while the Chief Inspector made a long speech about the progressive outlook of the L.C.C., about how they didn't have corporal punishment but could not tolerate anyone saying publicly that he didn't have corporal punishment; and he waved the brown booklet called *Punishment in Schools* at me and shouted, 'I don't suppose Miss Berg has seen this!'

When he had finished, I said I was sorry he had prevented me from speaking. I had merely wanted first to say that I resented his deliberate whipping up of hostility against me, and secondly, to give the heads the correct information that it was not *I* who had forced them to 'give up this beautiful summer morning', but the L.C.C. as the Chief Inspector knew perfectly well (though he had not realized I was already present and could refute his statement); and I recounted the steps that had led up to this meeting. Then I said 'I have, of course, seen the fairly pleasant brown booklet, that is fairly easily obtainable. I have also seen this, which is not so pleasant, not so easily obtainable, but was reissued seven years after that brown booklet was published,' and I held up a white double-leaflet headed *Corporal Punishment*.

'That is highly confidential!'

'I know. It says so on the outside. Why is it?'

'This is intolerable! This is grossly improper! I don't know who gave you that document! Nobody has any right – '

'Why do you call it improper for anyone to know that their children in our schools can be hit with a cane of the approved pattern? Why do you think I, a parent and a citizen, have no right to know – '

I will spare a full report of this ·'informal, friendly meeting' discussion. I have rarely been filled with such a weight of despair, but fortunately I was angry, too, and there are times, I have found, when anger is the only emotion worth having.

One head after another said 'Of course we don't have corporal punishment.' But one after another, they made it very clear that they regarded a head who told the children he wasn't going to use corporal punishment as a traitor – they used the same words as Anglo-Indians use of an Englishman who gets too friendly with the natives. A little while later, the head who didn't use corporal punishment would be saying 'Of course, I use it for ... swearing' (or it might be talking, or running, or lying, or coming late, or stealing ...). Quite soon, one of these picked heads who didn't have corporal punishment, was saying 'The cane must be used when with some children you don't get the appropriate response to stimuli'; this head also said, twice, 'Corporal punishment gives a child something.'

He then said that his boy went to a well-known public school (pausing, and looking here at the Chief Inspector, the two of them nodding to each other) and one day during the vacation he was having a bath, and he, the father, said, 'Can I come in, my boy', and entering, saw that his son's back was covered in red weals; so he said, 'Ah, my boy, I see you have been in some trouble. What was the cause of it?' His son did not want to tell him because he did not consider it important; but he said 'Tell me, my boy.' And at last his son told him that he had helped a friend who had got into trouble to write out his 'lines'. And his father said 'Yes, of course you must be punished for that.'

I looked round at the other heads. Surely there would be disgust and horror on their faces? Surely they would repudiate him? There was not a flicker of emotion.

And he concluded 'I am sure it did him good. Yes, I know that beating *gave* my boy something.' At this they broke into little smiles and nodded knowingly and looked pleased.

When I could speak, I said, 'It is evident that nothing good can come out of a meeting that has been called untruthfully. I suggest that we stop talking about corporal punishment, and instead talk about how pleasantly these heads run their own schools, since that is obviously what they have been asked to come here for; then at least we may get some experience of communication.'

The Chief Inspector looked at his watch, and said, 'I'll give you five minutes each.'

The first head took her five minutes. When she had finished, I said 'That does indeed sound very pleasant. I wonder what sort of a district your school is in. What school is it?'

A complete silence. Then looking towards the Chief Inspector, she said 'Well . . . I don't know if Dr Payling will allow me – '

'No,' said the Chief Inspector. 'We can't have names. No one is to give their name, or the name of their school!'

In the silence, perhaps Dr Payling began to wonder if he had gone a little too far. He had had no voiced opposition, but he muttered a little to himself, and then said that when each head had taken five minutes to speak about his school, he, the Chief Inspector, would consider again whether he might allow them to give the names of their schools; in the meantime they must be silent on this. I said 'That means I must listen to what they can tell me without any idea of the environment of the school, so most of it will be lost on me.' No matter. The Chief Inspector had decided. So I listened to the rapid speeches about pleasant, unnamed, unlocated schools, each hanging in its own meaningless social and geographical vacuum.

The Chief Inspector then closed the meeting. But I said, 'Dr Payling, I hope you haven't forgotten that you said you would consider again whether I might know the names and whereabouts of these delightful schools.'

He angrily burst out, 'I have just discovered that you already *know* two of these heads!'* (It was scarcely surprising – except, of course, to a member of the L.C.C.) He struggled for words. 'I'm not going to take any decision about this! I shall leave it to each individual head! Each head will decide whether or not to give the name of their school!'

In the silence that followed, I sat there wondering if they were all afraid of having their pensions stopped, their schools closed down, their job gone, or what ? If you can keep your Head when all about you are losing theirs. . . . Then one elderly headmistress stood up. In that fantastic atmosphere it seemed conduct worthy of the Victoria Cross. She said 'I have decided I do not mind Miss Berg knowing my name. And I don't mind her knowing the name of my school.' So inspired one by one to a faltering bravery, everyone came up to me separately and revealed to me their secrets. I wrote them down and left. I was supposed to be a special guest, but the Chief Inspector did not open the door for me. Of course, I can open a door quite well for myself.

I walked down the Embankment with many things racing through my head. I thought: which is the more civilized behaviour ? For a parent to look at his child's marked body and say, 'My boy, I am sure that did you good' – or to say, 'Who the hell did that to you ?' For a parent to say, 'Certainly you must be beaten if you helped a friend' – or to say, 'Of course you were right to help a friend in trouble!' I knew who I would put my money on. The human being who reacts, who feels his own feelings and thinks his own thoughts and has not delegated his personal relationships to an outside authority.

I thought of those heads, who cane '*only* for swearing', '*only* for stealing'. I thought of the Risinghill mother who said 'I don't know where he gets his fucking language from!' And stealing! Some kids at Risinghill could whip a bicycle, and have it dismantled and the parts all distributed to different people and halfway to being sold before anyone noticed it was missing.

---

*I did know one – from my own district. The other was the head I had 'met' on the phone.

They knew how to do it because their fathers taught them.

You can't beat a child for doing what his parents do. This was the first rule ever forged at Risinghill. You can discuss it with him, yes; you can show him other ways of behaving, and if they appeal to him – or if *you* appeal to him or if he develops concern for other people – he may learn from you. But you can't force a child, on pain of beating, to spit on his parents. Or, if you do, heaven help the child, and society.

And I thought, too – and for a long time I could not fathom this – of those *picked* heads, who had been chosen to prove to me that L.C.C. schools didn't have corporal punishment, and of the things they had said. I was appalled to think that they were the most progressive of our heads. But I was right off the track. Much later it dawned on me that they had been chosen simply because they were good image-presenters . . . only I didn't play that game. Whatever the questions were going to be about – 'I don't like corporal punishment. Do you use it?' 'I do like corporal punishment. Do you use it?' 'I use Omo. Do you use it?' – these Heads would be chosen to answer because they were reckoned as good public relations people, good soothers, reassuring figures who said everything was under control – not because they had necessarily anything to contribute to education or the understanding of children. There may well have been people who *could* contribute these things, there may even have been heads who really did not have corporal punishment, but if they were not good image-presenters then it would not occur to the L.C.C. for one moment to trot them forward.

It was now May, and the government decision had still not arrived. There was still time for one last bang from Mr Sebag-Montefiore. At a meeting of the L.C.C., which was actually about merging two Islington boys' schools into one comprehensive school, Mr Sebag-Montefiore and a colleague (Conservative Councillor Mrs Townsend) waved the red rag of Risinghill. Mrs Townsend said that on a recent visit there she had been appalled at what she had seen . . . table legs torn off, walls scribbled on from top to bottom, tables in the staff room covered with cigarette burns, and in the prefects' room a notice that prefects caught gambling would have their badges removed.

It was in the last Easter holidays, when only the school care-taker was there, doing his school-holiday chore of collecting together all things needing repair, that Mrs Townsend visited Risinghill. She had been on the advisory committee of Risinghill before Risinghill had opened, but had not been elected a governor. She was, however, one of the governors of Starcross – who had unanimously voted against moving into Risinghill. She came on behalf of Starcross School to inspect the premises that the L.C.C., disregarding their expressed feelings, was wishing on them. It was perhaps therefore understandable that she should have gazed at the walls of a top-floor art room, drawn on by the considered policy of just one capable art master, while disregarding the mag-nificent murals painted by the children in rooms on the way up.

At this meeting it was stated that the cost of new items needed by Starcross – because, it was clearly inferred, of the damage done at Risinghill – would be £31,600; the furniture and fittings for Risinghill itself in 1960 had been £40,000. It seemed just possible that some businessmen were going to get some rich pickings out of the Risinghill affair, for I later discovered the £31,600 covered such items as £5,544 for completely unnecessary replacements of furniture, carpets and equipment in excellent condition, some of which were in fact actually new (when I inquired about this I was told 'Well, naturally people's tastes in carpets differ'), and £8,674 for total replacement of furniture that was worn but sound, apart from various expenses due to the change from a mixed school to a girls' school, and to the fact that Starcross was going to be given things – such as a sixth-form common room – which Risinghill had asked for and been refused. When you added the cost of such things as converting Risinghill's bookstore into twenty-four new lavatories, converting the caretaker's room into a new bookstore, making a new caretaker's office, the total came near to £100,000. And this did not include such matters as turning the Risinghill boys' workshops into girls' arts and crafts rooms, and making additional boys' workshops at a secon-dary school to which the boys were being transferred.

It therefore did not entirely surprise me when, the L.C.C. having decided to buy the decrepit rat-ridden houses in Rising-hill Street, in order to propitiate Starcross with a better frontage (another of the things Risinghill had asked for, which they had not obtained), a Conservative Councillor said these houses were sound and not slum property at all. Looking at the figures of thousands of pounds which the L.C.C. was now handing out to aid the reshuffling that wiped out Risinghill, it was interesting that the L.C.C. had said their basic reason was – 'economy'. Later I learned that the head of Starcross had been told 'no expense will be spared'.

On 3 June, it was announced that the government had agreed to close Risinghill.

Death 1965

Dissolution

Boys' and girls' behaviour, confidence and attitude to work can all be shaped by successful relations with individual teachers: what ultimately counts is a person.

In 1960, the first year of Risinghill (formed from four secondary-modern-level schools), eighteen pupils had entered for G.C.E. O level examinations, and five had passed.

In 1961, thirty-two had entered and sixteen passed.

In 1962, thirty-nine entered and twenty passed.

In 1963, fifty-nine entered and thirty-four passed.

In 1964, eighty had entered and forty-two passed (in one to six subjects); three pupils took A level examinations, and two went on to universities.

In 1960, there were ninety-eight children already on probation. In 1964, there were nine.

In 1965, the Ministry of Education decided to close the school.

*

All the deputations to the government of both children and parents, all the clauses of the Education Act hopefully intoned, all the meetings and the letters and the signatures collected in the pouring rain had been just something that filled in the time, while authority got on with what it intended to do in the first place. A headmaster at another school had said to a Risinghill mother 'You surely don't think these deputations will get you anywhere? The decision has already been taken. This three months for the appeal to be considered, these kind invitations to state your case, that's just papering over the cracks in the walls of democracy.' No one had wanted to listen to him. Of course he was right.

There had not even been any point in wondering whether a Labour government with such a tiny majority dare offend its most powerful Labour local authority. The old-boy network stretched along the Thames from County Hall to Westminster and on to Curzon Street, maybe on to Hampstead; but it never touched Chapel Market.

I came up from the Angel, saying to myself – the people of Islington are as reasonable as anyone. If the Education Act is a farce, let the government tell them. Let them tell everybody. Then we will all stop taking it seriously. If the right of a child to be educated in accordance with the wishes of his parents is not meant to be believed in, then tell us. If the right it lays down that parents can appeal against unreasonableness, if this right and any other right is just a joke, let the government say so. We are all reasonable. We only expect what we are promised. If we do not have these rights, then let us tear up the Act.

Islington parents have a background of belting, yet only one child has been withdrawn from Risinghill in these five years. (His father was afraid of what the toughs, uncaned, would do to his child; but his child was not afraid.) All the parents wanted to send their younger children too. They moved from the district and still continued to send the children to Risinghill. They came daily from Romford, Wembley. . . .

Teachers always say that the uneducated parents never care about a school, never come to school meetings. At Risinghill they came. Two hundred and fifty sometimes, sometimes one hundred, sometimes fifty. The L.C.C. said this was not enough, that they were negligible.

How can an education authority – a Socialist authority at that – count two hundred, even fifty, parents from violent slums, who have yet been stirred into response by a philosophy of gentleness, as 'negligible'? When the inhabitants of these rotting homes tried to crawl out and stand up like free men and women, feeling their own humanity and revelling in their strength, it was the Socialist authorities who crushed them down and told them they were of no account. And in months to come – and the time may come quicker than they think – they will doubtless complain of 'apathy' and 'cynicism' among these people who once had high hopes and thought they controlled their own future.

*

I walked up the black clattering hill towards the school. In the market it was half-day closing, and Bob Redrupp, the leader of the parents and a borough councillor, was packing up his potato stall in the market. He said he would send off a telegram to the Ministry demanding the inquiry that the parents asked for back in January. He was choked, and he worked and talked in jerks.

I used to hit my kid. Now I don't. I don't need to. I didn't have people from Oxford or Cambridge to teach me that. Duane taught me. This may not matter to people high up in education, but it matters to me. If someone says he won't hit children, he's a trouble-maker. From what I've seen of back-biting among people of education, I'm glad I left school at fourteen and work in the market. I'm an average person. I'm not too clever and I'm not too dim. The higher in the scale you go, the bloodier the rat-race is. I don't want to go any higher. This thing stinks. We're completely disregarded. We had an average of 150 to 250 people to our parents' meetings. At the borough council meeting, not more than ten people turned up to hear about twelve million pounds being spent on rates on their behalf. And the L.C.C. said that our parents' meeting did not represent parents. If I thought I could help Duane, I'd go to the end of the bloody earth for him.

He was too angry to talk much to anyone, and too full of betrayal to talk to anyone as well-spoken as I.

Miles's mother met me in the market. She said she would teach as many children as she could at home – she knew she was allowed a maximum of five. She is not an officially-trained teacher, but reckons she is perfectly competent. This is valiant of her, I thought, but who else can do it?

In this area the people are least equipped to fight back. Under the Education Act, they can keep their children at home provided they educate them. What a mockery. Hardly any parents here have any education. It was Risinghill that for the first time opened their eyes to education.

And even if the mothers were educated, they are most of them working. Sometimes they are the only wage-earner. How could they keep the children at home, giving up their job? Those who are not working, because their rents are lower than the council flats, are living in stinking hovels unfit for human beings to live and sleep in; shall these hovels become schools as well?

But what pounds at one is that these people have not only no education to pass on, but none of the self-confidence, the self-esteem, the belief that they have any rights that will be recognized, that goes with education and that enables an educated person to fight for what he wants. And the fate of Risinghill is only one more incident that confirms to them their worthlessness. A sense of history might have saved them, but their elementary schooling saw they didn't have that.

*

At Risinghill, visitors were always aware of the friendliness of the children towards strangers. These children were getting beyond themselves, beyond egotism. The children I saw in the head's study were concerned for Terry; and they were concerned for him because they knew people were concerned for them. Human beings move from themselves outward; they have to feel themselves, appreciate themselves, and feel respected and loved by others, before they genuinely move out; and this, then, they will do, *spontaneously*. This was apparent at Risinghill.

I do not know whether it was by chance, but when I went to Risinghill after the Ministry decision this feeling was gone. In the playground, in the corridors, children glanced at me with cold indifference and looked away again. No one came voluntarily to me and said 'Can I help?' A boy was *asked* to help me, and did so without a smile; he did not keep pace with me and chat with me, as he would have done in the earlier days, but strode ahead and waited for me from time to time as if I were frustrating him. He did not open doors for me. I had to open them myself. This was scarcely surprising. The trust these children had put in democracy, the faith they had had that they would be considered, had been treated contemptuously.

One boy told me that some of the teachers, three or four of them, had laughed when the Ministry decision was announced at assembly. Perhaps it was a nervous reaction, because the teacher who announced the decision broke down. . . .

The day after the decision had been announced, Mr Duane asked the school assembly to pray that everyone, children and teachers, would find new schools where they would be happy, and where they would be able to love people. He told the children that they should not worry about going to a different school. He and the teachers would make very full reports for every one of them, so that they should not go into their new school as strangers.

I wrote in my notebook that day 'This is the first time I have been in his study when it has not been a continuous procession of parents and children, asking for help and advice. Today, perhaps, there has seemed no point.'

But two girls phoned, one after the other. They had each left the school a little while ago. Do sixteen-year-olds generally worry over the future of their ex-headmasters or grieve over his present ?

I spoke to them both. One said:

I think it's terrible. Mr Duane used to treat us lovely. We weren't frightened to go to him when we were in trouble. We used to talk to him about things like why sometimes we didn't get on with coloured children. He was a person you could talk very frankly to. I was at a very strict school before. The only time you went to your head there was when you got the cane. Risinghill gave me a different outlook on life. Mr Duane was a person who made you feel happy.

And the other said:

I left three terms ago. I thought that in the end they would leave the school as it was. I didn't think they'd really close it. It was quite a lovely school because you could learn a lot of things there that would help you when you left school. Some of the boys were a bit rough at first. I'm a coloured girl, but you could always go to Mr Duane and talk to him as frank as you like. Then your mind would feel more at rest, because you knew he would try to sort things out. Before Risinghill, I went to another school till I was eleven, and then to Risinghill when it was new. At that school, you couldn't go to the headmistress.

The only reason you went to her was to get told off or caned. The teachers were much more strict than at Risinghill. They didn't sit and listen to your problems. Here lots of teachers try to help you. It was good to be at school, and you weren't frightened all the time you'd get into trouble.

Then a shop phoned. The shop had mended a school silver cup without giving an estimate first as Mr Duane had asked; and he was horrified at the bill. So he suggested, on the phone, it might be more sensible to sell the cup because with the proceeds he could send some Risinghill children to the Lake District. The shopkeeper said he would only get three pounds for the cup melted down; but he offered to give it back, repaired, for nothing.

While this was going on, I read the letter from the Ministry. I read it through twice. It could have been written before either of the delegations, invited and received with such democratic courtesy, had left their work to come and plead for their school; it could have been written before any of the petitions had been signed – written long ago, and left on the desk or in a drawer until the democratic machinery had wound its way through and it could be decently posted.

Later on, a friend of mine told me he had applied for a job at Kingsway a long time before the Ministry decision, and had been told then that Kingsway would be occupying the Starcross buildings.

I sat there for a while and I listened to an old lady – a genuine old-fashioned Socialist, who had lived in the worst part of this district all her life, not an image-worshipper – talking about Mr Duane.

You only have to look at that man to see he has a soul. Without knowing he's a teacher, you can see from his face he's a man to lead people.

Our mothers used to say 'Knock one devil out, knock ten in.' They knew even in those days.

He was doing something about delinquency. Isn't that what we want? We're always talking about the need to do something about delinquency, and when someone does it we throw him out.

I suppose the L.C.C. wants to hush up what the Risinghill district is really like. Every other country has its problems, prostitutes or whatever you like. But we haven't. Britain hates to admit any problem.

As she talked, I heard through the thin walls a teacher snap out in a voice like a whipcrack 'Get back to your class!' It was the voice of a tamer of wild animals, tight and deadly and full of hate and fear, not the voice of a woman talking to children. It was not the sort of voice Mr Duane must have wanted to hear at Risinghill. I wondered how the man had managed to get as far as he did, with such teachers and such politicians.

Later I took a group of twelve-year-olds; they had only been at Risinghill a year. Geraldine said 'I feel horrible. They tell too many lies about Risinghill, and if their own children were here they'd talk different.' Milly said 'The headmaster, if you're ever in trouble, he'll always help.' And all the class shouted 'Yes, he's a good geezer!'

Suddenly Andreos said 'It is Mr Duane's fault the school is closing!' The children were silent and shocked. Andreos went on 'Some people stay in the toilets instead of doing lessons.'

The children were very angry that he should speak against Mr Duane, but I quietened them, and asked them if what Andreos said was true and some people did stay in the toilets, and they said 'Yes.' We talked about this for a while, and then I asked them which of them thought children needed to be punished in some way to get them to behave properly. Every child but one put up his hand.

I have been struck by this several times at Risinghill, particularly with the younger ones who had not been at the school long; that they were afraid of themselves. 'I must be stopped from being bad. Left alone I am bound to be bad. Yet my friends make me bad. Separate me from my friends. Separate me from myself. Stand over me with an upraised fist and keep me from harm.' But what is this 'harm' they are afraid freedom will lead them into? Only the harm of the upraised fist. When they say 'Left alone I am bound to be bad', they mean 'Time and again I have proved that if I take a decision of my own, if I use any initiative, I am bound to be punished for it. It is safer for me if it is impossible for me to do anything on my own.'

In this class, on this day, the one child who did not put her hand up with the rest was a little coloured girl. But after a few minutes' discussion, other children were beginning to say things like 'If you get hit from the beginning for every little thing, then you start being bad all the time.'

All this while Andreos had been staring fiercely at his desk. Suddenly he said 'It's not Mr Duane's fault. It's the children's.' He got up and came over to me, and got hold of my notebook urgently. 'Cross that out,' he said. 'Cross out where you put down I said it was Mr Duane's fault. In Mr Duane's class we do work. I do work because I want to be an engineer, and I promised my

mother I would. It was wrong, what I said. Cross it out.' I was
reluctant to cross it out, because I wanted a full record of what
the children said, and each of his statements was equally important
to me; but it was a matter of his own integrity. I crossed it out,
but faintly, so that I should later remember what had happened.
At times like this, as a recorder, I get troubled.

The discussion was brief and noisy – because our state classroom furniture is not geared to discussion – and undisciplined;
but it was a discussion on things that mattered to these children.
They were all tired of uncertainty. Some had been confirmed in
the belief that everyone was against them. Very few of them had
genuine confidence, in a placid way, that what they said was
important. Oddly enough the ones who had most inner dignity
were the immigrant children, the Greeks and the Turks and the
West Indians; I had noticed this before.

Susan was saying that people always hated her – at any school.
I asked whether this was because the grown-ups that she met were
always horrible people; or was it that she had a way of doing
things that always irritated people, wherever they were; or was
it that she was forgetting the people who were nice? She thought
a moment, and said 'Perhaps it's just that I don't like school.'

One thing Risinghill has done for these children, even those
who have been there a short time. It has made it possible for them
to think about what they are doing and what they are feeling, and
what other people think and feel. This is no small piece of education. Risinghill children can express themselves.

They have become used to reasoning things out. They did not
arrive at the school like this. This was a quite deliberate education
they received at Risinghill. It was 'deliberate' not in the sense
that it took part only at certain times and in certain rooms, for
it had often been quite spontaneous, but in the sense that the
discussion might be instigated and was certainly encouraged by
people who thought that what these children were feeling and
thinking was important. And it was 'education' not in the sense
of conditioning, of controlling the child's conclusions, but in the
true sense of drawing out of the child the potentialities that were
already there. This is something that many grammar schools
now do not do, and know they do not do; if you ask them why they

don't do it, they will say 'We have no time for that kind of thing; we have examinations and a syllabus to keep to; people don't come to schools to enjoy themselves.' It is also something many other schools do not do either, simply because authoritarianism in any form does not take kindly to free discussion and free conclusions.

Geraldine and Carol said they would write down what they thought so that I should have it to keep. Whispering and consulting together, they wrote a joint document.

Risinghill should not have closed because we have got used to Risinghill. . . . I think this school is great. It is — School that is worser than ours. It is all lies that they say. It upset our senior master and headmaster and most of the teachers. It is not Mr Duane's fault that we behave like we do. People all over say it should close because they think that people smoke and swear. Some pupils might smoke and swear. But not everyone. Because Mr Duane doesn't cane us they think they can close the school. A couple of teachers hit us but not every teacher. Mr Duane can lose his temper sometimes. All the children in Risinghill School has thought it very heartbreaking to have it closed. Why should it be our school that has to be closed. All schools are the same not only ours.

When all the children had gone, Andreos stayed behind. He said fiercely and insistently 'Did you cross it out, that it was Mr Duane's fault?' I reassured him – not that he felt dependent on me – and said I did.

The same day that the decision came through about Risinghill, the *Evening News* reported that a grammar school headmaster had 'banned holding hands'. According to the *Evening News*, the 800 boys and 600 girls at this Ipswich state secondary school were told by their head that he had received 'complaints from influential people about pupils walking hand-in-hand while wearing the school uniform'; it must stop. Here was 'the approved pattern'. It was heartening to read in the paper that when the head made his announcement 'everyone laughed so much that he had to stop talking'.

*

A week later I went to Risinghill again, and the helpfulness was back to a certain extent, but not the warmth; it was more detached, more wary.

Twelve youngsters didn't bother to turn up for their G.C.E. examinations. The children were saying that the staff had stopped bothering, that they were saying 'Oh don't pester me now. I've got my new school to think about.'

At Easter, the equivalent of a whole sixth form left. (In July, the L.C.C. maintained to me that not one child now at Risinghill was giving up the idea of higher education. They could have looked back a little, for a whole form gave up when they first knew for sure that Risinghill was crumbling around them, and dropped back into the jungle again. They did not wait for July. Parents who had heard of jobs going did not want to miss the opportunity. They had acted against tradition in letting their children stay at school; now tradition had taken over again. Even in July, even pedantically, the L.C.C. were not accurate, for on the very last day I myself talked to a boy who was giving up the extra year of education he had promised himself and getting a job instead.)

The school was emptying. Michael Duane concentrated on getting the children off on various excursions all over the country as soon as their examinations were finished, to get their minds off smashing up the school. (This seemed a strong possibility. Two children had said to their mother that they weren't going to go to school on the last day, because they would find it too upsetting, and because the children were planning to smash everything up and they didn't want to get involved in it.) He seized the chance to show them how they could use spare time creatively. He told them about youth hostels, about camping, and climbing. He started raffles and other money-raising plans to help the kids who were really stuck for money.

Bobby Barton, actually twelve but a tiny shrimp of a kid, painted a picture in Mr Benson's art class and told Mr Benson he could have it for a present, to remember him by. Then someone came along and admired it and offered Bobby three pounds for it. Bobby was very bothered. He comes from a chronically hard-up family and with the three pounds he could go away camping. He put the problem before Mr Benson, who said 'Go on boy, if you can sell it for three quid, you do it.' So Bobby did – and then insisted on Mr Benson taking a pound for himself. How many schools have children who will give a teacher a pound that they have earned ? And how many have teachers that have the respect to take it ? Now Bobby, still bothered, is painting Mr Benson another picture. Bobby is a boy who will not let any adult shout at him and get away with it. He swears back. The authoritarians hate him.

One day, when that last bit of time was trickling away, Mr Duane was out in the market hunting for Stevie Thomas, who had run away from home – searching among all the children playing there, for they play in the market till eleven at night. He found the child at last, and since his mother had shut him out and wanted no more to do with him, and his father lived some-where else, he took the kid home with him, bathed him, washed his clothes several times over, and put him to bed.

In the morning he took him to school, but the same day Stevie had disappeared again. He searched for him again all day, and late at night found him walking towards his hide-out. For it turned out Stevie lived, at times of crisis, in a disused loft in a disused factory, furnished and fitted out with such things as a broken alarm clock and part of a chair and a few potato chips and pieces of bread that his school-friends had secretly brought him. He was not playing at being adventurous, as one of the children in Hampstead whom the governor spoke of ('Why can't they play like children in Hampstead!') might have been doing. He was fighting for his survival.

Stevie's life had scarcely begun to be sorted out, when, one afternoon, five boys came up to Mr Duane's room and said that a man had stopped them outside the school and offered them £5 to throw a stone through the school windows while he photographed them. He said it was for a newspaper. Instead they smashed his camera, or Jimmy Lee said they did.

That same week, Mr Duane was fighting to keep a member of his staff – not a particular friend of his – from disgrace. I would not mention this – and certainly I will not reveal any of the detail that I know – if it were not that I have come across people who believe that Mr Duane cared only for his children and not for his staff. I have said earlier that you could ask him about any child, and he would know; it was the same if you asked him about a teacher; with them too he knew what personal worries or problems contributed to their worries or problems at school. But of course many people who say he did not care for his staff do not mean he did not go out of his way to help any teacher who was in trouble; they mean 'he did not rule them with an iron hand, which is what they expect and all they are fit for'.

That weekend, on the Sunday, Mr Duane came to our house. There were adults and children of different ages here, as there often are, and he had a gardenful of them playing 'British Bulldog' and 'Sly Fox' and all the other games of everyone's childhood. The parents, of different temperaments, some quiet, some stolid, some ebullient, all went staggering home, delighted to find they still had it in them; and the children, three of whom we realized afterwards, three little ones, were sickening for something and had been crotchety when they arrived, had dropped their tearfulness like handkerchiefs on the grass, and been lifted into delight. One of the older children, a thirteen-year-old boy from an orphanage who has not yet learned to read, said afterwards out of the blue 'I could learn to read with somebody like *him* to teach me.' Then, thinking about it, and about what he had heard of Michael Duane's difficulties, and about the adults he had known in his institutional world, he added, 'Of course, it's true what they say. Headmasters aren't like that' . . . meaning, with the resignation of an institution child, you just can't win.

*

One evening I went to see one of the parents who lives on the seventh floor of a council block at the back of the school. I stood by the lift at ground-floor level and pressed the button . . . pressed and pressed. Nothing came. Once it came past me, but wouldn't stop, and carried on up. And once it went past me, wouldn't stop, and carried on down. I kept my finger on, on and on and on, grimly, till I got it. I got in, pressed the button for the seventh floor, and as soon as I closed the gate the lift shot down to the basement.

There stood two small boys, Cockney shrimps of boys. 'Oh,'

I said, with a laugh, 'it's you who've been stopping me going where I want to, all this time. Are you coming in?' They grinned and stepped in, but they were definitely in charge. 'Where do you want to go, Miss?' said one, looking severe. 'The seventh floor, please.'

As he closed the gate, he left his fingers where the door would clang to. I cried out 'Look out, you'll trap your hand!' The door clanged as I shouted – and I saw it left a gap just big enough for his fingers. It was a cool, deliberate and effective piece of style. I was knocked flat. 'Cor!' I said, letting out my breath and rolling my eyes. The other kid looked up at me, sideways, and grinned.

The first shot the lift up, and, important and splendid and silently savouring his triumph, ignored me. As I got out he said 'What number flat do you want?' I said 'It's all right, thank you. It's this first one, right near the lift.' They waited to make sure someone was coming to open the door. If no one had come, I know they would have advised me what to do. Then they shot down in the lift again. I smiled to myself, warmed by their friendliness and their independent capability. And then suddenly I thought – what would one of those authoritarian teachers at Risinghill have felt? They would have seen it quite differently. And suddenly I saw them, and heard them: 'Stopping people using the lift! Putting themselves in danger! Not minding their own business! Interfering with grown-ups!' And yet I positively enjoyed it. That is the trouble; there are two opposite ways of looking at children.

Inside the flat, Mrs Armstrong said over cups of coffee:

'You know, my choice wasn't Risinghill for Janey. I was one of those narrow-minded parents who wanted a single-sex school. [She laughed.] I tried for —, then for —; then in the end I chose Risinghill because it was near enough for me to know what time she was leaving school and what time I could expect her home, and to keep an eye on her.

But very soon I saw a change in her. She seemed to begin to understand life. I don't mean giggling about boys and things like that; she became mature. The boys and girls had learnt to accept each other socially. They didn't smirk and giggle, they were happy and natural together – just as they accepted the West Indians and the Greeks and put us all to shame. There was one boy in Janey's class, a horrible, really nasty boy, and instead of making a hero of him the children didn't like him and spoke very angrily of him, especially when he called a coloured teacher a 'nigger'.

Janey, young as she was, was terribly upset about Mr Duane. She'd come home and say he was on the platform and he looked very sad, or he put his head between his hands and shook his head from side to side . . . you know? Janey was only in her first year.

Someone nominated me to go on to the committee, but as soon as I started the trouble began, and instead of getting all the fun out of the school that we were looking forward to – we were going to buy a bus, you know, to take the children abroad – we had all the trouble. I felt from the word go, we were fighting a losing battle – even though I stood in the pouring rain getting signatures for the petitions, I felt it.

I think Mr Duane is one of the finest people I have ever met – but not for this neighbourhood. He believes you can do everything with kindness. I know there are a lot of children round here who need kindness, but never having had it they take advantage of him and think it weakness. I think it's broken him inside. He's offended people in very high places.

I would like Mr Duane to do the same thing again in a better neighbourhood. And yet, in this neighbourhood it got him the love and respect of the children and of the parents – maybe not the teachers, though there were some who were very good and loyal.

When you went there in the evenings, the teenagers were always there at the gate to greet you and take you round, and I've yet to meet a nicer bunch of teenagers. Young men and young women they were, decent young people we saw when we went to the meetings. They won't get the big shock we got when we went out into the world for our first job. They'll go out with confidence. And I don't think they'll experiment so much sexually – they've talked about it already, discussed it, got rid of their fears, and they're calm about it.

A wonderful thing for the children – it was a big thing in my daughter's life – was the pets. We can't have pets in our flats.

The teacher said to Janey 'We're going to paint a carnival.' She said 'What's that?' Teacher said 'Well, do you get the Sunday *Observer*?' She said 'Yes.' The teacher said 'Well, in the colour supplement you'll see a picture of a carnival.' At any other school, they'd never have thought we'd get the *Observer*. But we do. They'd have laughed at her, or said she was lying, or told her off for not knowing what a carnival was. I told her to take it with her next day, just to show she really did have it; a West Indian carnival it was.

Yes, we were going to get money for a bus. I thought this was marvellous, going abroad and all that. I went along that first time, and he impressed me very much, Mr Duane. I thought there's something here I can learn for myself. In fact, I even tried to have a look to see what books he was reading. I think he'd been a bit of a bugger himself when he was a kid, and he understood all about it. I'd like to see him with children again. The kids'd be squatting on the ground, gambling, you know, and he'd walk past and pretend he didn't see – wouldn't bat an eyelid.

I shan't join the P.T.A. at the new school now. I know that sounds like sour grapes; but I joined at Risinghill because I had something to learn there.

I feel he'll be wasted doing anything else but teaching children. I hear they're trying to make him teach training college students; but at that age they're already set. Children haven't been twisted. He has a lot to offer children.

I can see a lot of trouble at first with the change-over. It won't last with the younger ones. They can bounce back. But the older ones, thirteen and fourteen, they're not going to like the school they'll get now. There's a lot of talk about unsettled teenagers – they'll be unsettled all right. I don't think the older children will wear the old kind of teacher now. They've got used to being treated as individuals, and being expected to pull together. Another two years and he'd have seen the real climax, the fruits of his labour.

I get very sad when I think about the school. Very sad. He tried so hard. He tried to bring a bit of light into their life when it's so dull.

You know, you can't squash children. When Janey went for her interview at her new school – I'd warned her to be on her best be-haviour – they asked her 'Are you looking forward to coming here?' And she said 'No, I'm not!' Collapse of mother.

There's an old lady here. I went across to help her once. She's all crippled with arthritis, and you know, when I saw her, I saw it was my old Sunday-school teacher! At Christmas time there was a knock at her door. It was children from Risinghill with a big basket of fruit and groceries for her. They knew about her at the school. She wasn't a parent, she was an old maiden lady. She was very sad when she heard it was closing.

They talk a lot of rot about people going out to work, and they blame a lot of children's bad behaviour on that. But when it's a case of £5 for a flat, you have to go to work. Some of the people live in horrible places, but even in those places in one way the kids are luckier because their mothers stay at home; they don't have to go to work to pay the rent; and at least they get the warmth of their mothers. But they're not very bad, the majority of kids round here. And if you meet them on their own level and are prepared to accept them for what they are, they're very nice.

You heard about the kid who ran away? You know the other kids looked after him – they'd been protecting him, hiding him, feeding him. What other man would have spent his time searching for him, and looking after him in his own home at the weekend?

If the kids nicked something from a teacher, Mr Duane would put it round on the grapevine. 'So-and-so's lost something. It's not of great value. Give it back.' If the kids liked that teacher, that thing would be back on Mr Duane's desk within a few minutes.

Do you know, the children had been to Whipsnade and two of them came to Mr Duane and said 'Sir, we've got this bird. We brought it back from Whipsnade yesterday.' Mr Duane said 'Good God, we're for it now.' He told us at the parents' meeting, 'I gave the kids half a crown and told them to go to the London Zoo and explain, and ask if they would look after the bird for the holidays.' He got a letter back from them, very polite, saying 'This is a yellow-hammer. It would not have been kept in captivity at Whipsnade. It is a wild bird. We are treating it as a donation. Thank you.' And they enclosed a special certificate saying thank you!

He was wonderful at dealing with what with anyone else would have been terrible. If the ceiling had fallen in, he'd just have said 'Come on, we'll move into the next room.' Yet he doesn't dash round trying to impress you.

I went one morning in the middle of this trouble to talk to Mr Brown, our newly appointed M.P. After five minutes, we walked out, Mr Duane and me. He said to me 'What do you think?' I said 'A waste of time.' He said 'That's what I think too.' That was a big blow to me.

What does the L.C.C. think it's done? I think every comprehensive school will be watched from now on.

I was terrified of my teachers. They called it respect. And I thought it was respect. But now I know it was hate. I was always in trouble, because although I was terrified I had self-respect.

Did you ever hear anyone speak to Mr Duane disrespectfully? I never did. It was always 'Sir'. But it was a nice 'Sir' – a 'Sir' that might have been 'Dad'. They didn't just have respect – they had love for him – all the kids had. All that work, it hasn't gone for nothing.

These kids when they're grown-up will think about it. They'll think about it when they have their own kids too.

At first, when Janey came home and told me things, I thought 'How cheeky to say that to a teacher.' But after a while I got used to it. I could see she respected them, and I thought how wonderful to be on such friendly terms with teachers. I hated my teachers. I hated and loathed them, *and* my school, and I'll never forget them or forgive them, never. But that's not a bad thing for a child to copy – to think 'Sir's mod!' or 'Miss is mod!' I loathed my school so much. I wish I'd had a school like that to go to. I might have made something.

*

Prize-giving day came, and Jan Thatcher, husband of one of the teachers, said to me afterwards, 'The first thing I saw of those kids was a group of boys pulling down a derelict wall outside the school. And the last thing I've seen was the prize-giving, and they were all done up to the nines, pleased, proud and happy, and every one of them getting prizes, for something; and their parents were happy and proud of them and done up to the nines too.'

No prominent people in London official education circles ever visited Risinghill Prize Days, which was perhaps fortunate, for they would not at all have cared to hear Mr Duane, on that last Prize Day, informing the children in his light casual tone that the report he had to give was rather like the report you give at an inquest over a dead body, when you try to find out whether the cause of death is natural, is brought about by neglect and starvation, or is murder. He talked warmly of the work of the children and of his good teachers – the children who were helped to be vital by 'the work of a core of real professionals, who put the children's needs before their own convenience and their ideas of what children ought to be, and who had to cope with the idle lay-abouts dressed up as teachers whom the teacher shortage brought to the profession.' His tone was always light and conversational, and I think this too disturbed the authoritarians who would have masochistically preferred to be denounced in a god-almighty voice.

Was this frankness bad for the children? Was Mr Duane stirring things up? In cold print it may look so, to people who have no personal knowledge of Mr Duane or his school. A sixteen-year-old girl said to me, when she came back from a pupils' deputation to the Ministry of Education, 'People don't understand about this school. You can't understand if you don't know Mr Duane'; I think this was an important and valid remark.

Had he said these things in a furious rage, I believe it would have been bad. But he did not. How it did in fact affect the children was something you could see in the children themselves; and I saw in many of these adolescents a degree of human understanding, of tolerance in the positive sense which is not the way we normally speak of it, of making allowances, of acknowledging the weakness in a person while at the same time appreciating the strength, that in my experience is unusual in sixteen-year-olds evaluating adults, particularly sixteen-year-olds who have no background of books and theatre and family discussions. As for the younger ones, there is nothing more terrifying to a child than a raging hostility that is not explained or even acknowledged. When the spoken words of an adult do not match the tension of the adult's face, body, and tone, a child is lost and silently terrified. Of course it would have been very much better if the children could have been, at any rate during their school day, in an atmosphere of serenity. But since they had been apt at any moment to witness a furious attack by one teacher on another – to see, for instance (and I am describing an actual incident), a man teacher calling a woman teacher a fool and an idiot, deliberately in front of the children, and the woman teacher then calling on the children to make as much noise as possible to pay the man teacher back (neither of these teachers, by the way, being supporters of Mr Duane's policy) – it was far better that they should understand why this was happening, so that they could make allowances for people, rather than pretend the conflicts did not exist.

It was good for them too, I am sure, to understand how history is made. If the conflicts had been concealed from them, they would never have absorbed this very valuable understanding.

If we really wanted schoolchildren to understand about history we would set them to find out the truth behind some contemporary event. I think by the time the school was closed, Risinghill children understood history more than any other children. I do not think for them history can ever be again an arbitrary string of events like a string of beads, or something inhuman and unchangeable like the seasons. They may be cynical – and some of them are – but they know that history has something to do with the planning of people, people with problems and power. That is why history is not normally taught in this way, in State schools.

*

And now it was the last day of all. Someone had heard Alec Brown and his friends planning to wreck the place – 'If Mr Duane can't have the school, then no one will,' said Alec – and Mr Duane had got them all together and told them there was no sense in causing more trouble and wouldn't it be better to talk to me, someone who was writing a book about Risinghill, so that what they felt could be written down and understood by the hundreds of people who would read it.

We sat down and talked. And two things above all came over from this group poised on the edge of destruction, but now very quiet and calm. They knew that whatever they made, whatever they were loyal to, would be despised, and would be broken up.

However they acted they would be indicted. This they knew from experience, and it is wisdom, we say, to learn from experience.

Roger Smith said:

There's more rough schools than this. This school's reputation is bad. When you go for a job, a part-time job in the market, if you say you've been to Risinghill they say 'Ever been in trouble with the police?' It's the first question they ask.

And Bill Cross said:

Yes, I got a part-time job the other week. He said 'What school did you go to?' I said 'Risinghill.' He said 'Is it true what they say about it?' I told him 'No, it isn't true.'

And Ronald Jones said:

Last year we had a visit to Fords'. First thing we got was a warning. 'That machine costs . . . so many thousand pounds. Don't you touch it.' Just because in the first year of the school some kids turned off a machine, and everything piled up.

(That first year – the puppy born with a tin can tied to its tail, again.)

Alec himself said:

When I came in '61, it was a very rough place. All sorts of geezers used to come round and bash us up. If you didn't hit 'em back, they used to come round and bash you again, and take your money. Four used to get on one person. There's hardly any of that now. We used to get old Bill* coming round every day. Now they don't come round at all, or hardly ever.

We talked about all this quite calmly. Later, one of the Rising-hill ex-head-boys was to say to me:

We had a relief inspector at our evening institute tennis club and he started to talk about Risinghill, and we said 'Oh, we went there.' And he said 'Oh, I didn't know anyone respectable went to it' – as if it was a den of thieves or something.

(And later still I was to hear about Bobby, who always said the police picked on him and followed him around, and whose mother always said the police picked on him and followed him around; and I found, with a sense of shock, that several of the police *did* pick on him and follow him around. I had read psychology, and I lived in a good-class suburb, so I thought it was paranoia. Bobby incidentally is now in borstal; in the end it was simpler to go there.)

Mark Robson said:

Most of us are using our chance of getting a good job. We're just going to get a job instead. We don't know what we're going to do. We'll just do anything. I was going to stay on another year and decide what I was going to do then. Now I'll just get anything.

And this was the other point that came over. It is not just that they don't know what they want to do – many adolescents don't, and there is no reason whatever why they should, except that our society lays down that it is immoral (which only means, not customary) for anyone fit, healthy, and under a certain income, not to be stuck into working for someone. It is that they don't

*Police.

know what they *can* do. And their parents can't help them because they themselves had no choice.

Mr Duane gave a farewell address on the last day that some people will not have cared for, though they probably did not bother to come and hear it. He said in a tone that was always friendly 'What is important is not examination results but our concern for each other.' And he went on:

When we started here I had to inquire in a dozen different directions at once when I wanted to find out how something had gone wrong. Now I ask 'Did you do this?' and in nine cases out of ten I get the answer 'Yes I did'. If you behave like this, people will treat you as a person; not as a thing.

And he ended:

In this school, we have had good teachers, some of the best I have ever met in my life. And we have had bad ones, the worst I have ever met, who have brought us a lot of trouble. The good ones are the ones who treat people with respect, as friends. The bad ones are the ones who push children about, who have no respect for them.

You will go into other schools, and meet good teachers and bad teachers. But how you behave will not depend on them; it will depend on you. I hope you will take from the good teachers you have had here the understanding that respect for other people, and for other people's ideas – whether you agree with them or not – is the main thing that matters.

At this point, he said the younger ones could go, but that he had a few words more to say to the older ones. He waited patiently for the young ones to go, without any nagging at them for noise or dilatoriness. When only the top forms were left, he said,

I couldn't say this to the kids because they are too young. From a number of you I gather you feel resentful at what has happened. I know how you feel. But the decision has been made and finished with. We now have to show we can accept it, and not let it affect ourselves. Sometimes a man is killed by another man. Sometimes if he is a friend of ours we are so angry we want to kill the murderer. But perhaps we discover that the man who killed him is sick. What he has done is bad, but to do an evil thing like striking a sick man would be even worse. All the people concerned share the responsibility. Stupidity, ignorance, prejudice, sheer spite have been at work. But *we* don't start lashing out, hurting other people because they have done that to us. You will go to other schools, or you will go to work, and you'll meet other people who will try to take it out of you because you have been to Risinghill. Talk straight to them about the school. Tell them honestly, if you like, the bad things. But don't forget the good things.

Weeks later, I talked to a mother, and she said to me 'Mr Duane helped an awful lot to get the children to accept the move. Roger came home and told me about it, that they were not to go with malice, and were to show that Risinghill could breed gentlemen.' I was amazed. I had not sat among the children, and had not absorbed their response. Up in the front row of the gallery, I could scarcely hear the quiet, conversational tone. I had been moved, but out of an adult's experience. Yet fourteen-year-old Roger, who at first had flatly announced that he would 'not go to any new school', had brought this message home to his mother.

On that last day at Risinghill no one did break up the school. The people who came to move the piano said another school had smashed theirs to smithereens. A teacher said that at a Lambeth school the children tore the school apart on the last day. Another said that at a Paddington school all the doors were taken off their hinges. At a school near Risinghill, the staff had been pelted with tomatoes and the staff room set on fire, though on the last day itself things had been quieter. And at another school, equally near, the children were rehearsing their brass band with the music teacher, and another *teacher* said they were making too much noise and furiously threw a bucket of water over them all.

But Risinghill closed quietly, with crowds of children talking in Mr Duane's study, and the toughest kids of all crying in the lavatories.

Waste

The children of these areas, because of their surroundings, are severely handicapped at the outset of their education, and they stand in need of specially gifted teachers.

The L.C.C. offered Mr Duane an inspectorship in Nigeria.

*

A little while later, Mr Gwyn phoned me, surprised and disturbed. A friend of his, a trained sociologist doing care-committee work for the L.C.C., had just said to him, 'We have all been instructed not to tell Leila Berg anything.'

Up to this point I had done nothing whatever as far as Risinghill was concerned except spend some time there, and write one feature article for the *Guardian* about it. (I was fairly well known as a writer for children and about children, and I had written and had published in the *Teacher* during this period a short story for children and an article for adults, both about children in a huge L.C.C. Home; just possibly it was this that had roused their anger.)

Mr Gwyn said 'I cannot tell you how horrified I am. Surely it seems reasonable to think that public bodies must be answerable to public scrutiny? I am appalled to find the extent to which the L.C.C. is prepared to go to stop your inquiry. I will stand by whatever I said, no matter what the consequences. If I have to leave London, then all right I'll leave London.'

The staff of Risinghill had been promised 'comparable posts' in London, with their Risinghill salary guaranteed.

The first job the L.C.C. offered Mr Duane, through the London Teachers' Association Secretary, was a post as 'Lecturer in English' at a certain London training college where the English library is very small and where he was firmly told, in an interview with the principal, that he would do no lecturing. In fact the job was to consist of correcting the English of Commonwealth students in their technical work; and for this very junior post he would continue to draw his Risinghill salary, which was more than the salary of two department heads at the college put together. He had already been puzzled at being sent for interview at a college that trained people for teaching adults, not children, but he was even more puzzled when he found that no one else on the staff knew that such a post existed or was about to be invented. Indeed I discovered later from a friend of mine who works at this college that the rumour that Mr Duane was offered a job there was an uproarious staff-room joke; he was startled when I said it was true. It was evident that this job would continue to exist just as long as the L.C.C. thought it necessary – which, at my guess, would not have been very long. But he politely turned it down.

He was then offered the job in Nigeria.

Both these jobs were offered by the L.C.C. through the London Teachers' Association, and over the telephone. The L.C.C. was aware it mightn't be so good for 'the image' to have them offered in writing under the County Hall letterhead.

Yet during this time there had been three 'comparable' headships open, all of them bordering Islington and in similar districts to Risinghill.

*

I had been struck by a clause in the 'Articles of Government of a London Secondary School', which says that when a headmastership falls vacant, the governors 'may be required, unless they can show good reasons to the contrary, to agree to the appointment of a headmaster . . . who is under obligation to move from his present post owing to the reorganization or closure of the school.'

I phoned Leila Campbell (Mrs Campbell is chairman of the Schools Sub-committee under the new organization) and asked if I could have a talk with her.

It seems to be the L.C.C.'s policy not to allow one person to meet another face to face unguarded, especially if one of the two wants to ask questions. When I reached County Hall, I found Mr

Turner, Assistant Education Officer, and the Reverend H. W. Hinds, Mrs Campbell's deputy, waiting together with Mrs Campbell; and it became clear this was not because they wanted to give me additional information.

It was a very angry meeting, and since I had got up from a sick-bed to keep the appointment and was due to enter hospital for a major operation I was not so quick off the mark as perhaps I might otherwise have been. However, I took detailed notes of everything said, as it was said. Here are extracts.

I said I had a vague recollection, which might be completely wrong, that there was one section in the Articles of Government which seemed to say that a displaced head could be almost automatically taken on at another school, unless the governors had some specific objection.

Mr Turner said immediately and quite definitely that there was no such clause – nothing anything like it.

I looked doubtful.

Mrs Campbell, who had only just joined the department, said helpfully 'Have we got one of the Articles of Government here?'

'No!' said Mr Turner.

'Then shall I send for one?' said Mrs Campbell. (Poor Mrs Campbell. I was beginning to feel worried for her.)

Mr Turner was struggling for control. In the end he had to agree that Mrs Campbell should send for one. It took a long time to arrive, and when it came I took care to accept it and to hold on to it. (Not that it would have mattered much really if Mr Turner had beaten me to it. I had brought a copy with me.)

Mr Turner said 'I'll take it. I'll look through it.'

Holding on, and taking my time (though in fact I knew exactly where the clause was – the bottom of the first page), I said, 'No, it's all right . . . I've found it now.'

I read it out.

Mr Turner said 'It can't possibly mean what you think it means.'

I said 'But there *is* a section about this, isn't there, even if it doesn't mean anything?'

Mrs Campbell came in sweetly again. 'Yes, of course you are right. Mr Turner was not quite correct. There *is* a clause dealing with this. But I think what Mr Turner is trying to say is – '

Mr Turner recovered. 'There are many heads displaced, because of all the reorganization we are doing. They all have to be considered, not merely Mr Duane. . . . The L.C.C. cannot possibly influence the appointment of heads. That is for the governors to decide. It would be outrageous if the L.C.C. brought pressure to bear on governors.'

A little later on, when discussion had ranged further, I said 'But I really only wanted to know from you what this clause means. First you say no such clause exists. Then you say it doesn't mean anything.'

Mr Turner said 'I have only known this clause to be brought up once in seven years. Mr Duane has had possibilities of appointments put before him at County Hall at least a dozen times. He knows very well that every displaced head, and he is not the only one, gets priority of treatment. We *insist* that the governors send them to County Hall for the Staff Sub-committee to decide. The authority is paying his salary. It is safeguarded for ever, which other authorities who are not so progressive as the L.C.C. do not do.'

I said, in gentle disbelief, 'For ever?'

Mr Turner, shouting, 'Yes! For ever and ever and ever and ever!'

I solemnly wrote this down.

We talked of other matters. Mr Turner said 'It is absolute nonsense that no other schools have stopped corporal punishment. There are dozens of heads in London who are just as much against corporal punishment as Mr Duane.'

I said two mothers had told me they had toured the Islington district and could not find one other such school. One of them had asked at the Area Education Office and been told 'We can't tell you.'

Mr Turner said 'It is not true. The Education Office could not possibly have told her that, because it wouldn't have been true. And the heads in the district would say the same.'

I said 'Probation officers have told me what great difficulties they have because the schools cane the children; then the children run away and get into trouble.'

Mr Turner said 'I know the probation officer you are talking about.' (Actually he didn't. He was thinking of another one.) 'What he has told you is not true. Schools do not cane. The probation officers are lying.'

Mr Hinds said, kindly and informatively, 'You can't believe probation officers' clients. The clients learn to sum up a situation pretty well, and know what they can say.'

I said 'I think probation officers also learn to sum up a situation pretty well.'

I then said to Mr Turner 'Are you saying that corporal punishment has been abolished in London schools?'

He struggled, and finally said 'Corporal punishment has not been abolished in schools.'

'But the Council would like to see it abolished?'

He struggled more. Then, picking his words with care, he said 'This authority does not attempt to punish any head who does not use corporal punishment.'

The other two, both new to the department, were a little uneasy. Mrs Campbell said 'Is that perhaps a little negative?' And Mr Hinds said 'The encouragement of the inspectorate is towards the doing away with corporal punishment. Corporal punishment, most here agree, is the last resort. . . . The head, knowing the child best, must be the judge.'

I said 'Better than the parents? I have had for some time a copy of the rules for administering corporal punishment in London schools with one of two canes of an approved pattern. Why aren't parents shown these rules? Don't they have a right to know?'

Mr Hinds said 'The retaining weight of parents is for the cane. So often one hears complaints of parents that the teacher is not hard enough. Parents must take things on trust. To tell parents would be destructive of trust.'

Mr Turner was a little impatient of this religious mysticism. He said 'It is exactly on the same level as reading. We don't bother parents with the particular reading method the school uses. In the same way, we don't bother them with the rules for corporal punishment.'

We talked also of other things. Mr Turner, for instance, said that Risinghill was no different from any other school; it was an *average* school; it started under very good auspices. Mrs Campbell said putting schools together was something that had happened over and over again, that made for excitement not difficulty. I said 'Even when one of the schools had been without a head for a very long time?'

At this, Mr Turner burst out, 'Gifford *did* have a head! Do you know who that head was? It was Mr Duane! You didn't know that, did you? He hasn't told you that!'

I said no, I didn't; I would make a note of it, and ask him about it. The other two were very excited, and discussed in lively fashion whether Mr Duane had been head of Gifford for a year or for nine months. In fact, as I checked when I got home, he had never been head of Gifford, though the L.C.C. had tried to make him. And the L.C.C. visitation report (1962) on Risinghill, describing in its first paragraph the coming together of the four small schools, had said 'Gifford had declined rapidly since the departure of its last headmaster.'

We spoke too of the Minister's letter. Mr Hinds said soothingly 'I have seen the Minister's letter myself. And I can assure you it took great account of what the parents said.' I was by now rather irritated at the way I was assumed to be ignorant. I said, '*I* have seen the Minister's letter *my*self. And it took no account whatever of what the parents said. It did not raise even one of the points they made.' After this Mr Hinds said no more.

I have not given all the statements the L.C.C. representatives made, nor am I going to bother to refute the ones I have quoted. The refutations are already here elsewhere in these pages.

One thing however I will say. Wherever Michael Duane has been headmaster, officials have always maintained stubbornly, in the face of all evidence, that these children 'are not deprived in any way', that the circumstances are 'exactly the same as with any other school', that this is 'not a difficult area'. Michael Duane, when I mentioned it to him, thought that this was just the usual reaction of authority to any suggestions that, in authority's paranoid view, might reflect on their efficiency.

But I think there was something additional here. It seemed to me that the official attitude was, 'If we grant that these children have specially disadvantageous circumstances, we may find we are forced to agree – since our "image" is one of enlightenment – that you need not beat them. In any case, we may find ourselves looking at the children as individual human beings, when the same dangerous inference may be drawn. Therefore we will insist that they are in every way "normal", since to us "normal" means "able to be looked at in bulk" and "able to be beaten".' This is what they mean when they say 'There must be no danger of departing from the traditional.'

*

Some time in July, Mr Duane was asked to give the prizes at a school outside London. They wanted him to take over the headship. The headmistress thinks very highly of him and so do several of the governors. He liked the school very much. But, he said to me back at Risinghill, 'a place like that is already on the way to solving its problems. I want to work in an area where the problems have not yet been solved, where the children are being pulled by their environment into completely impossible shapes. I have to be in a job where I can be used and burnt out, with nothing left in reserve. This means London. London is the battlefront.'

I read a letter from a couple of parents to Mr Duane.

I would like to take this opportunity to thank you for all the kindness and patience you have shown to Joey, my wife and myself.

We realize that Joey has been quite a problem to you at times, but your immediate response to help him in and out of court, your testimonials to the good side of his character, has been and will be always appreciated by us all for a long time to come.

We sincerely hope that wherever your destiny takes you or whatever appointment you take up, you will be both very happy and successful.

I *personally* hope that whatever the future holds, you will never lose sight of your ideals and your faith in human nature. For these things make you, Mr Duane, in my opinion humanitarian.

Yours with deepest respect. . . .

But other people, more educated people, were speaking in a different style. I wrote to a university lecturer who had made very good use of Risinghill's facilities and Mr Duane's helpfulness, and had considered the school important enough, and pioneering enough, to warrant taking groups of students there, and had become interested enough as a result to become a Governor of the school; and I suggested a meeting. The reply was a refusal. 'In my view it would be quite irregular for any governor to express any opinion about the matter, and like many other people I feel it should be allowed to die a natural death.' And let us avoid, in our well-bred way, looking at the knife sticking out of the corpse.

In the middle of July, the L.C.C. suggested to Mr Duane (impressing on him that this was very confidential since the post did not even exist yet) that he run for them a small remedial group, perhaps with one other teacher, of children who have simply been thrown out of other schools for bad behaviour.* Coming from the L.C.C. this suggestion was amazing. Mr Duane turned it down, saying the continual segregation of children in different kinds of schools was entirely wrong.

But they did not let this matter drop for a long time. The next month saw the publication of the government White Paper on *The Child, the Family, and the Young Offender*; the part of the schools was completely ignored. Maybe the L.C.C. felt the image was slipping; or maybe they had simply been asked awkward questions by reporters; or it might just possibly have had something to do with the fact that Mr Duane had himself applied for the two local headships, and the L.C.C. was afraid the press might notice if they turned him down.

At any rate, they began to step up this small remedial group until they were agreeing completely with Mr Duane when he said that the only way such work could be done was in conjunction with other children from their families and from the streets around who should be able to use the centre and share its cultural and social facilities, that no child would be transferred there against the wishes of the parents, that it would be in no sense a penal institution, that if a child did not want to return to his old school he would not be made to, that Mr Duane, whatever he wished to

*The L.C.C. – and many heads – maintain that London children are not expelled; they are excluded. The unsophisticated children, and their parents, continue to think they are expelled. And apparently there were enough of them roaming the streets at this date, and thereby getting into trouble, to constitute a job for Mr Duane and an assistant.

do in the unit, would have the L.C.C.'s complete support against the heads in the traditional schools in which the children were when they were rejected and to which they might perhaps return. They were now making statements that were only possible if the L.C.C. was contemplating reorganizing and restaffing itself and all its linked institutions from head to foot, and however much they might like Mr Duane this would be difficult and would take time. As he hesitated, lost in wonder, they then also happened to say that he would have to take what they offered him, even if it was not a headmaster's job, because they couldn't go on paying his salary while he did nothing. (How brief is 'for ever and ever and ever and ever'!)

Mr Duane considered this carefully, then wrote a long, detailed and thoughtful memorandum on the subject of such children and his own alternative plans for educating them, which he thought might be a useful contribution. Then, saying that after discussions with lecturers in university Institutes of Education and the staffs of special schools he had been confirmed in his view that the normal secondary school, given some specialist help on the staff, was capable of handling all children, including children thought to be in need of special schools, and that, given mature and understanding adults, all children were the better for it – he rejected the suggestion.

A few weeks later he made his position very clear on this subject in a letter to the *Guardian*, referring to an article they had published on delinquents:

These boys are the 'end-products' – still sensitive, human and young – of the combined effects of family, school, job, neighbourhood and country at a particular point in place and time. Would it not be more revealing to have each of these institutions examined in depth so that we might see their impact on the emerging individuality of the young? Perhaps we could then better assess whether our cultural standards set before the young, whether the examples of our leading politicians and entertainers, so assiduously thrust before their eyes, are worthy of emulation; whether the accepted practices of business and industry conform to any reasonable definition of 'civilized' or 'democratic'; or whether, in fact, the common reactions of violence and aggression by the young towards our pretensions that we have

'God on our side' may not be the healthy, if crude, protest of those who crave for integrity in action as well as talk.

By now I could not think the L.C.C. considered this letter a good reference for a headmaster. And they were now in the position they had tried to avoid. They were going to have to refuse to give him another headship.

*

He had applied for three. One application he later withdrew because one of his own staff applied for it – and got it.

The second school informed him that there were not enough other applicants. Obviously they could not give the job to Mr Duane simply because he was the only person who wanted it; it would have to be readvertised.

It was readvertised, and more applicants appeared. They were then interviewed by the school governors, and three, one of them Mr Duane, were chosen to appear before the Staff Sub-committee at County Hall for final selection. The L.C.C. panel asked Mr Duane his views on corporal punishment. They then turned him down.

For the third school, a school known through the district for the ferocity of its caning, Mr Duane was again one of the three selected by the governors to appear at County Hall. Again the L.C.C. asked Mr Duane what his views were on corporal punishment. Again he was turned down – and not, incidentally, in favour of another displaced head.

The member of the L.C.C. panel who was so insistent about corporal punishment asked Mr Duane 'what sanctions' he would use against the children, and 'what sanctions' he would use against the staff who, for instance, he had seen with horror on a recent visit to Risinghill had defaced the table with cigarette burns. (He seemed to think that the 'appalling' way the staff behaved was due to Risinghill being a no-caning school; either he had forgotten the staff had all been educated at caning schools, or he thought Mr Duane should carry on caning them now.)

*

On 19 October, *The Times* had quite a lot to say about Mr Duane –

quoting Robin Pedley, author of *The Comprehensive School* (Penguin), who had recently said, 'Mr Duane's sincerity and honesty of approach were too much for the L.C.C.' *The Times*, after going in some detail into Mr Duane's ideas and results, said 'Much of Mr Duane's impressiveness is that he is so concrete and down-to-earth', and concluded that the L.C.C., while paying his salary and rejecting his applications for headships, was wasting both talent and money.

This article stung the L.C.C. who leapt into battle again, waving the brown booklet *Punishment in Schools* like a knitted banner. Mrs Helen Bentwich, in a published letter, demanded

Is it likely that in 1965 the L.C.C. would close a school because the headmaster carried out their own declared policy, despite an indiscreet remark by an official of the council? [Readers speculated which she meant.] The question of corporal punishment was never mentioned when the closure of the school was discussed by the schools sub-committee, of which I was then the chairman.

Mr Duane, frustrated, depressed and unemployed, and humiliated at being paid so much for doing nothing, had already suggested to the L.C.C. that until they found him a headship he would be prepared to fill in for absent training college lecturers. There now evolved the suggestion from the L.C.C. of 'peripatetic lecturer'; he would be based at one training college and administratively attached to it, and would try to arrange lectures and seminars with various London colleges. This job, on the understanding that it was temporary, he accepted.

I did not see the L.C.C. press hand-out, since I am not attached to any newspaper; but I did, like everyone else, see the newspaper reports the next day which reprinted this hand-out. The word 'temporary' was not mentioned.

When this job fades away, as it is likely to, unless the London training colleges sturdily ignore the paralysing hint they have received that the L.C.C. does not approve of Mr Duane, the L.C.C. will have no further obligation, for Mr Duane is no longer a 'displaced head' (set on a spike, as a warning), but a 'peripatetic lecturer'.

*

I wandered through Islington, up from the Angel, and through the littered Chapel Market. 'Don't you touch my fucking apples!' roared a stall-holder at a customer; and she, with dignity and outrage, shouted back 'Do you think I'll be a customer of yours when you use such language! Keep your fucking apples!' This was the beginning of Risinghill.

I talked to a mother. She had covered not only Islington, but the three divisions surrounding her, without being able to find one school that didn't have corporal punishment. She told me that the head of the school to which she had finally decided to send her daughter told her that even though he himself does use the cane he thought it very wrong Risinghill should have been closed; parents should have the right to choose, he had said, and Risinghill was the only school he knew of that did not have corporal punishment.

I met some old Risinghill boys, and asked how they liked their new school.

'This school we're at now, you *resent* the teacher,' said Roger. 'Working's not fun any more. At Risinghill you did your work and you got enjoyment out of it. Here you don't want to get up in the morning and have a go – there's no interest in it. We *enjoyed* working, at Risinghill.'

Dicky said his kid brother came home from his new school every day with weals across his backside.

John said that he was sent to the head to be caned, but 'I just said what Mr Duane told us to say – "You're not going to cane me" – and the head said "Oh run along, run along", and never mentioned it again'.

They asked me if Mr Duane had another school yet, and when I said 'No', Bob said, 'If he sticks to his principles, they won't give him a job. They'll only let him work if he does what he doesn't believe.'

*

January 1966. The sign *Risinghill Street* has been permitted to stay. But the school notice-board says *Starcross School*.

The school is single-sex, and the girls are uniformed. The Risinghill girls who only had one year to go at Starcross and were assured they would not be bothered about uniform have been pulled out of line because they were not wearing 'the right attire'. One of them, a coloured girl, said to me later 'The company are different. The girls don't mix like they used to. And the teachers like the A-level girls, not the others. I liked Risinghill.' Inside the school, the pegs that Mr Duane had repeatedly asked for are at last installed, and an inspector who has come to see how education is progressing is congratulating the staff because 'the children's coats are on pegs at last and are not being brought into the classroom' (but in at least one room at the top of the block missed by the pleased inspector the children are still hanging on to them).

A group of girls, furious and distressed, come up to a sympathetic teacher. They tell her that a clergyman invited to their religious instruction class said there was only one God and only one religion and anyone who did not belong to it worshipped the devil. These girls are Turkish, West Indian, Greek and Irish Catholic.

I hear that many fourth-year girls have left without taking their G.C.E. – so many that the leavers are now put into one class. Many teachers too are leaving – even the one who worked hardest to close Risinghill.

And in one of the lavatories the old frightened words are scribbled on the wall again – 'Fuck' – 'Cunt'. Only in case anyone assumes it must have been done by ex-Risinghill girls, I'll reveal that a lavatory at the old Starcross building had to be closed for a fortnight till the wall was washed down.

*

In January 1966, Inspector Clark was awarded the O.B.E.

Obituary

Last words – for the moment

I talked to many people in the last days of Risinghill. Here are some of the things they said. When I first wrote them down, people said I must have invented them; this is because people rarely listen to other people, particularly if they speak with a different accent. I have therefore given a brief description of each speaker, enough to establish their reality.

PARENTS

A mother. An artist. Herself child of two university lecturers and educationists. They were atheists, she herself is religious; her daughter is religious too, and enjoyed Risinghill's humanist assemblies.

I always get involved in the troubles of the kids in the district, because I like kids, and, having a better accent than most, parents think I can cope. This particular kid was called Paul, a very bright boy, loved studying. But he'd been unexpected; all his brothers and sisters were grown up with children Paul's age or older. He got to grammar school but he was terribly teased there; he was very small, with glasses, and always studying, just the kind who is often picked on by the others.

Someone said to him 'You'd better behave yourself, or you'll get kicked out.' So he started to try to get kicked out because he was unhappy. He stopped working. He got into trouble with the police. Eventually he was going to court once a fortnight, mostly, I think, for things he wasn't guilty of – but if the magistrate sees you often enough, you get sent away. By now he was playing truant, because on Tuesday if he went to school, he'd have to explain why he hadn't been at school on Monday; and on Monday he'd been at court. On Wednesday it would be even worse. Well, he did get thrown out of his grammar school, and he was sent to Risinghill.

I said to him 'Paul, you and I will go together to see the head of your new school. If you can't get on with him, you can come home with me.' I didn't know then what an easy task I'd given myself.

We spent the whole morning there, and *five* members of staff were called in to see if they could contribute to thinking out how Paul could be made happy.

Mr Duane said to him, 'Come in, and get your mark. After that, you can go into the library, and you can type. If you really can't bear it, come and tell me and I'll let you go home; but come in and get your mark so that you get into no further trouble.'

He even went into the class where Paul was, and asked if any child was friendly with him. One boy said he was. This boy was in trouble with the police. Some of the staff thought this was a mistake. But Mr Duane said no. He believed responsibility of the right kind helped a child. He said to the boy 'Try and help Paul to like the school, to see it's worth while.'

When I saw this man would take so much trouble for one child, I said this is the school for my own children.

I've done about eight years' teaching myself. I know that one child can upset a whole class. I know that the way to remain in control is to put everything out for the sake of one child. This is better than to allow one child to upset the whole class. I saw Mr Duane was prepared to do this on the scale of the whole school.

The people of our own locality are pretty level-headed about 'sex rumours' and so on, and they know jolly well what goes on in other schools. We all used to joke about Sh— School having the highest birthrate in London. One of my daughters is eighteen, and almost all her old school-friends have children. One at seventeen has two, and one at eighteen has four. These were all children who were with her at Sh— School.

No, I'm wrong about the seventeen-year-old. She didn't in fact go to Sh— comprehensive school. She had to go to a secondary modern in the end; and she was a bright child. She went for an interview at Sh—, and *she* was all right, but then her mother spoke and she couldn't say a sentence without an f. in it, and so the head wouldn't have her. And this was her last chance. Risinghill didn't exist then.

We knew her well, because her parents were in the pub all the time when she was little, and she was locked out, so we used to take her in. She was a child who was passionately fond of reading. Most of the family have been in trouble with the police.

Michael Duane's children had far worse backgrounds than the other schools because he was the only person who would take them in. Even so, Ann's education at Risinghill was very much higher than Lisa's at Sh—.

My parents started their own school, a very well-known school. All these progressive schools were known as 'nudist schools' and goodness knows what. All sorts of labels went on, because people thought if a school had one unconventional thing, it had them all. It wouldn't surprise me at all to hear Risinghill described as a 'nudist school', though I haven't heard that one yet.

They could close fifty thousand other schools, but not Risinghill. This is a school that is trying to do things other schools are not, and so it caters for people who are not otherwise catered for. From the point of view of education, it is absolutely deplorable to close it. Risinghill was one of the experimental schools, and if you don't have experimental schools, education can't live.

A father, drying plates in his cafe in Islington . . . men eating in overalls, tables covered with ashtrays like craters of the moon.

He'd been playing the piano-accordion since he was about seven. We knew nothing then about opportunities for kids, like people think you can't go to universities without lots of loot. We found the accordion wasn't recognized; he'd have to play something else to get into college. So he went on to the clarinet.

There weren't many people at Risinghill interested then in music, and the ordinary music classes that the other kids were having were elementary for him; so Mr Strong gave him special extra classes after school, special tuition. And for his audition for the National Youth Orchestra, Mr Strong not only accompanied him – some kids don't do very well, you know, with an accompanist they're not used to – but he actually wrote something for him to play, and that's really something, you know. This teacher and Mr Duane gave him every possible encouragement. Why, once when he wanted to get into an orchestra, Mr Duane spent days telephoning for him, and in the end took him round to the place himself.

When he was due to go for his audition, there was a big school football match on, their Cup Final as a matter of fact, and Joe was the star and he was heart-broken. We felt it was a nasty situation, because if he went for the audition he'd be worrying about the Cup Final, and vice versa. We thought the only thing to do was to go round and ask *him*, Mr Duane as usual, to get us out of trouble. Well, he simply phoned the bloke up and asked him to change the date of the audition, just like that, and the chap was very sympathetic and said 'Yes, of course.'

We're too reticent about dealing with what we think are important people, and we find ourselves bowing and scraping. He encouraged people to do what they want to do, what's important to them, not what they were expected to do – to do things the straight simple way.

Joe started at Risinghill in its second term. I'm glad he had the opportunity to work under a bloke like Mr Duane. I'm sure in later life there are many things he'll have learnt through association with Mr Duane and some of his teachers. The approach was fine. None of this kiddywinky stuff. They became grown-up emotionally and mentally well in advance of their years because of this approach.

If it'd been as bad as they said, we'd have taken Joe away, wouldn't we? Why, kids were coming from as far as Woodford, and Wembley. They'd moved, and they didn't want to leave Risinghill, so they came all that way.

We went to see our Member of Parliament. He was one of those blokes who had the art of speaking sewn up tight; he never left a gap between phrases for you to get a word in. That was the first time I've ever been to see a Member of Parliament and it's the last. I'll never go again. . . . If any one parent had been clever enough, or could speak well enough, I don't believe the authorities would have got away with it.

Mr Duane sent a kid here for a good meal – to my cafe here. He'd found the kid hadn't had anything to eat for three days. He phoned me through, said, 'Look after him. I'll pay you for it tonight, Sam.'

Nothing was too much for him to do for a kid. He was round these streets at seven in the morning and again at eleven at night. Nothing was too much.

A mother, talking in her council flat. Her husband is an engineer.

He did fairly well in his eleven-plus, but the head at his junior school told me that because he'd had so much time off in hospital he'd find it a strain to be at a grammar school, and he suggested a comprehensive school, particularly recommending Risinghill. He did exceptionally well at Risinghill, even though he was constantly away ill – the teachers were kind and sympathetic. They didn't make kids feel they'd lost their bit of teaching and that was that. A coloured teacher he had was exceptionally good.

The whole atmosphere was so *friendly*. They were respectful to-wards the teachers and yet the teachers were so friendly with them. You could always go up and see the house master or mistress or any other teacher any time, and say 'I don't like Roger doing this or not doing that', and they would explain it to you. Once I didn't think

Roger was doing well in the practical side of engineering, and I didn't think it worth him stopping for a two-year course, but they reassured me, and afterwards I was pleased.

[Father interrupted here: 'The engineering curriculum was first-class. I've been an engineer for thirty years, and I know what I'm talking about.']

The youth employment officer said a firm told him they wouldn't take any more engineering apprentices; they were full up – they didn't want to know; but he said yes, he'd take them from Rising-hill.

He had a thankless task at the beginning, Mr Duane. You couldn't help but have trouble. But another couple of years would have shown the tremendous change. All the stories had a little bit added every time you heard them. At one time people were saying there were forty girls pregnant.

He's fourteen now, Roger. He said 'I'm not going to any new school.' The children all felt that with the bad publicity they would have a bad deal. But Mr Duane helped an awful lot to get the children to accept the move. Roger came home and told me about it, that they weren't to go with malice, and to show that Risinghill could breed gentlemen.

The old Risinghill was infant and junior. Roger moved from it when they started to build; moved to Penton. Lots of children were told – in those days – if they got into trouble 'Oh you're one of those Risinghill kids. We never had any trouble till we had Risinghill hooligans.' I went to Risinghill myself when a child, and before it was bombed it had a dreadful reputation. The street was a terrible tenement street. Once you've experienced this, you're afraid of it again. . . .

A father. An artist, Australian. In Australia, state schools are best. He assumed it would be the same in England.

He's a wonderfully charming chap, a very intelligent bloke, no cant, no rot, a complete lack of affectation, absolutely direct, very likeable. Very unusual in headmasters, who are generally stuffy and pompous, following books of rules so closely they have no time for imagination, and you cannot talk to them about the vision of education. He was a rare person. I have never encountered anyone in this field so full of imagination. What impressed me most was the freedom with which the children approached him – they didn't stand in awe of him – and his approach to them, gentle but firm.

My daughter said he was liked by the whole school. Certainly he was not despised by anyone.

The children didn't hold him in awe at all; they trusted him. They were never insolent or cheeky. They regarded him as their friend, not as a monster waiting in his study with a cane. When people come across such a direct simple person in such a job, they are appalled.

When I first went to the school, to enrol my eldest daughter, Mr Duane showed me round. When we were leaving the arts section, there were some obscenities scrawled on the wall; and we talked about them. It seemed he had done nothing about them. No one had been reprimanded or punished. He just ignored them. And consequently there was no tremendous spate of it, as you often get. When they found it made no impression, it simply stopped.

It is not going to stop the problems in a depressed area to close the school. Educating the young ones was a way of overcoming it.

Most of the kids in this part of the world want to get out of school and earn some money. But Mr Duane was coping with this very well, and had made quite a bit of progress: he was getting academic results. Of course, it would take years, with only one school like this in such a large area. If they had made detailed observations while Mr Duane was building up his school, the whole area would have been better off for it, and much happier.

Even if the intake dropped for ten years, who is to say it wouldn't pick up again? Given the right amount of encouragement, the right publicity, it would become a school everyone was trying to get into.

The L.C.C. bureaucrats probably have a measure by which they reckon up everything and anyone outside it they come down on. If they really supported Mr Duane, nothing would have made them close the school.

He's an educationist. He should be kept active. So many people are resisting growth: 'What's good enough for my father is good enough for me'. I expect there were people in education who supported him, but the machinery was so cumbersome they gave up.

My daughter didn't want to go to any other school, after Risinghill closed. She knew children who go to other schools in the neighbourhood. She's a normally intelligent child, and she is very much in favour of co-education. I think, too, that it's a good idea for the sexes to grow up together. There is no school in the area that we now think will suit her, no school that is conducting an experiment like Mr Duane's.

A father. Parents' leader. Borough councillor. Potato-seller in Chapel Market.

I knew my kid, regardless of ability, would be helped to do something worth while. I believe Mr Duane's aim is to make better citizens, and I believe he will do so.

I think he was far too advanced for our present educational system. Ultimately the brutality will go, and Duane will be respected wherever he goes. He is a person with such a pleasant personality he is easy to like. He is not a yes-man. He will not accept criticisms of his methods, just to be called a good chap. But he's at all times reasonable. He will argue and explain and perhaps make enemies, when it would be easy for him to agree.

I've only known him for about two years, and my only regret is that I didn't know him sooner.

PARENTS AND PUPILS

Family of fourteen, in scabrous basement. Joey is fourteen.

JOEY: That teacher sent terrible reports on children to the courts. It was always the same with her. Said the worst things about you she could. Things you'd done years ago. You know what – she practically accused me of setting the school on fire! And my dad's in the fire-brigade!

MOTHER: I've made Mr Duane my most unforgettable character – like in the *Reader's Digest*.

JOEY: You know what the kids used to call Mr Benson? They used to call him J.B.

FATHER: They owe it to us to keep Mr Duane.

JOEY: She wanted to be head. She wanted to punish everyone.

FATHER: He's a very fine man, Mr Duane, humanitarian. His methods are a bit far advanced. He'll make a success but he has to have the right staff.

JOEY: If he could start with primary school pupils, and then keep them all the way up, without corporal punishment – then it would work.

FATHER: I think it needed more time. Racial fights were getting less. The kids were mellowing. Another couple of years. I think with a smaller school where he could have absolute control, and not have to go through other teachers all the time, it would work fine. You can't mix a policy; it has to be a hundred per cent. . . . He never turned his back on a child in trouble. He was very down to earth, Mr Duane. He had all sorts of ideas, and he was educated of course, but he wasn't out of touch with ordinary children – he knew what was going on all the time.

MOTHER: Kids came into his room all the time, when they were in trouble.

FATHER: I don't think he'd ever back down to anyone. He had the courage of his convictions and that's a good thing to instil into children. We only met a few times and that was under stress and strain, but I thought a lot of him. He could talk to anyone, the roughest of the rough, and the highest. The L.C.C. lose sight of the fact that they're here to serve us. The decision had been made a long time before the school was closed. They came down to tell us – not to listen to us.

JOEY: It was all sorted out at Risinghill. The boys from — and the boys from — had stopped fighting. Now this will all start over again at the new school.

FATHER: Why didn't they leave the school, the teachers who disagreed? They could have got other jobs, easily enough.

JOEY: Mr Carr and some others had the idea they could straighten the kids out. One of them used to stand us in a half circle and swish his cane backwards and forwards, and if you got in the way of it, that was your look-out. . . . Mr Duane, if ever there was trouble, he talked it out with you. I did a kid in the street here because he called me a —* and then he chased me round the school with a chopper. Mr Duane took us both out in his car, and then talked to us. We never had a fight again.

FATHER: I had an old motor-cycle combination outside my place. I never used it. Mr Duane was chatting to me about boys being interested in engineering. I said to him you could have this for them if you like. He was chuffed – he said he'd collect it right away. He had a bit of ground where the kids could ride it without getting on the road. He wanted them to enjoy themselves.

JOEY: I'm going camping with Mr Duane when he gets back from Ireland.

FATHER: I think he'll always meet opposition from people who believe in the iron fist. They're always afraid kids will turn into mods and rockers. . . . I don't think he'd ever get a door slammed in his face, not by parents.

JOEY: In this school he only had time to help kids who were already in trouble; he never turned away from them. If he had a smaller

*The gap here occurs simply because I never could get clear what the insult was.

school, he could help children *before* they got into trouble.

FATHER: When I was a kid at school, I never saw the head except to get the cane.

JOEY: Were you there on the last day? Did you see that crowd of boys and girls in Mr Duane's room? And the toilets were packed with boys crying – did you know that?

[A pause.]

JOEY: Mr Duane and J.B. used to give the kids money to buy rolls when they'd lost or forgotten their dinner money. That other teacher was very against your young brothers or young sisters looking round the school, but Mr Duane liked it.

FATHER: Mr Brown and Mr Gervis both came from Gifford. That was a very severe school. Yet they both changed and fitted in at Risinghill. They were two that adjusted. Yet when I had him at Gifford, you daren't look at him sideways.

JOEY: If a strict teacher like Mr Carr says 'You shut up or I'll hit you', you say 'You do and I'll hit you back.' It's natural. But if Mr Duane or Mr Benson said it, you'd keep quiet and take it.

FATHER: It strikes me there's a lot of esprit de corps among the kids, even though they are fighting each other. . . . If Mr Duane had another school with a staff behind him, I'd send my kid.

PUPILS

Head boy at Risinghill, previous year. Now a bank-clerk. About eighteen.

I've been to functions at many schools, but I've never seen anyone give performances like we did. At Risinghill everyone's talent was developed. Joe Tonello, whose father has a cafe on the Pentonville Road, his musical talents were encouraged in every possible way . . . and people like Katerina who might have been submerged in another school though she was so intelligent. He helped so many people whom other schools might just have thought naughty.

Some of us, the older pupils, formed a committee. We limited it to the fifth and sixth formers who had stayed on for exams. We drew up a petition and collected 300 signatures. And don't forget these were people who had come from those four schools and had therefore known another school to compare it with. This was completely separate from the other pupils' petitions. We didn't march, because we thought the press might make us look like trouble-makers, so we dealt with it very quietly. We had to decide whether to let the press know and maybe get misrepresented, or not to and let it pass almost unnoticed.

There were so many activities at that school. They did so much for the old people . . . fairs, parties. . . . The staff were always so busy. The magnificent nativity play . . . it used the different nationalities *as* the nationalities, with dances and songs of their own. Here again I think the school excelled. It didn't try to make other nationalities English. It drew whatever they had to give to enrich the rest of us.

They did a marvellous thing at one assembly about slavery and John Brown. It linked up with the colour bar. The whole of it was read, with music rising in the background and then taking over. It was very moving.

All our assemblies were like this. At assemblies Mr Duane's talk was always in tune with the times, often on things that adults never discuss with children . . . capital punishment and so on.

He made it clear to the children that some of the staff disagreed with him – he was very frank – he told the children he would not cane them.

We suffered so much from a shortage of teachers – we had so many incapable supply teachers. If we'd had a whole staff like some of our really first-class senior permanent staff we'd have been fine. The frequent changes in the staff right through the five years – and now the second change of the school within such a short time . . . and Islington isn't such an easy area anyway.

The lack of teachers at Risinghill made it difficult for the A streams, who had to fight for their G.C.E.s. I know from my own lessons. My teacher had me at break, dinnertime, anytime she could, to get me through the exams. We were terribly under-staffed and therefore the fifth and sixth forms got smaller and smaller, and therefore we got even less teachers and had to be fitted in with other classes. At one time, a maths teacher was taking three classes, totalling eighty, together. We couldn't take all the subjects we wanted because there just wasn't the staff.

Mr Duane was first-rate, always ready to help. People who did put Mr Duane's policy into practice found it worked and never found it necessary even to threaten.

I think the school started off badly. They started at Easter, which meant that some people had only one term, and had no interest in the school. There was resentment between the schools too. But after that things got easier. Most of the equipment was very fragile; later we got some things remedied. You wouldn't have got this in an older school where things are more solid. There were some silly things –

hose-pipes littered all over the school, a temptation to everyone. The glass everywhere was terrible; it was very dangerous; the putty was like plasticine and never set. Only at the very end of the school did the L.C.C. put in those banisters in the corridors . . . you know the ones ?

The assembly hall was far from sensibly designed. So many entrances – an invitation to romp around. So the prefects used to be on duty there; and we never had any difficulty in controlling children.

There were so many broken homes in the school. The teachers had to be social workers as well, and spent a lot of time on problems of this kind. So many immigrant children brought particular problems. When the press reported that a number of children were on probation when the school opened, even though they went on to say that with Mr Duane the number had lessened, this didn't encourage people to send children to Risinghill. But other schools in the neighbourhood have great difficulties. There are some very rough schools. Islington has always been a very tough area; it's only in recent years it's risen as high as it is.

The L.C.C. obviously didn't see eye to eye with Mr Duane. This was very clear. The publicity was very bad for the school, and the L.C.C. didn't like it, and it also affected the intake, which the L.C.C. didn't like either. There were lots of reports that mightn't have been meant to do the school harm, and shouldn't have done the school harm, but that in the circumstances did. If you read the reports, even when they are favourable – we did read the reports and we found many of them were really friendly – but just the fact that there's a report at all is unfavourable. I think it was the publicity that forced the L.C.C. to move.

We made a very good target for a Conservative County Councillor to aim at – 'This is an example of what the Labour Party wants.' We were an election platform for him. He didn't know anything at all about the school.

The school has turned out a great many people who have got good jobs. But it has been a great strain on them that they went to Risinghill. I have experienced this often myself. We who went to Risinghill think a lot of the school and of Mr Duane; but when a firm asks you what school you went to – this was in an accountant's office, or an advertising office – they say 'Oh that's where all that trouble was. I didn't think any nice people went there.' We had a relief inspector at our evening institute tennis club and he started to talk about Risinghill, and we said 'Oh, we went there.' And he said 'Oh, I didn't know anyone respectable went to it' – as if it was a den of thieves or something. It's not only hard on the children – it's hard on the staff too; they're finding it difficult to get jobs too.

Working at Risinghill and being used to doing things for children there, I'd have liked to have gone to work for the L.C.C.; but the jobs are mostly voluntary and unpaid. While I was at the school, I worked in the holidays at play centres. I worked three evenings a week, and enjoyed it very much. We mainly got the difficult children, a lot of them from the rest centre where families were being resettled. Some of the children were very difficult and played absolute havoc – much more difficult than the children at Risinghill – but it was very rewarding work.

I think the fact that so many of the stall-holders in the market fought to keep Risinghill open proves something. Children are often a nuisance to people living nearby. But in our case it was people living nearby who supported the school.

Boy, sixteen, going to be an engineer.

These people who talk against comprehensive schools don't know what it is to be labelled a failure at eleven.

Teachers talk about hooligans. But I know, personally, some of the children who were called hooligans. They weren't hooligans, they were just ordinary. The teachers thought they were hooligans because the teachers got fifteen of them together in a bunch among their class, egging each other on. But I only saw them one at a time and then they weren't hooligans.

Parents have no idea really how hard teachers work. Good teachers, I mean. One of the teachers here took his class all the way up to Bristol for the weekend, for their geography work, and then had to start work in school when he got back on Monday morning. They give up their spare time to the job. They train for years before they can teach. And then a labourer earns more than they do. They ought to have more pay. Then we'd have more teachers, and smaller classes, and better teaching.

You remember the 'Seven Plus' *World in Action* programme on television? You remember how the prep school kids all knew what university they were going to when they left school? And you remember what that working-class kid said – 'What's a university?' Their whole future was mapped out. But this kid, he didn't even know there was something he could go to after he left school, he didn't even know such a thing existed. And from the way he talked, it didn't sound as if anyone would ever have bothered to tell him.

Sixteen-year-old Greek girl, prefect. Father was cook in the barracks.

I have a brother, fourteen years old. He's been here three years. He could only speak Greek. Now he speaks English. And he's learning Italian, because his friend is Italian. In a school like this, they learn about other people, and they learn to love other people. You learn about other people's country, their customs, the language. And you learn a lot about life, if there are boys in the school too.

I used to go to a private school.* I think if I had stayed there, when I came out I would have done many things wrong. I am grateful to my parents for sending me to Risinghill. I used to hate the coloured people. Now I have many coloured friends. And of course I know that coloured people have unpleasant people just like white people do.

I have played a great part in helping other pupils with their difficulties. We used to have a Greek girl . . . Her father left her mother, and things like that. She was very unhappy. I had to translate her problems to the teachers. I have helped many Greek pupils and many parents with their problems. Sometimes they will not listen to a teacher. They say, of course a teacher would say that. But when a Greek pupil says it, they believe it. I have taken Greek children in trouble to my house. My parents have helped them and been like parents to them. I have helped them with money, with clothes. . . .

I hope to get into college. I've taken six G.C.E.s, O level. I'm hoping to pass in four. As long as I study, my parents will give me as much money as I need. They want me to be a teacher. They are good parents. They were both very satisfied with this school. I learnt English so fast just by mixing with the English children.

TEACHERS

Man, Greek. Married during the last days of Risinghill; Mr Duane went to the traditional huge Greek wedding, which is festooned with dancing children.

I remember in the early days English boys would fight Greek boys, all with their belts. A teacher once had to hold a boy down for half an hour to get him calm. Trouble came from both sides. Greek boys would gather in the corner of the school and discuss their problems, in their own language. In another corner, Greek girls, keeping away, traditionally, from Greek boys.

*I think she meant by this one of the schools immigrants set up for themselves, in church halls for instance.

Our main effort was to help these children to realize that the English, the West Indians, and so on, were all the same human beings. Mr Duane, I and the Greek Embassy worked together to sort this out.

Risinghill gave some warmth to these children. They realized they had people in the school who cared about them. People wouldn't turn on them and say 'Go back to your own country.' Having many staff who were non-English helped them and encouraged them.

Often during assembly Mr Duane would read passages from Greek – from Homer, for example – and he encouraged other teachers to teach them Greek folk songs. During assembly they would play folk music, breaking the monotony of quietness or prayers.

Greek girls used to be made prefects, which encouraged them and made their parents proud and more secure. Children were given a chance, especially at the beginning, to speak their own language, and to be interpreted. Therefore they could tell the truth in their own words.

Also when we had to send messages to the parents, they were translated into Greek. When their children needed free dinners, or school uniforms, we visited their homes and helped them fill in the forms. This encouraged the parents to feel we cared not only for the children but for the whole family.

This made Risinghill a very popular school among the whole Greek community. Greek people who had no children at the school would visit the school for help. Someone who wanted a bathroom and had to go to the Town Hall for it would come for help.

Mr Duane would spend out-of-school time with me visiting homes – mothers who had trouble with their husbands, fathers who had trouble with their daughters, and so on. Our school used to be the centre of information for education. Parents would come and ask about schools for their younger children. Even from Cyprus, I would get letters asking for advice. The Educational Attaché at the Embassy and the Welfare Officer at the Embassy were very interested in what the school was doing, and visited it. There is nothing to take its place.

To the Greek parents, the word education has a better meaning than to English children (and I do not only speak of Islington). I think parents here neglect their children a lot – they do not teach them ordinary simple manners. The necessity of education in our country is very high. A parent who will not educate his child in our country is regarded as someone who neglects his children. I think English people's attitude to education is not so good – they think in terms of earning good money, not being educated. The fact that teachers are so badly paid contributes to this. English people despise them. I said to a Risinghill boy 'Why do you think it is you don't want to learn anything?' The boy said 'Well, sir, what do you earn?' I told him. And the boy said 'My father's a dustman; and he gets twice as much.'

We attended court, Mr Duane and I and a child in trouble, and gave evidence. A child might be accused of breaking open a gas-meter. Mr Duane would get a clear statement from the child. This was very important.

He once, I remember, bought sandwiches and chocolate for a child, hungry, waiting for his case to come up. I was very moved. I felt Mr Duane was not English but Greek.

Zvia. Artist and sculptor.

A child can't frighten an adult who likes him. But these teachers were frightened and they hated the children.

When I first went to Risinghill, I was warned it would be difficult to teach there. But I didn't find it difficult at all. They simply didn't have the right kind of teacher. You need a very special kind of teacher – or rather, what is considered in this country to be a special kind of teacher.

It was this bad relationship between teacher and children that was the main trouble at Risinghill.

When I first came to the school, the atmosphere was electric. You felt a bomb was going to go off at any moment. I must say, I enjoyed it! Afterwards, everything calmed down and became quite different.

Art is full of so many things – it wasn't necessary for them to be doing nothing but painting. I did masks with them, and squares of murals. At the end of three weeks we held an art exhibition.

I gathered the worst trouble-makers together and asked them to help me. They protected me and would not allow anyone to spoil any of the exhibits. I had no discipline troubles at all.

The children I found very exciting – very open to learn if you didn't give them middle-class lies. They were very enthusiastic, very grateful that you like them and want to teach them. They didn't mess up the lessons at all.

There were just one or two incidents. One kid, half-coloured, very thin and tall, about fourteen, very frightened-looking eyes, he was the leader of a gang. . . . After the second lesson at masks, I asked him with one or two others, to clean the tables. He said 'Me!' and walked away in disgust.

I said nothing. But at the next lesson I asked the boy would he please go to the other art class and change places with someone else. He was surprised, and said 'Why?' I said 'Because I haven't time to argue about matters. The masks have to be done quickly. We need people to work on them, not to play with the teacher.'

He was very indignant. He marched away, came back with a Greek boy who couldn't speak a word of English; I think he picked him specially. I produced the very beautiful mask that this boy had made, and asked the Greek boy would he do the last stage on it. Then the boy pulled a knife on me.

So I lectured him. I said it was ridiculous that a boy so talented, who could make such a good mask, did not know how to behave if someone treated him as an equal, and not as a boss which I had no intention of doing. When I had finished, he said 'All right, I'll clean your bloody fucking table like it's never been cleaned before.'

I said 'Fine. Obviously it would be much better if you finished the mask yourself, since you have made it', and I sent the Greek boy away. He finished the mask, and was no further trouble.

Later I found out his mother was a prostitute. She was living at the time with a man who was not the boy's father, and who beat the boy savagely. He had run away from home several times.

He has left school now. And whenever the Hampstead Fair is on, he stands by the bow-and-arrow stall – he has arranged this with me permanently – and waits for me. I find a few minutes to go and talk to him.

He arranged with Mr Duane to go to evening classes to learn the guitar. I said I didn't mind what he learned, as long as he wanted to go on learning something.

Once a Greek boy, very small and under-developed, slipped his hand between the legs of a big, blonde, buxom English girl, in front of the class, simply to test me. I had a lot of this testing at the beginning. Never later on, when they knew I liked them.

The girl turned very pale, and lifted her hand to give him a terrific wallop. I said 'Just a minute.' The whole class went dead quiet, waiting.

I said 'Why did you do that?'

He said 'Because I like it' (in a very high-pitched voice).

I said 'I'm delighted to hear it. If you said you didn't, I'd be very disturbed. But I suggest you find someone who wants to do it with you, and then do it in private; it is much pleasanter.'

I had no more trouble with him. He used to come and ask me questions sometimes.

I had discussions with the girls.

'Did you ever live alone?' one girl asked me.

'Yes.'

'Did you like it?'

'Sometimes yes, sometimes no. I was lonely sometimes, but on the other hand I was freer.'

'Did you ever get into trouble?'

'No. I knew about contraceptives.'

'I don't care if I get into trouble. My sister did, and my brother took her and the baby to live with him, and his wife and their baby. I'll do the same.'

'But will this be a good idea? You'll have to work and you won't be able to spend any time with your baby.'

'Well, if I'm not married by eighteen I'll be a nun.' What a point of view!

I came back to the school later on. I had some large plastic sculpture to do and Mr Duane said 'You could use the large studio, and in return take the boys on probation, so that they will not disturb the other classes; they can work with you like apprentices.'

I learnt a great deal from these five boys, who, because I was not part of the Establishment, spoke frankly to me.

The only person that they trusted in the school was Mr Duane. They told me a lot of their experiences with other teachers who hit the children and treated them very badly behind his back. In him they had complete faith. The only thing they didn't tell him was intentional law-breaking beforehand, because they felt it would put him in a delicate position; this they told me. I made an agreement with them that as long as they were working with me, they would not break the law, because I found them very good workers and did not want to lose them to borstal.

An Italian boy, Vittorio, was in my class. He used to come in very smart exquisite clothes, and write on the walls 'Vittorio is the most handsome boy in the world', and dance round me brushing me with his hips.

One day he walked out of my class. I said nothing. I was very aware they were always in a dangerous emotional state.

He came back very very pale. I said 'Vittorio! What has happened?' He said 'I went to get a broom to sweep the room.'

I was amazed he should think of doing such a thing. He had gone to this teacher's room where the broom was kept, and asked if he could take it. The teacher told him to get out of the room, knock on the door, and wait till he was told to come in. So he told the teacher where to stick his broom.

Then the teacher came into my room, screaming with rage, and shaking.

After a few incidents like this, I called the boys together. I told them that if they wanted to swear they could all get together in my room and swear as often and as loudly as they liked. But I said there is a certain language used by teachers, and you must talk to them in it, just as you talk to a French person in French. It is stupid to talk to a person in a language that isn't his. The school is made for teaching, I said to them, not for my sculpture, nor for your special arrangements; and if you annoy everybody I will simply be asked to leave the school, and you will have to go back to your ordinary lessons. This they accepted.

One day, I said 'Terry, I am terribly tired of you saying the same word all the time. Why do you always say "fuck"? Don't you know any other swear words?'

He said 'Yes. I know another one.'

'What is it?'

'Cunt.'

'Well, say that for a while.'

'No.'

'Why not?'

'Because my mother says "fuck" all the time, but she doesn't say "cunt". I don't think she likes it. If I get used to saying it with you, I might say it by accident with her, and she might be upset.'

This boy's father was always drunk. He used to beat his mother savagely – Terry often found her unconscious. Terry was very attached to his mother. Once she had concussion and the morning after this happened that same teacher met him in the corridor and went for him furiously about something.

This sort of incident was typical. The teachers seemed to have no idea of the kind of things that were going on at home. They made demands that were wildly irrelevant.

Terry used to arrive in the studio, flop on the floor, and while I was working, put his head on my lap, excusing himself with 'Oh, I'm so tired' or something of the kind. Vittorio would get very jealous. They would walk with me in the playground, and if another child bumped into me by accident they would be ready to knock the child down. I had to say 'It is not necessary for you to protect me so carefully. I'm quite able to look after myself.'

'I took Kim [her small daughter] with me to the school. Mr Duane encouraged it. The children were very sweet to her. But when I was doing sculpture there, and I had all the boys on probation in with me, they tested me, to see, if they teased Kim, whose side I would be on. This became very delicate for all of us. It was building up. So I stopped taking her with me.

It is not enough to do things with children. The other half is the parents. It is no good giving children something they are not given at home. Eventually they are bound to break the law and everyone – law court, police, magistrates, probation officers are involved, expensively, with the child. I felt a group of social workers should go from house to house, explaining to the parents what education is. They do not believe children will be any good unless they are beaten. Such a group will be less expensive than the law process afterwards.

Some things in education are obvious. I was sitting in the staff room. My English wasn't very hot at the time. The children loved it. They corrected me, and taught me. There was a group of about fifteen teachers there; I was writing something. I noticed they looked round to see who was there and then someone said 'Yes, those Jews are a pest. Thank goodness we don't have many of them in the school.' I think they thought I was French. People like this always believe Jews have enormous hooked noses, and so on. I was shocked. These were teachers in a school of numerous nationalities. Then I discovered the educational authority was not horrified at such attitudes at all.

In Israel, it is against the law to send a child out of the class, or to lift a hand against the child. You can't leave a child in a class more than a year because he isn't good enough to go up – you must give him special coaching.

It would be good for English teachers to be aware of some of these things. They are not aware everyone does not think in the English way, and may sometimes be thinking more intelligently.

I think I had better not identify the rest of the speakers too closely. Just – a man.

When I get home, I'm afraid to sit down, because I know I'll fall straight asleep. I think tiredness is inherent in teaching. But at Rising-hill it's exaggerated, because the children are so demanding.

They have problems and want them solved *instantly*. And they come up to you before lessons. They want recognition. They are not used to ordinary discipline, as children are in grammar schools.

It has always been a great problem getting teachers for Risinghill. No one wants to teach in this district. We have part-time, temporary, supply teachers. It all adds to the strain. You never get any free time during the day, and you find yourself teaching thirty-five periods a week.

Teaching here is difficult, but it gets better as you go along. Basically it is a question of knowing the children. (Always provided you're
reasonably competent, and are making teaching your career – many
teachers are just filling in time.) The children won't accept just anyone
standing in front of them. In this school you can't be authoritarian,
because it rouses the aggressiveness itself. You have to know shrewdly
what you can and can't do. Some people – especially supply teachers –
think you can just let them do as they like; but most are authoritarian;
each lot are as bad. Many teachers are so insecure they cannot stand
children answering back, most particularly when they realize they've
made a mistake.

Many of the children here should be in special schools. In these
cases the relationship between you and the child deteriorates.

In my last school, they had houses – but only for football; and there
was no machinery for knowing the children's backgrounds. Sometimes
I was severe with a child because I didn't know the backgrounds.
Once I had been very severe, and then discovered afterwards that
the child's grandmother, whom she loved very much, had died.
People say you can't get to know children in a large comprehensive.
I have found it just the opposite. I have never known my children so
well as I do in this school.

One of my main problems has always been what to do with a child
who wrecks a lesson, and does it week after week. In my last class
there were four who had had psychiatric treatment, and at least three
others who should have had. Or it may be a child who is very backward. We have *one* trained remedial teacher for the whole school –
and he says a quarter of the children in the school need remedial
teaching. I had one class where only *two* had normal reading ages,
stretching right down to illiterate. We have forty-six per cent in the
lowest intelligence grade. . . .

As for corporal punishment, the L.C.C. puts you in an impossible
position. No teacher in his first year is supposed to administer it.
But suppose you find yourself in a school where everyone else is using
it. At the end you feel if you don't hit them they will hit you. In the
end, in my first year, I hit one, and then I went home and sat on
the end of the bed and cried. But in my last term there I hardly hit at
all. When children are hit by other teachers, they expect you to hit
them. They believe you aren't a proper teacher unless you hit them –
and this is the most horrible thing of all.

A head who keeps a cane in his cupboard believes in corporal
punishment.

You can't get anywhere in the educational situation by being a good teacher. The higher up you go, the less teaching you do and the less teaching experience is asked for. Teaching is the lowest rung of the educational ladder. Teachers are the people who are kicked around – by the training college which conditions them, by the government, by the inspectorate. The derisive way our salary claims are treated – this is just a follow-up to the contemptuous way we are treated in training colleges. You know, two girls from Risinghill got jobs yesterday, as secretaries at £10 a week – about the level of what a twenty-one-year-old teacher takes home.

At that last school, I had some brilliant children. I took them all the way up till they were at the end of their fourth year. Then the head there decided they should take G.C.E. a year earlier. I had been doing all kinds of things with the kids – they were being *educated*. I protested. But I had to take it. I told the class 'It has been decided I must stop educating you and get you through exams.' It ruined them. They lost all interest. And although the head had envisaged them having an extra year in the sixth and all going to university in consequence, in fact most of them left without doing any higher education at all.

A man.

I was working as a joiner's labourer. I didn't like it very much. I'd had a grammar school education, and one day I decided I'd like to teach art. I went to fix it up, to get a training, but it was in August. They told me I wouldn't be able to start training till September, but they said 'If you're so keen, we're desperately short of teachers, why don't you go to your local secondary school and get a job there right away?' So I went.

The head said 'When can you start?' I said 'Any time.' He said 'Fine. This afternoon then.'

I handed in my cards at one o'clock, and started teaching geography to a class of thirty-five to forty kids at 1.30. It was chaos. I hadn't a clue. So I started lashing about, hitting them all. And the boys came to heel. I thought 'This is the salvation of teaching. I've got the key at last.'

Now I've been at Risinghill, I've learned differently. But many teachers, thrown young and immature like that into the middle of large classes, never do learn differently. They find 'the key' and use it for ever. It's fear, purely and simply. Do away with the large classes, get teaching on to a personal basis, and you can't go wrong.

But people say 'If an order works, why change it?' They say if standing in front of a class dishing out words works, why change it.

When I came here, work in the art room was not lively, yet the children had every appearance of being lively. In my other school in Gloucestershire, the whole art room was a place where children could go and do whatever they liked. They just came and did their own personal work. Or did nothing if they had no personal ideas. I wanted to do that here. I came here and found these walls bare, all the cupboards locked. I decided I wanted everything out. I was told by some people that it would be pinched. So what? What if I lose one dozen claspknives at one-and-six each, but eight hundred children have free use of them?

They think if they draw anything funny, they'll be hit for it. A kid here drew a funny man, and a teacher hit him for it. They think in school everything has to be serious. Many teachers are always afraid the child is taking the micky out of them.

Fifty per cent of teachers – higher at this school – have their own ideas about when children should stand up, when they should sit down, and so on. The trouble's in training colleges – especially single-sex ones. People who have gone to a co-educational college are much more relaxed.

In this school you have an incredibly varied staff. Some of them, in a limited way, are good. But they don't think in terms of developing and learning from new situations. They just stick. The wrong people are teachers.

Calling a boy by his surname is ridiculous. You get a much better response from him if you call him by his first name. You do in the family.

They need physical contact with a grown-up. And sometimes they can only get it by punishment. By eleven, this is probably – with these children here – the only physical contact they have ever been able to get. They have such irrational treatment – banging them one second, kissing them the next.

Some of them come up here on a Tuesday evening, when I come; but not many. I would like it to be more like a club. But a teacher can't be here every evening. You'd be pressed into the ground. You'd need someone else. It'd have to be someone you had very good relations with. In a boarding school run that way, the kids would be in the art room every evening; here it's too separate from home.

When I'm lecturing at this training college I'm going to, I want people to come to me to recognize what this creative bug in themselves is; then they can go away. When they recognize the bug is in everybody, then you can bring them down from the cold floors of the Tate.

Our visits there – from Risinghill – always ended in a barney – the warden yelling 'Don't you touch that Henry Moore!'

A woman.

In America, all the children have dreams, of being important one day. In Risinghill the children talked to me about jobs. I told them the sort of things they could do when they left school, the kind of money they could make. 'What would I do with all that money?' they said. 'It's no good having money.' And 'What's the use of trying to get on? As soon as I open my mouth they'll know what I am' – and this was from a very bright child.

In America we have local accents, but they just tell us where a person comes from geographically. Here it tells you how the person is going to behave, if you will like him, and so on. You attract to teaching here in London the same people as we get in Mississippi. Even though they have three years' training, they're only one step above clerks in mentality. The teacher's attitude is 'Here comes the miserable child with a completely blank mind which I must fill up.' But a child – say a child at Risinghill – comes not with a blank mind but with certain attitudes. Unless you tie up teaching with his attitudes, he won't learn anything.

If I so much as laid a hand on a child in the U.S.A., I would be charged. Nor can a child hit a teacher. Both are illegal. I saw a letter recently from an English teacher, teaching in America. He was shocked that disciplinary matters were out of his hands, and talked of loss of 'power' in the classroom.

I find it almost impossible to run a discussion in a class in England; they are not used to it. In America, children in schools discuss things all the time. We believe they must get a lot of practice in expressing their viewpoint. You cannot treat a child as a blank, receiving knowledge, and throw them out at sixteen expecting them to express a viewpoint. Children need to be encouraged from the beginning to question, to be taught the difference between fact and opinion. Textbooks are often mainly opinion.

I took the fourth-year English class at Risinghill. After a short time, I found I had a good average class, and taught them as such. So we did Shakespeare. They were grateful, and they were upset when I went. They said 'You don't treat us as if we were different. You teach us.' They knew that most of the teachers wouldn't bother with them. They'd just concentrate on keeping them occupied and quiet.

My father – he is a headmaster – started a new job at an American school where the boys and girls ate separately, and when he started, the school newspaper carried a sarcastic leader about it. The School Council Committee came to him with a request to change it. He said 'We'll have a discussion and vote on it.' The school voted and changed the ruling. Now boys and girls eat together. A Student Council in New York could never be dissolved because teachers had been criticized. If you give children a stake in the school you are bound to get a better reaction, and all-round work becomes more pleasant.

I was with the 'foreign contingent' in the Risinghill staff room. The English staff didn't speak to Americans, Australians, Greeks, Turkish people and so on.

We were all shocked by the same thing. Their attitude towards what they were doing sounded to me as if from another period of time. The things I heard them say about the children didn't belong to the twentieth century.

Their attitude to immigrant children – their *ignorance* of them – is fantastic. One Italian child, very proud, was constantly getting into trouble, because they treated him like dirt because he couldn't speak English; they knew nothing of his national background. I was very amused because my subject is really European History, but I found here you can only teach *English* history.

It is ludicrous that teachers want secrecy in a *state* school – a school that is run for the people. The staff were furious at the head going on television and explaining.

In England, schools are not for the children. Nor are they for the parents. The teachers who disagreed with Mr Duane, their reaction to the children made education impossible. They would say 'For most of these children, school is a waste of time. They come from a rotten home; they will be rotten people.' They used to mock at the parents 'This little market stall-holder thinks he can have an opinion!'

A woman.

There were so many desperate kids. And scarcely anyone on the whole staff who understood what Mr Duane was doing. I've never known Mr Duane when he didn't have time for any child. And not only the children – he had time for the staff and their troubles too.

Did you hear about Tim ? He spent a lot of time with me. Came to our house for a weekend. The first night he wandered all round the house, locking all the doors and windows; never lay down at all. In the morning he came to breakfast carrying an enormous carving-fork. He said 'I always take a weapon to bed with me.' The second night he lay down in the corner of the room. Only on the third night did that kid dare to sleep in the bed.

Mrs Brown downstairs – she's a pleasant woman really – complained about something he did. And Tim went downstairs to her *in tears* and said 'Why are you making trouble between Mary and me?'

But the other teachers couldn't stick him. He wouldn't stay in their lessons. . . . He's in borstal now.

I taught at a school once where the headmistress used to grab hold of a girl – 'You've got a frilly petticoat on!' – pull off her skirt, pull down her frilly petticoat, and whack her. It was quite common there. 'You've got a tint in your hair!' Whack! The children used to creep round the corridors, they used to cry for no reason. It was considered a very good school.

A woman.

I'm an old-fashioned teacher. A child has to do as it's told for me. I go to great lengths to understand it; to know the background; but beyond that I don't think it's kind to the child to go. I shut my door and get on with things my own way. I know the background well – I've taught in this particular district twenty years. No, I don't know their families. I know perhaps two of their parents. The background of these children is exceptionally difficult. But they have to know before they go into the world what their limitations are. The world is a hard place. Many of them are going to find things very difficult next year, when they are not going to be allowed to do as they like. I believe a child *likes* discipline, knowing that if it oversteps the mark it is a calculated risk. I don't think children are capable of deciding for themselves the difference between right and wrong.

A woman.

We have the right to be led . . . and to be told.

The head should know the children through us, not on his own, or what are we for? We can tell him what the children are like, and he should take our word for it; otherwise he is demoting us. He should see the children through the teachers. Otherwise, if the teacher is not very successful, he demotes them.

You can't help one person at the expense of others, as has happened here.

A man.

Do I believe the L.C.C. closed the school because of accommodation problems? I must believe what I am told.

TEACHING STUDENT

A man. He lives in Islington. He spoke lightly, not bitterly.

I was always being reminded at grammar school how my Dad was working overtime so I could go to grammar school, and wear a school uniform, and all that. Got on my nerves. As far as I could see, all a grammar school ever did was alienate you from the other kids in the flats. I packed it up. Got a job. Later on I suddenly decided I wanted to teach, and got myself some O Levels.

My parents resent me enjoying myself for three years at college. Playing football, they say, just a lay-about. And they resent my college friends. They're not so lively as my outside-college friends to them. The girls – my mother liked them at first because she's a snob – now she thinks they're drippy, and soppy and don't stick up for themselves, and the men are dreary and ignorant of what life is about. 'Who'd give *him* a job?' And they don't work during the vacation which is something my parents thoroughly disapprove of. 'Living off his parents!' And they don't like me leaving home – I've escaped! This is something I've had to give a lot of thought to. How can I lead up to wanting to teach in another district, maybe even in another town? Most working-class kids don't escape.

Why do I want to teach? Well, I like children and they like me. We get on well together. And I want to do something socially useful. And I'd like to have some effect on the future. I think you could do that by teaching, don't you?

But I know that people who go into teaching are often people who've failed in other things. So they're people without self-confidence, who go *wham* into the power situation as soon as they're challenged.

Teachers are not a part of the community. They are rootless people. I talked to a young teacher the other day. I said to him, 'Would you talk to the parents?' He said 'No, not on your life.' 'Why not, then?' I said. 'They'd only interfere,' he said. I said 'Well, isn't that what they're for, in a way? Would you give your car over to a mechanic without chatting to him about it?' He thought I was mad. 'No, of course I wouldn't. What's a car got to do with it?'

You know, the other day I bumped into someone I used to know at primary school. He was one of the kids who scored nought in every paper in the rehearsal for the eleven-plus. This boy at eleven couldn't read. Yet when I bumped into him he was a Post Office engineer studying for his Higher National Certificate. I was amazed. I said to him 'I hope you don't mind me asking you, but when I last saw you you couldn't read. What's going on now? What did you do?' 'Oh well,' he said, 'I left school at fourteen or something – they never kept a check on you, you know, never asked to see your birth certificate . . . I got a job as errand boy with old Jackson.' I said, 'That twister! Everyone thought he was a mean old bastard. You must have had it tough!'

'Well, as a matter of fact,' this chap said, 'he took a fancy to me. He taught me how to read.'

'Go on?' I said. 'How did he do it?'

'Oh, he got books and that,' he said. 'And then his daughter, she taught me too. And then, when I could read anything at all he sacked me – said I was too intelligent for a job like that, and fixed me up in the Post Office. I've been taking all the exams.'

My girl-friend's a teacher too. When she started at this school she's at, the kids asked her where she lived, which way did she come. Then they said 'That's not the way, Miss! It'd only take you ten minutes if you cut through the bomb sites.' She tried the way they said. She was a bit relieved, to tell you the truth, to find them all waiting to escort her. She's a bit absent-minded; she could never find her way by herself; I reckon she *needs* them. But the staff, you know, they say such vicious things about her, coming to school with 'a horde of children'. They say she must be neurotic. So she's thinking she'll have to go back to the long way round.

EDUCATION LECTURERS

A woman.

If Risinghill were a country place, the natural conditions of rural life would throw the teacher into the community, but in London social conditions do not do this; unless you see this as a need, you would go along quite happily thinking the community is no part of your job.

When students of mine had to get out, because they weren't up to it, they often themselves realized that what they really wanted was a steady job without responsibility, just with a routine. We need people like this – where should we be without them? – but not in teaching. . . .

A friend of mine did a survey on the capacities you look for in a teaching student. I think myself vitality is tremendously important – an optimistic attitude to life. And sensitivity. You need patience but not at the top of the list; the too patient person may fail, by offering no incentive. And *respect* for children, respect for them as fellow human beings, this is vital for a teacher. I have seen many children destroyed by the lack of it.

Some teachers think listening to a story is too passive – 'Oughtn't they to be *doing* something?' they say, meaning well. They have no idea of the extraordinary magic unity, the mutual creativeness, that goes into telling and listening to a story.

Some teachers tell the children what they *ought* to experience. If you say 'why not help them to write about their own experiences?' they say 'But children have no experiences!'

Physical relationship with the children is enormously important – sitting *among* them, whispering to them. Only a teacher who is interested in the children, who knows about their life or who wants to know about it, will be able to get them to talk, and from that, to write. It is a *shock* for staff to see a head being friendly with children like Mick was.

The teachers who came after the war, men and women from the forces, were superb. They were so socially aware. And they talked to the children with mutual respect.

I remember Mick as a student. I remember him taking a class of boys and being impressed much with his handling of the lads. And he was ready to take anything from anyone with delight if it was going to help him learn more about teaching. He started out with a great flair, meaning to do something that had never been done in a state school before.

He knew the children when they didn't know themselves. In one of his schools he said to me 'That boy is a thief, and that boy is sexually warped.' I said 'How do you know?' He said 'I can tell, without seeing it in action.' And with this he was so relaxed and treating them always with genuine warm friendliness, and a gentlemanly courtesy in not interfering with their private lives.

Someone said recently 'Children want to learn, but they hate being pushed around.' Some teachers do not understand what teaching is. They reach a point where it is 'His will against mine.' They *must* beat the child down. It need not be brutality – it is sometimes despair. The alternative is to burst into tears of rage. That is what his teachers felt – 'You have taken away from us the only means of control.'

We talk about physical punishment not being used in schools. It *is* being used. And it is being used without any control. It is a terrible sight to see the faces of the assailed and the assailant. The answer to 'You *have* to beat them' is 'Why don't you teach better? You can't teach anyone unless you give, and make them realize they have something to give' . . .

And they inherit enmity against children. . . . But mostly they have no faith in what they are doing.

Yet a teacher, just one teacher, can come into a class and the atmosphere changes. The children cluster round the desk like lambs round a feeding shepherd – and that is what such a teacher is. . . .

These parents, they are new. They really care about education. In a rather 'better' area, they would be talking about exams, not about education. . . .

A woman.

I am shocked at the way even the people who wrote to him have done nothing to help him. Everyone is afraid. I am sickened by what has happened. I think now the way his friends can help him best is by preaching what he stands for.

SOCIAL WORKERS AND PROBATION OFFICERS

A woman.

I have sent unhappy deprived children who have got into trouble to Risinghill, and they have become happy. Children on probation come to me. 'How's school?' 'All right.' 'Happy there?' 'They hit you a lot. For nothing.' But a Risinghill schoolchild comes in: 'How's school?' 'It's smashing. I like the head. Treats you all right.'

I had one boy on probation, a very intelligent boy. He was a boy who couldn't stand the cane. He ran away from his school and was put in a remand home for inquiries. I asked Mr Duane if he would take him. He did, and he never truanted again. Whatever has happened to him now, he could not fail to have benefited from the maturity, warmth and sympathy he got from Mr Duane.

Lip-service is paid to doing something about delinquency. When someone really does something about it, and tries to make people look clearly at uncomfortable facts, they don't like it at all. The fact that he even got a Parent–Teacher Association going at all was amazing. The fact that he had taken active steps to integrate – that the coloured children could be completely themselves – this was tremendous. Given time, people would have come from all over the world to see what he had done.

I think a lot of children would get over their maladjustment, given warmth, without having to have special schools. That is why Michael Duane was so wonderful.

Some heads are fine. You can hear, as soon as they pick up the phone, you are talking to the right person. But two schools in — we can't do anything with at all. In fact we are frightened to mention a child, in case we make things worse for him.

I was at a school, once, in the head's study, when a child knocked timidly on the door. No answer. The child knocked again. Still no answer. At last the child put a head in. . . . 'Oh please, sir . . .' 'How dare you enter my room before I have given you permission!' thundered the head. Then, turning to me, 'These children have no manners.'

Someone ran a meeting for probation officers and some teachers came along too. Mr Duane was there and he said there was something very wrong with training colleges that turned out teachers with no knowledge of the reality of the children they'd be teaching, no understanding of their districts and their homes. The teachers were flaming. Later he said teachers 'provoked' children. And the teachers again flamed up and said 'Scandalous disloyalty to the teaching profession! Absolutely untrue!' The rest of the meeting roared with laughter, and shouted 'Do you want instances? We can give you plenty!' But the teachers didn't want any. An independent child with a sense of justice is continually in trouble.

One young teacher caned all twenty-six children in her class some years ago. Children copy what adults round them do – they see adults' violence and as soon as they are strong enough they imitate it. What is the difference between our nation, our children and our teachers, and Norway, Holland, America, Israel, that our children have to be beaten?

Children need success. A few schools understand this. Sometimes you just need to be a person to talk to, wherever that is needed . . . someone to fill a gap. If more schools were like Risinghill, we wouldn't have all these children on probation. The children are beaten, they truant, then immediately a Fit Person Order is taken out and they are sent away – only because they are unhappy. Why shouldn't they truant from a school that treats them so dreadfully?

Michael Duane was the answer to our prayer.

A woman.

When I went to Risinghill I was absolutely amazed that Mr Duane was willing to see me. Why should I be amazed?, I asked myself afterwards. I was.

I saw him in his study. Children came in, a few staff came in, a grandmother came in – everyone he had time for. I was so astounded that I asked myself '*Why* am I astounded? What are my standards?'

The children laughed, talked to me, helped me. They threw snow-balls in the playground, and he leaned out of the window and shouted to them in a friendly way, and they stopped. . . .

I find so much feeling among children of 'Well, it's the way teachers treat you!' You can sit in the back row. As long as you're quiet and don't make much trouble, you can sit in the back row. At some stage, adolescent boys and girls are ready with a response to almost anything, some with a tremendous enthusiasm, some just with a willingness to participate. What is it then they're lacking there that makes them not even want to go to school? I want to find out what happens. I keep asking questions. It seems that some teachers in some schools have not been worn down by the effort; maybe they have special skills that rub off on the children, maybe they have more experience, I don't know. . . . But what I know from my girls is that it matters the way they treat you, the way they look at you. And if you know they like you, they get a response from you that no one, looking at your I.Q., would expect to happen.

I took some girls out skating, and one of them was at Risinghill. She sprained her ankle and, while I was talking to her, suddenly Risinghill came up, and she said 'I love it! I don't want to leave!' There's no man in her family, just one that comes in and out. That girl could well have been a girl who wouldn't go to school, because her mother wanted to possess her emotionally. Talking to her, I felt that whatever happened at Risinghill was for her good.

I think of another of our children who is at Risinghill. Her father was alcoholic, her mother was mentally disturbed and eventually left the home. The girl was twelve or thirteen, and there were two younger ones. Now the girl is responsible for them. There was a difficult mother-in-law upstairs, who punishes the father for driving the mother away. The girl, coping with all this, would still be expected by most teachers to go to school, make a good attendance, learn, and pass examinations. You can get teachers who just can't afford to know. I think we must show we are not blaming teachers. But here is a problem. How are we going to solve it? Only by pooling knowledge and experience.

Daisy was at Risinghill too. Again there was no man in the family. This girl was completely apathetic. I think she truanted. But if you're aggressive and get into trouble, you get noticed. Some of my girls behave very badly at school and get noticed; but some seem to be very good, and perhaps they manage to get to school, but from what I know of them this is an apathetic attitude at school; they are no trouble and sit at the back. But I am faced with this – when they are adolescent, what is going to happen to them?

Can they in that last year at school somehow be made to feel that life – getting a job – is interesting and exciting, when in fact the job they are going to get is so damn dreary that no one could blame them for drifting around in and out of it?

I know another family, rather a sophisticated family. Their father ran a cafe and they might easily have gone to Risinghill but they didn't. There was no mother. Molly has just left school. She has never been in the same job three days running. The father doesn't know how to cope, but he was concerned about Molly and her younger sister. So I rang the school for him, to talk about Jenny, and said 'Jenny is going to leave school now. Will she see the Youth Employment Officer?' Instead of discussing this with me, the head then involved me in a long talk about Molly, the elder girl who had 'dyed her hair and you know what that means!'

I saw there was a tremendous amount of criticism of them. When I talked to Molly about her school – she was an intelligent girl who liked to go round to the Geffrye Museum – she said 'Well, they didn't want to know me.' Could anything have happened at that school that could have reached this girl before I reached her?

Some girls say they get fined a penny if they come to school with painted nails, and have to go and clean it off. I don't know whether there's any reason to bother about painted nails. It would seem to me that the fact that they take an interest in their appearance is something to seize on. What can they be taught in these last years that will help them to be proud of the people they are? If the families don't teach them, why don't the schools? Is there anything inherent in the set-up of a school that prohibits a different attitude to these children?

You know the boy I told you about earlier? Well, his mother, who was mentally disturbed, was pregnant again, after a very long gap, and I took her to the ante-natal clinic. The doctor interrogated her and she had a fit of hysteria because, she said, 'They said they'd probably keep me in, and you know what that means. I'll end up at that mental hospital where my husband is.' I tried to calm her.

A nurse appeared and said 'Where's *Barker* then?' A few years ago my feelings would have choked me. But now I was calm, and I said 'Are you speaking of Mrs Barker, who has just had this attack?' 'Who are you then?' 'I happen to be a social worker, and also a friend of Mrs Barker.' 'Oh. Will you come this way then?'

When she actually went into the hospital, she met with tremendous kindness. Yet here she had met someone from the hierarchy. She said to me afterwards 'What would have happened to me if you hadn't been there? – if you hadn't been educated.'

Children should be leaving school with a conception of themselves as someone worthwhile – by giving and receiving.

What they learn at most schools is a *subject*. It has nothing to do with life. These girls I know, they learned about hygiene, but it means nothing. Well, maybe it doesn't matter if they learn about hygiene and food values and live on chips and baked beans. But they talk about boy-friends. And you say 'Do you learn about things like this at school?' They say 'Oh, you mean hygiene?' or 'Oh, you mean about males and females?' 'No I don't,' I said angrily to one of them, 'I mean about you and Robert.' Now she has a boy-friend and is in trouble; but she is having a *warm* relationship – not a clinical one. Isn't this important?

You know, a doctor friend told me he had a woman come to see him about birth control. She was married, about twenty-five years old. He was struck by her tenseness and rigidity, which showed very strong emotional difficulties. He talked to her, to try to get her to relax. And he found she was a teacher of sex education and biology!

I went to Risinghill because I was interested to see what happens in a school where the barriers come down. A school is a community. How many barriers of inadequacy are there between members of the staff, between teachers and children? In an office job, except for your colleagues, you are only dealing with pen and paper. If in a school the people are still battling towards maturity, the children are bound to be involved. If the teachers are torn out of the hierarchy which protects them, and are *exposed*, are they mature enough to cope?

Some teachers only want clean tidy corridors, not friendly chatter and a warm noisiness. Why shouldn't the children work off a bit of steam going from one classroom to another? A friend of mine is at a grammar school that had a good head who didn't mind noise; recently this head left and my friend was talking to me about the change. 'Inside the classroom, those girls were teachable,' she said. 'Now we have quiet classrooms but the children are not so teachable.' Now the girls are coming to the staff room bringing her their problems, pregnancies.

Yet such a person is afraid of speaking up openly. She would not say this except, privately, to me. Why?

Too many people like things to be tidy and not to give trouble and to be quick.

Young people terribly want to talk – but to someone who will listen.

It is all of us who need educating.

A man.

I had some boys whom I transferred to Risinghill school. One was a Turkish-Cypriot boy. It is a culture that is very different to ours, a culture that is very disciplined indeed. And he happened to go to a school where the same thing applied. He detested both. He was caned a great deal, and for that reason started not going to school, and then began to commit offences. It was possible to get him transferred to Risinghill. He stopped being a truant – because Mr Duane took interest in him. If he'd stayed on at his old school these eighteen months, I know he'd have gone right round the bend. He very nearly stayed on another year to take an engineering course. He has in fact become an engineer and is now on good terms with his father.

I have been to so many schools where the child is sent to the head's study, and the head says 'How many?' the child says 'Three' or 'Four', the head says 'Get the cane', the child gets it, and is given the three or the four – no questions asked, not even what is it for?

At one, perhaps two, of our local schools, without harming the children, I can talk to the head about things the children have told me.

It was always a matter of treating each child individually.

A man.

I was out in a car with a mother from the school, taking her somewhere. A policeman stopped us. He said nobody could turn right. All I wanted to do was to go to a house on the right, and I wasn't going to go two miles round to get to it. I stopped the car, and just stayed there. He kept waving me on. I would not go. Eventually the policeman came over. I explained – several times. In the end the policeman said 'Well, I suppose it's all right', and let me go where I wanted. The mother said, as we drove on, 'Isn't Education wonderful!'

Yesterday, I went to the Gas Board to pay a bill for someone. The official said 'What's his number? You should have a card with his number on it.' I said 'I don't know what his number is. But here's his money.' So he went into a tremendous flim-flam saying he couldn't accept the money without being given a particular number.

I stood my ground. I was as objectionable as he was. And in the end I forced him to take the money. The person whose bill it was would not have known the number, would not have dared to be as objectionable as the official, would not have been allowed to pay the money, and would have had his gas cut off – because he hadn't had an education.

Appendix 1

Pages from an official document

Confidential within the London Teaching Service

LONDON COUNTY COUNCIL

CORPORAL PUNISHMENT IN PRIMARY AND SECONDARY SCHOOLS

The regulation, rules and conditions, which have been made after discussions with representatives of teachers' associations through the Consultative Committee on Educational Matters, are set out below:

COUNCIL REGULATION G144

Corporal punishment in county, voluntary controlled and special agreement primary and secondary (including special) schools and in schools in residential establishments conducted under the Children Act, 1948, shall be administered as determined by the Education Committee.

CONDITIONS

These are confidential within the London Teaching Service

The conditions under which corporal punishment may be administered, as prescribed by the Primary and Secondary Schools Sub-Committee for primary and secondary schools and by the Special Education Sub-Committee for special schools, are as follows:

(i) Corporal punishment shall be given only with the open hand of the teacher used on the arm or the hand or with a cane of approved pattern. Two canes, a larger and a smaller, are approved. The smaller cane only may be used for boys below 11 years of age and for all girls, irrespective of age. The larger or the smaller cane may be used for boys above 11 years of age at the discretion of the head master or head mistress. Corporal punishment of girls shall not be administered by a head master or assistant master.

(ii) Corporal punishment of children below the age of 8 shall be given only in very exceptional circumstances, and then as a rule only by the open hand of the teacher used on the arm or the hand.

(iii) Head masters and head mistresses may, where they think necessary, delegate to such of their assistants* as they consider to be fit and proper persons to be so entrusted the power to give corporal punishment. This power shall be delegated only to assistants who have had at least one year's experience as a qualified teacher. Head masters and head mistresses who either give to or withdraw from their assistants the power to give corporal punishment shall do so in writing and shall record the fact at the time in the school record book. If the head master or head mistress of a special school delegates the power to administer corporal punishment to an assistant teacher he/she shall be present when the punishment is administered.

(iv) Except as may be required under paragraph (v), the canes and the punishment book, in which details of any corporal punishment shall be entered in accordance with . . .

*Delegation should be restricted to permanently appointed teachers.

These are the first two pages of the document [L.B.].

Appendix 2

Risinghill and the problem before us

(*Michael Duane*)   [Extract]

I am under no illusion about the size of the task faced by this Staff. Some problems we have in common with other schools, e.g.

(a) Shortage of normally qualified and experienced Staff, and high turnover of Staff, though our pupil/Staff ratio is the best in London.*

(b) A school population of widely varying abilities and with very mixed ethnic and cultural backgrounds.

Some problems we suffer with other schools though perhaps to a more intense degree:

(c) A complex site that is difficult to administer and to supervise.

(d) An open site with playgrounds and classrooms often in full view of the outside world and where any misdemeanour is likely to become the subject of exaggerated rumour in the locality.

(e) An immediate environment in which, during the past four years, three murders have actually taken place, where prostitution, larceny and violence are commonplace in the lives of many of the children and where the hangings that take place at Pentonville Prison periodically create deep disquiet in the minds of all our children.

(f) A locality where a large number of the parents are antagonistic to the values and purposes represented by the school.

(g) A dearth of children with high levels of ability (.8 of 1%) and a plenitude of children (nearly 50%) in the lowest levels and including children already deemed E.S.N. with a corresponding difficulty of providing a full educational programme for both.

*This was true in the first two years of Risinghill, before the staff began to be cut' but not afterwards. When Mr Duane wrote this, he had not checked the figures.

I am also in no doubt about the amount of devoted hard work that has gone on during the last four years. No headmaster could have wished for more.

What is happening now, in my opinion, is that although clear progress can be seen to have taken place in many ways (academic achievement has exceeded our expectations; we have eliminated the 'nasty violence' of the early days; the abandonment of physical punishment is now generally accepted as no longer a major issue), the changes that have occurred are changes in quantity only (more instances of good rapport between individual teachers and children; fewer acts of wanton destruction; more participation of children in House activities) but these changes are not yet numerous enough to have brought about a better overall tone in the relationships in the school. Children who are amenable and co-operative are still regarded as somewhat unusual both by the Staff and by other children. There is not the feeling of hostility towards them that was prevalent in 1960 and 1961, nor the widespread antipathy felt towards prefects and monitors and the organised 'beat-ups' of that time.

We want something more than just this. We want a climate of co-operation, hard work, a tranquil atmosphere during lessons and an end to the wearing guerilla tactics against truancy, dirt, litter, noise and vulgarity. We know that success is possible even in this neighbourhood, but after four years the confidence of even the most experienced of the Staff is less strong. The departure of eight outstandingly capable Staff to positions of greater responsibility last year hit us very hard at a time when we might have begun to hope for an accelerating rate of improvement.

The reasons for the decline in confidence and the greater feeling of strain, evident in the recent series of outbursts by individual members of Staff to one another and to me about colleagues, are, as I see them,

(a) The exceptionally uninhibited behaviour of our children, rendered the more fearless by their realisation soon after the school opened that the cane was not to be used on any account.

(b) The continued rejection by so many of the children of the moral, ethical, cultural, linguistic and other standards accepted as fundamental by most teachers with middle-class or artisan backgrounds. The attack by the children on these standards is, of course, quite unconscious. They think and feel in terms of their upbringing and of the standards set by those most dear to them, their parents. But their attack has become the more insidious for the very reason that as children they are attractive to us and the personal bonds that have grown between so many Staff and children make it impossible to be insensitively rigid in our demands on them to live up to standards largely alien.

For teachers whose own ethical, moral or other standards have been inculcated by friendly conditioning even if not by fear, rather than having been acquired as a result of experience and personal verification, such continuous rejection can cause grave personal problems of integration amounting in certain cases to 'nervous breakdown', so called, or in less serious cases, outbursts of temper, periods of irritability and fits of depression. That those values and standards are already under fire in the adult world does not simplify the problem for such teachers.

In the third and fourth years, with the main onset of puberty, the attack on these standards takes on a new intensity, especially in the field of sexual behaviour and the activities associated with sex: dress, relations with members of the opposite sex, manners towards adults of the same or opposite sex. Where the attitude of the parents or teachers has been unduly repressive; where great insistence has been laid on 'manners'; on obedience as such; on conformity for its own sake or for reasons that are irrational, there will be many complaints by parents and teachers about an upsurge of 'cheek'. The young adolescent has begun to resent being still treated and spoken to as a child. The physical changes that are taking place give rise to new emotions, new feelings of competence and power and an irrepressible urge to live and feel as an adult. Where the adults ignore these quite natural desires or fail to deal sympathetically with their expression, they will create resentment and hostility.

Correspondingly, this period of new emotions and needs opens up an immense range of materials in nearly all subjects, certainly in English, Art, Housecraft, Needlework, Science, Physical Education, Music and Religious Education. If we can utilise their craving to come to grips with the adult world now opening for them, and show them that because we ourselves underwent these same feelings and experiences we are sympathetic and prepared to be of help, we shall find that a totally new relationship will emerge. Work in most subjects will cease to be a fight to maintain attention.

(c) A third reason for this greater feeling of strain is that the high proportion of specialist and technical teaching, with its tendency to see the child in a compartmentalised fashion, the scattered layout of the buildings, isolating workshop, gym, house-craft, needlecraft and science Staffs for long periods, and the alternation between House and school activities make it difficult for both Staff and children to see a clear pattern in each day. Communication is spasmodic, difficult and requires conscious effort. In small schools to which most of the Staff were accustomed, with a majority of form-teachers taking a group of subjects, with the staff-room the one main meeting point for Staff, and with most Staff knowing every child in the school, communication is continuous, easy and informal. The Head and the Staff meet frequently.

(d) A fourth reason for strain is that, whereas in the small school responsibility for direction and control rest inescapably on one person, the Head – with perhaps the Deputy accepting some responsibility for timetabling and discipline but always in close consultation with the Head – and administration is simple because it has grown round the small school, and the small school has come to be designed for easy administration, such centralisation of direction and control in one person is totally impossible in a large school that is not designed like an old-fashioned prison.

Delegation, except in trivial matters, is almost non-existent in the small school. It is inevitable in a large school of seventeen departments and six Houses with many specialists far better qualified in their subjects than the Head. The delegation of responsibility to which I now refer means the delegation of responsibility for judgement and decision in matters of human conduct and entails the possibility of considerable variation in interpretation and action. To the teacher trained in small schools there was only one person with the power of decision beyond his own, the Head, or, in his absence, the Deputy. In this school it may be one of twenty-eight people according to circumstances. In the small school the Head can give an immediate decision in most things if so required by a member of Staff. Here such simple decision may require negotiation with several departments or the alteration of a complicated timetable before it is possible, and the amount of work so involved may make an apparently desirable objective questionable.

All this detracts from the 'image' of the all-powerful Head common among not only many members of Staff but among parents, themselves mostly educated in small schools. Staff accustomed to rely on the Head for effective decision feel terribly insecure, or 'let down', or 'not backed up' when such 'effective' decision is not evident. The Head is often accused of 'evading the issue' or of 'not giving a straight answer'.

(e) A fifth reason for strain which is really an extension of the problem of communication, is the difficulty, in the crowded day of the large school, of finding enough time for discussion among individuals, groups of Staff or among the Staff as a whole. This is made more difficult by the fairly high rate of Staff turnover. Of the original Staff barely 20 have survived the four years.

(f) A sixth reason for strain comes from the heavy demands on physical and nervous energy made on the Staff by our children, so many of whom need the affection, the care and the concern for them as individuals that the normal child gets in his own family, but which for so many of our children, in their broken and disordered families, is lacking. . . .

The Comprehensive School

Robin Pedley

Nearly everyone interested in education today wants
to abolish the 11 + examination, but few people
are clear what the alternatives are.

The best alternative is some form of comprehensive
school, and in this new appraisal the Director of the
Exeter University Institute of Education gives
a clear and critical picture of the comprehensive
school as it exists in England and Wales today. Dr.
Pedley first describes just what the 11 + is and does.
Then, after dispelling the bogey that comprehensive
schools need at least two thousand pupils in
order to function, he goes on to demonstrate,
by statistics, that those in existence are already
rivalling the tripartite system in academic
achievements. Finally, and most important, he
argues that a good comprehensive school can both
focus and mirror a community as can no
other school.

Of all our educational establishments the
comprehensive school is the least understood. This
book, which contains a glossary of educational
terms and a list of comprehensive schools, offers
to interested readers – especially parents – all the
facts.